**Stories
they wouldn't
let me do
on TV**

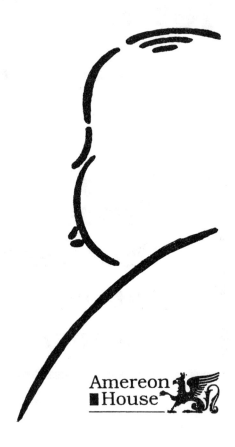

Stories they wouldn't let me do on TV

Edited by

ALFRED HITCHCOCK

To order, contact
Amereon House,
the publishing division of
Amereon Ltd.
Post Office Box 1200
Mattituck, New York 11952-9500

CONTENTS

PREFACE

Good evening, ladies and gentlemen, this is Alfred Hitchcock speaking.

Being what is probably one of the most obtrusive producers on television has spoiled me. I cannot conceive of giving people stories without adding my own comments. The publishers of this book, being far wiser than my television sponsors, have limited my interference to this short preface.

First of all I should make it absolutely clear to you that these stories will not be interspersed with long-playing commercials. You may enjoy them while facing in any direction in any room in the house. Or outside, if you like. Furthermore, you may read them at any time, and if you take longer than half an hour for one of them you will not be penalized. Of course, this information is for those of you with poor memories and good television sets who may have forgotten some of the freedom allowed a reader.

An anthology of stories, like a soufflé, reflects the taste of the person who selects and mixes the ingredients. It matters a great deal, for example, whether onions or garlic are used and when the arsenic is added. I doubt that you will find much garlic or onions in this volume, but I am certain that you will find more than a little arsenic. I only hope that, like me, you have developed a taste for it.

This particular selection of tales is primarily aimed at those of you who find television fare too bland. You may not care for some of these stories because you think them too shocking, macabre or grotesque, but I am confident that you will not find any of them bland or dull.

The reason why some of these stories cannot be produced on the home screen will be obvious on reading. After all, actors are only human. (Debatable but true.) And this quality is a severe limitation for anyone attempting to produce Edward Lucas White's "Lukun-doo," William Hope Hodgson's "The Voice in the Night" or John Collier's "The Lady on the Grey."

These and several other eerie tales of the supernatural make up a part of the book, but the chief staple is that ever popular crime—murder. However, you will look in vain for a story of an underworld killing—homicide as practiced by hoodlums. I have nothing against gangsters, you understand. Some very delightful murders have been committed by professional criminals. By and large, however, the more interesting work in this field is done by amateurs. Highly gifted amateurs, but still amateurs. They are people who perform their work with dignity, good taste and originality, leavened with a sense of the grotesque. Furthermore, they do not bore you afterward by telling you how they got the way they are. Here is polite and whole-some mayhem as practiced by civilized people and I think it makes good reading.

I was Johnny-come-lately to television, and some persons have claimed that I was waiting for the screens to become wide enough to accommodate me (an allegation which I stoutly deny). However, I have become quite fond of the medium, and I trust that this book will not be interpreted as a criticism but merely an admission that there are a number of taboos and that there are some stories to which TV cannot do justice. As for my dear sponsor: he is really a rather toler-ant fellow, and on the program when I bite the hand that feeds me I really have my tongue firmly in my cheek. I am sure this is the neatest trick of the week, and if you want to see how it is done you are wel-come to tune in any Sunday evening.

But now I had better fade away while you select the first story to read.

Good night and good hunting.

ALFRED HITCHCOCK

BEING A MURDERER MYSELF

BY ARTHUR WILLIAMS

❦ BEING A MURDERER MYSELF, I was very interested in the statement recently made by a well-known reviewer of murder stories that "the best and most stimulating detective stories being written today are those that stress the puzzle of 'why' at least co-equally with 'who' and 'how.' "

It is gratifying to see, even if it is only in the field of fiction, that the character of a murderer is at last being considered worthy of more detailed analysis. In the past too much importance has been attached to discovering the identity of a murderer and the means of apprehending him. On the other hand, I do not consider wasted the time spent on the puzzle of "how," since after all, the method adopted is an indication of the type of man employing it; furthermore, it often decides whether the killer is to become famous, as a failure—or unknown, as a success.

I would also like to mention that we murderers do not *always* make a mistake. That fallacy has arisen because only those murderers who *have* made mistakes ever come to the notice of the police. On the whole, we are very efficient, and taking the number of known cases only, it is evident that we have got away with many murders, in spite of the very large organizations directed against us.

But the most common misconception held by most people is that a murderer is different from the ordinary man. Too often he is described in exaggerated terms such as "an insane monster" or "a cold-blooded brute." Such melodramatic ideas are far from the truth.

"Being a Murderer Myself" appeared originally in *Ellery Queen's Mystery Magazine*. Copyright 1948. Reprinted by permission of the author.

Actually, a murderer is quite normal, merely possessing greater courage to act on the universal conviction that the true golden rule is "Every man for himself."

It is for this reason, therefore—to provide authentic data for the detective-story writer—that I have decided to make public my experience of murder. I have been fortunate in being so clever that I am able to relate this experience without fear of unpleasant consequences.

I felt no animosity toward Susan Braithwaite, personally, when I killed her, though some might consider that I had reason to hate her. I had been very fond of her once and would have married her if she had not been so stupid as to choose Stanley Braithwaite for a husband. Still, as I consider myself a civilized man of the world, I had felt that if she wanted to marry money-bags, that was her own funeral.

I suppose it was the feminine in her which had attracted me, that was in turn more attracted to the obvious maleness of Braithwaite—a great lout of a fellow, but with the right sort of brains to make his way in the world. He had inherited a little money, and being a city man he was able to make the best use of it. He had made a fair income by dealing on the Stock Exchange, not by the haphazard methods of a gambler, but with the unspectacular method of the investor. It was typical of him that during the record boom on the Johannesburg Stock Exchange, brought about by the discovery of gold in the Orange Free State, he continued his phlegmatic way of taking a profit as soon as a deal showed any, in spite of the fever of optimism that raged on the Exchange. He was thus able to build up and consolidate a small fortune, and when the inevitable recession came, his funds were mostly liquid. Then, instead of being affected by the pervading depression, he quietly bought shares which had dropped to next to nothing and so almost doubled his already swollen fortune when the equally inevitable recovery took place. An infuriating man!

When I introduced him to Susan, she became greatly attracted by his masterful manner and the success which it spelled. In fact, she was carried away to such an extent that she flew to Europe with him—thus terminating our engagement.

I had hoped never to see her again.

Eighteen months later, on answering a knock at the back door of my house, I found Susan on the step, suitcase in hand. When she had comfortably settled herself on the Chesterfield couch in my study, she told me her story. I was not surprised at what she revealed. I could well imagine that Braithwaite's self-assured dominant maleness, which she had preferred to my modest intellectual qualities, would develop into a complacent egoism, ruling with efficient tyranny. When she could bear his insensitiveness no longer, she had walked out on him and had come to me, for she felt that I would help her for old times' sake.

She did not notice, however, that I was not enthusiastic at the prospect of helping her. Actually, I was highly displeased. After she had jilted me, I had worked her out of my system, at the same time making extensive improvements on my poultry farm. I had made the whole farm self-supporting, and with labor-saving devices and processes was able to run the whole place singlehanded, for I liked fowls and preferred to do all the work among them myself.

But with Susan there it would have been difficult to continue in the same satisfying way. I knew I would have to entertain her, which meant that I would have had to shelve some of the less important, yet essential work. My routine would probably have got interfered with, and the three thousand chickens, which were at the most awkward age, might have caught cold or contracted some other ailment they are susceptible to.

Unfortunately, I could not think of any valid-sounding excuse for refusing to help her. Also, she had timed her arrival well: she would have had to stay the night at least, for there was no place in the village where she could have found accommodation and there were no trains back to Johannesburg till the following morning. I knew that once the ice had been broken by letting her stay the night, it would have been even more difficult to send her away the next day. After all, I had once been very fond of her and during the delirium of that time I had told her that no matter what ultimately happened between us, if she was ever in trouble she was to count on my help; and as I pride myself on being a man of my word, I could not bear to think of her telling our common friends that in an emergency I proved to be a broken reed.

All this passed through my mind while she chattered away about the cruel things her husband had done to her; but under the pretense of listening I followed the trend of my own thoughts till I became annoyed at the calm way she took my sympathy for granted. From the bits of her conversation I did listen to, I guessed in what manner she wished me to help her, and my annoyance mounted.

I saw my little bit of money being spent on lawyers; my comfortable and satisfying life being disturbed; my future peace being threatened by complicated emotions; in short, the whole of my nicely settled life being completely upset. I became so enraged that I thought, "Really, I could wring her neck!"

The actual strangling was more difficult than one would have thought. But the inability to face her, which had led me to go round the back of the couch to get my hands round her throat, turned out to be an advantage. For by crouching behind the back of the couch I was able to press her neck and head firmly against it, and so, by hanging on like grim death, avoid my hands becoming dislodged by her violent kicking, hitting, and threshing for air. Also, when she went limp, I was in a comfortable enough position not to need to relax till I was sure she was dead.

Her face—dark blue with grotesquely protruding tongue—was rather shocking when contrasted with the pretty animated expression it had had a few minutes before; and her once glossy hair seemed to have lost its blue tints and had become a lifeless-looking black. Otherwise, the sight of Susan's body did not affect me much.

After making sure that Susan was dead, I pushed her tongue back into her mouth and proceeded to dispose of the body in the manner I had been stimulated to devise when reading of the difficulties other murderers had experienced in this respect. I started the process that night, for though there was no urgency, as it would be days or even weeks before there would be any serious inquiry as to Susan's whereabouts, I was keen on putting my idea to the test. The following morning I was up early as usual and busy at my farm routine.

One afternoon, about three weeks later, Sergeant Theron of the local police turned up at my place and wanted to know if I knew anything about a Mrs. Braithwaite.

Sergeant John Theron on duty was a different man from the of-duty Johnny Theron who occasionally, when suitably warmed, entertained us in the back yard of Wiggins' pub by giving a demonstration of Wild West six-shooting. He was a crack shot and crouching slightly, he would fire two guns from the hip with amazing accuracy, at the same time looking from side to side with melodramatic belligerency; then after each salvo he would spit on the muzzles of the revolvers to "cool" them, giving a thigh-slappingly funny impression of a cowboy hero surrounded by dastardly villains.

But Sergeant John Theron of the South African Police was an alert and intelligent policeman who took his work seriously, and I knew by the way his question was worded that he was sure I *did* know something about Mrs. Braithwaite.

I guessed that she had been reported missing and had been traced to my farm. I decided, therefore, to take Theron into my confidence. I told him briefly all about my association with Susan in the past, winding up by telling him that she had been to see me one evening about three weeks before, but that she had left again the same night.

He naturally wanted further particulars and also wanted to know why I had not come forward and reported to the police that I had seen her at a time later than that which the newspaper appeal had stated was the last time she had been seen. I explained that I never read newspapers, but even if I had read the appeal for information, I would not have reported her visit as she had been running away from her husband.

I went on to tell him that she had wanted me to help her, but that I had refused; that we had quarreled till she had finally got into such a rage that she had walked out of the house leaving her hat, gloves, and suitcase behind. In reply to his questions I said that I did not know where she had gone, or how she intended to manage without her suitcase, or whether she had had a handbag with her or not.

After exhausting the subject of Susan's visit, Theron asked to see her suitcase. I gave it to him. He found it unlocked and opened it. On top was a brown handbag, which on being turned out was found to contain some money, a pair of earrings, a pearl necklace, a diamond ring, the usual feminine requirements, and a few loose keys, one of which fitted the suitcase. After carefully examining the rest of the suitcase's contents, Theron then asked me what Mrs. Braithwaite had been wearing that night.

That question had come sooner than I had expected, but I gave him the previously thought-out answer which was a genuine-sounding yet worthlessly vague description of the clothes I had carefully packed, together with the handbag, in the suitcase three weeks before. I had opened the case with one of the keys I had found in the handbag. I had had to leave the suitcase unlocked as I did not want the problem of disposing of the key. Incidentally, I had done the packing of the clothes, shoes, etc., while wearing gloves. I had no intention of leaving fingerprints inside the case and so making the traditional mistake.

Theron listened closely to the description, then pulled out the one dress in the suitcase which had obviously been worn, and asked me if that was the dress Mrs. Braithwaite had worn that evening. Of course, I replied that it was not, but I knew that if that dress had already been described by anyone who had seen Susan going to my farm, that description would be more or less the same as the one I had given.

After asking a few more unimportant questions, Sergeant Theron left, taking the suitcase, and the hat and gloves with him.

The police did not visit me again for a few days. I went to the village for a drink on the evening of the week that Johnny Theron usually spent at the pub, but he did not put in an appearance that night.

But I knew that it would only be a matter of time before I saw him again, for Susan's trail definitely ended at my place, and the police would concentrate there until they had reason to look elsewhere. When Theron eventually came again, about a week later, he was accompanied by Constable Barry, a prematurely bald young man who had wooed and won the village belle, Renée Otto, by so maneuvering his courting that she never saw him without his helmet on—so the story went in the village, anyway. In charge of both Theron and Barry, however, was a man from the C.I.D. Headquarters in Johannesburg. This time the only words Sergeant Theron spoke throughout the morning were, "Mr. Williams, this is Inspector Ben Liebenberg."

I acknowledged the introduction and asked the Inspector what

I could do for him. He was a tall, handsome man, more like an actor than a detective. Afterward I learned that he was a very good mixer— of drinks. His hobby was inventing new recipes for cocktails and other mixed drinks. I was told this, and about his variation of a Green Mamba, which is as deadly as the snake, by Theron later, when he was able to have a drink with me again.

Inspector Liebenberg professed himself sorry to trouble me, but would I mind if he had a look around? Mrs. Braithwaite had definitely been seen coming to my place, and had equally definitely not been seen anywhere else; so he would like to satisfy himself that she was not hiding somewhere on my farm.

I assured him that I understood and that it would be a pleasure to show him over the farm.

As we examined the homestead, I explained to them that I liked to be independent of any outside assistance, so had made my house and farm as self-contained as possible. I showed them the coal bin in the kitchen, built like a small room and filled at the top from the outside, having a little square outlet flush with the floor, next to the coal-burning stove. Below the kitchen there was a concrete underground tank for storing rain water. It had a hand pump attached, and pipes were laid from it to the bathroom. The rest of my domestic water supply came from a large gravity tank on the roof, filled by a wind pump from a borehole.

I started the tour outside by taking them to the three-hundred-feet-long, subdivided, intensive-type poultry house where, judging by the sound, the thousands of Leghorn hens were riveting their eggs together. I showed the policemen the incubator room and the brooder house, which I also used for experimental batches of chickens or fowls.

I then took them to the large corrugated-iron barn which housed my machinery—a tractor, a threshing machine, a hammermill, and various smaller machines such as lucerne cutters, etc.; also my general farm equipment such as plows, harrows, steam drying tank, planters, cultivators, etc., and my stocks of food. For round the sides of the barn were rows of large storage tanks, variously containing whole and crushed maize, maize meal, meat meal, peanut meal, bone meal, lucerne meal, and the various other poultry and animal feed requirements I used for making up the different balanced rations.

I could see their eyes measuring the tanks, and the jotting down of copious mental notes.

In the open air again, I pointed out my cultivated lands—the lucerne fields green, owing to the water from the dam, but the maize and other lands a yellowy brown. In the distance we could just make out the few cows, oxen, and horses grazing on the uncultivated part of my farm.

When they had seen the whole farm, Inspector Liebenberg thanked me for my trouble and departed—rather depressed, I thought. I would have liked to suggest that perhaps twenty maids with twenty mops . . . but decided that it was unwise to trade on my security too much.

A week passed without event, though I began to get irritated by being under continuous surveillance. Even Constable Barry had altered his beat so that he was able to pass my gate which, though a fair distance from the homestead, enabled him to have a clear view across the lawns to the house and garage.

I decided to make a move and bring matters to a climax. My best plan, of course, was to make Crippen's mistake, and run away.

I therefore made preparations, and early one morning I departed in my car at high speed. I drove fast for about five miles, then abruptly slowed down, headed the car into the veld and hid it as much as possible in a bushy bit, well away from the road.

I walked the rest of the way to the underground caves not far from the famous Blyvooruitzicht gold mine. These caves, though extensive, are not beautiful and do not attract many visitors. I had decided that the police would have already searched them thoroughly, so the chances were that I would be undisturbed. I had brought a Coleman lamp, a camp Primus, and ample provisions, and soon settled comfortably in one of the smaller caverns.

I knew the fowls on the farm would be all right for a few days, as their food troughs held enough for about three days, and the water troughs with their ball valves would remain full. The eggs would accumulate in the batteries of nests and ultimately make a mess, but one cannot have murder without breaking eggs. The other animals would not starve and there was plenty of water lying about the place. The chickens were then old enough to do without artificial heat for warmth, only requiring a small economical glow from the lamps to collect them in groups at night.

So, with my mind at peace, I was able to relax and enjoy the two detective books which I had brought with me. The stories were very good, though I noticed, with satisfaction, that the various detectives required considerable assistance from their authors.

On the morning of the third day I imagined that things should be about ripe for me to put in an appearance again.

As luck would have it, it was Sergeant Theron who met me first when I stepped out of the car in front of my house. The human face is not designed to express amazement, excitement, satisfaction, curiosity, wonder, relief, official reserve, friendliness, and regret all at once, but Theron's did its best.

When he recovered he demanded to know where I had been. I told him that I had gone to the caves to see if Mrs. Braithwaite had not perhaps gone there and got lost and died there, and that I had become lost myself and had found my way out only that morning. He snapped his fingers in exasperation and I guessed that he had spread his net far and wide, but had not thought of looking for me so close at hand.

While he was thinking what he ought to do next, I looked around to get details of the impression of an upturned ant heap which I had received when I drove up.

I had expected to see signs of activity but nothing like what I saw then. Evidently the police had decided to use more than twenty maids, for the place was in a turmoil.

There were men everywhere—on the roof of the house, round the house, half under the house; there were men walking about with heads bent examining the ground, men digging at various places, men around the dam, round the borehole, in the fields, and on the lands. I could not see into the barn, but it must have been full of men, for outside the main double doors a collection of agricultural hardware was scattered like the throwback of a burrowing terrier.

But the most joyous sight was the long hen house. The hens had, very unwisely, all been chased outside so that the concrete floor inside could be examined. To lay the floor bare a six-inch layer of manured straw had first to be removed. This considerable task had already been mostly achieved, for the straw lay in large mounds outside, in front of the entrance doors.

Along the outside of the poultry house there were men trying to uncover the foundations, for whoever was in charge of the searching meant to leave no stone unturned. I write "trying" advisedly, for the diggers were being considerably hampered by the thousands of hens who had no place to go, but who were trying, with henlike persistence, to go back where they belonged. Hens are very conservative—besides, they had eggs to lay. There was a precarious and continually changing line of them along the narrow ledge between the mesh wire front of the house and the edge of the low front wall on which the wire front rested. And this was one of the walls the foundations of which the men were hoping to examine.

They were almost smothered in hens. When it wasn't hens, it was dust and dirt. A Leghorn is a very highly strung bird, and jumpy at the best of times. With Leghorns you have to keep up a continual chatter, or be forever silent. While I was watching, one of the men digging had to reply to a call from a distant policeman. His sudden shouted answer resulted in the thousands of hens leaping into the air as one bird, with, literally, a roaring of wings. The men became lost to view in a cloud consisting of a mixture of fine particles of manure, straw, earth, spilled food, and down.

I was not able to see more, for by then Theron had decided that I had better come along with him to the police station to answer some questions. At the station I was left in charge of Constable Hurndal, who received my nod of recognition rigidly. After a short delay Theron started questioning me, trying hard to give the impression that he did not attach much importance to my answers.

I was halfway through my third cigarette when a constable burst into the room and shouted, "We've found the body!"

I jumped up, and exclaimed, "How exciting! Where?"—a remark thoroughly in bad taste considering that I had known Mrs. Braithwaite well, but one that could not be interpreted as coming from a guilty and apprehensive mind. I turned to Theron who had been watching me closely and saw doubt in his eyes.

Not that it mattered whether I betrayed guilt or not. I was perfectly safe and could never give myself away no matter what trick they tried. But if I had shown any signs of a guilty conscience, Theron would have known definitely that I was a murderer. This I wanted to avoid, or there would not have been much future pleasure in visiting the pub. I did not mind his official suspicion, but his private certainty would have been different.

Theron continued the farce and also asked the constable where the body had been found. The latter went on, with less enthusiasm, to describe vaguely some spot in the uncultivated land. They both looked at me with a last hope that I might indicate they were getting warm. I said, "Fancy, I wouldn't have thought that was a good place to bury a body. This means that she was murdered, doesn't it?"

Of course they never found Susan's body on my farm, or anywhere else. Nor any trace of it. They examined the stove for any signs of human ash, they swept the chimney for the same purpose. They dug up the drains to see if I had possibly dissolved the body in a bath of chemicals. In short, they looked everywhere and tried every box of tricks possessed by the Johannesburg C.I.D. All to no avail.

Finally, they had to give up, baffled, and no matter how much they suspected that Susan had been murdered, they had no proof. In spite of a most thorough search of my farm, no body was found, and this fact plus no obvious motive on my part resulted in the cloud of suspicion hanging over my head gradually becoming dispersed.

That Christmas, to show that there was no ill feeling, I sent Sergeant Theron a brace of cockerels.

The months passed in uninterrupted peace. My content was marred only by the news that Sergeant Theron was leaving to join the Rhodesian Police.

We gave him a fine farewell party, Bill Wiggins providing the drinks, while I contributed the poultry. Poor Johnny was not able to give us a last demonstration of six-shooting that night, for when we went out into the yard the fresh air had a bad effect on him, and it took him all his time to stay relatively upright, hanging on to the swaying washing lines.

The building of a new brooder house began to occupy all my thoughts. But doing it by myself took all my time, with the result that I could not keep my house clean and tidy. So after much indecision, I engaged a housekeeper—a blonde, tall, but giving the impression of childlike plumpness. She is most efficient, yet her warm smile suggests that she could be very kind and affectionate.

It is because she runs the house so well that I now have time in the evening to write this record of my experience with homicide.

I am looking forward to having an interesting time should I get this published. I am particularly curious about Theron's reaction should he read this and so learn the make-up and constitution of those plump chickens he so enjoyed.

I suppose he will be disgusted, though he need not be. After all, how was he to know that those chickens had been feeding on the body of Susan Braithwaite?

I do not mean by crudely pecking at it. On the contrary, the fowls ate Susan in well-balanced rations. Every bit of her body had been through the hammermill, to be ground into fine bone meal and meat meal. A separate process made blood meal.

These processes entailed no difficulty as I had learned how to do it from an article in the *Farmers' Magazine*, and had been doing it with animal carcasses long before. And as far as the hammermill process is concerned, human bodies, not requiring to be skinned and having smaller bones, are much easier to manage.

I had only to take extra care that every single piece of the body was powdered. The teeth I had to put through the milling process a couple of times till they became indistinguishable from the rest of the bone meal. The hair I burned on the head, making a sort of charcoal.

After I had processed the body, I wiped everything that it had touched with handfuls of green lucerne, which in turn was ground fine. Animal carcasses were then put through the mill, followed by heaps of lucerne and bags of maize, so that all traces of human cells were completely removed from the machine.

The meat meal, bone meal, and blood meal were made into a ration with other foodstuffs and were fed to my experimental batch of chicks—and what fine chickens they grew into, as Theron can testify. As a matter of fact, I have established quite a reputation for fine pullets and cockerels, and other poultry farmers have pestered me for the recipe of my balanced ration.

This will surely be brought to the attention of Inspector Liebenberg, who now, knowing where to look, may try to find some proof that there was once a human body on my farm. But I am certain he will not succeed. It would be no use slaughtering fowls wholesale, in an attempt to find the ones that have partaken of Susan—with the object of testing them for any traces of human cells in their make-up. I have seen to it that every fowl that shared that human ration has itself been consumed by other humans.

As people do not eat the bones of fowls, I made a point of selling, or giving, the dressed fowls only on condition that I was allowed to collect the bones afterward. My explanation of this was that I was short of bone meal. These bones then went through the mill with other bones. A nice example of *ad infinitum*. Also, there are a large number of anonymous people who, in a remoter degree, took part in this deplorable cannibalism. I mean those who ate the eggs that were laid by the hens.

Then Inspector Liebenberg will no doubt think of the manure. I wouldn't bother if I were he. Every bit of it has been spread over my uncultivated land and thoroughly plowed in. Alas for the Inspector, the plucked feathers, heads, legs, feet, and innards of the dressed fowls sold or given away, after being burned or steam dried, also did not escape a hammering from the relentless mill.

I hope the good Inspector is not driven to trying to make this story of mine have the value of a legal confession. It would be a great pity if an ardent student of detective fiction, desirous of seeing a story of his own published, should be arrested because he invented a feasible explanation to account for the disappearance of a woman he happened to know.

I suppose I must also expect a certain amount of unpleasantness if this is read in our village. Some narrow-minded people will no doubt look upon me with horror and others will fear me. Since the main result of such attitudes will be that I shall no longer be pestered by casual callers, I shall be only too pleased.

A new development has occurred. My housekeeper, Ann Lissen, may turn out to be a disappointment after all. She is evidently falling, or has already fallen, in love with me and is becoming tiresome. Her solicitude on my behalf is overwhelming and I now seem to have no privacy left, for she is always fussing about doing things to add to my comfort.

I would not like to hurt her feelings by telling her to stop doing what she does out of the kindness of her heart. And as she has no technical qualifications, it would be a shame to send her away to battle for a job again.

I have suggested to her that she should go out more, especially in the evenings, but she said it was dull going about alone. She has no friends, or even relations.

Poor thing! She has no one to miss her, and I am most eager to rear especially good stock next season, fed with rich and well-balanced rations. The President of the National Poultry Society has expressed a desire to see my farm and the fine pullets and cockerels for which I am now so justly famous.

LUKUNDOO

BY EDWARD LUCAS WHITE

❑ "IT STANDS TO REASON," said Twombly, "that a man must accept the evidence of his own eyes, and when eyes and ears agree, there can be no doubt. He has to believe what he has both seen and heard."

"Not always," put in Singleton, softly.

Every man turned toward Singleton. Twombly was standing on the hearth rug, his back to the grate, his legs spread out, with his habitual air of dominating the room. Singleton, as usual, was as much as possible effaced in a corner. But when Singleton spoke he said something. We faced him in that flattering spontaneity of expectant silence which invites utterance.

"I was thinking," he said, after an interval, "of something I both saw and heard in Africa."

Now, if there was one thing we had found impossible it had been to elicit from Singleton anything definite about his African experiences. As with the Alpinist in the story, who could tell only that he went up and came down, the sum of Singleton's revelations had been that he went there and came away. His words now riveted our attention at once. Twombly faded from the hearth rug, but not one of us could ever recall having seen him go. The room readjusted itself, focused on Singleton, and there was some hasty and furtive lighting of fresh cigars. Singleton lit one also, but it went out immediately, and he never relit it.

From *Lukundoo and Other Stories,* published by George H. Doran Company, copyright 1927.

I

We were in the Great Forest, exploring for Pygmies. Van Rieten had a theory that the dwarfs found by Stanley and others were a mere cross-breed between ordinary Negroes and the real Pygmies. He hoped to discover a race of men three feet tall at most, or shorter. We had found no trace of any such beings.

Natives were few, game scarce; food, except game, there was none; and the deepest, dankest, drippingest forest all about. We were the only novelty in the country, no native we met had even seen a white man before, most had never heard of white men. All of a sudden, late one afternoon, there came into our camp an Englishman, and pretty well used up he was, too. We had heard no rumor of him; he had not only heard of us but had made an amazing five-day march to reach us. His guide and two bearers were nearly as done up as he. Even though he was in tatters and had five days' beard on, you could see he was naturally dapper and neat and the sort of man to shave daily. He was small, but wiry. His face was the sort of British face from which emotion has been so carefully banished that a foreigner is apt to think the wearer of the face incapable of any sort of feeling; the kind of face which, if it has any expression at all, expresses principally the resolution to go through the world decorously, without intruding upon or annoying anyone.

His name was Etcham. He introduced himself modestly, and ate with us so deliberately that we should never have suspected, if our bearers had not had it from his bearers, that he had had but three meals in the five days, and those small. After we had lit up he told us why he had come.

"My chief is ve'y seedy," he said between puffs. "He is bound to go out if he keeps this way. I thought perhaps . . ."

He spoke quietly in a soft, even tone, but I could see little beads of sweat oozing out on his upper lip under his stubby mustache, and there was a tingle of repressed emotion in his tone, a veiled eagerness in his eye, a palpitating inward solicitude in his demeanor that moved me at once. Van Rieten had no sentiment in him; if he was moved he did not show it. But he listened. I was surprised at that. He was just

the man to refuse at once. But he listened to Etcham's halting, diffi-
dent hints. He even asked questions.

"Who is your chief?"

"Stone," Etcham lisped.

That electrified both of us.

"Ralph Stone?" we ejaculated together.

Etcham nodded.

For some minutes Van Rieten and I were silent. Van Rieten had
never seen him, but I had been a classmate of Stone's, and Van Rieten
and I had discussed him over many a campfire. We had heard of him
two years before, south of Luebo in the Balunda country, which had
been ringing with his theatrical strife against a Balunda witch doctor,
ending in the sorcerer's complete discomfiture and the abasement of
his tribe before Stone. They had even broken the fetish-man's whistle
and given Stone the pieces. It had been like the triumph of Elijah over
the prophets of Baal, only more real to the Balunda.

We had thought of Stone as far off, if still in Africa at all, and
here he turned up ahead of us and probably forestalling our quest.

II

Etcham's naming of Stone brought back to us all his tantalizing
story, his fascinating parents, their tragic death; the brilliance of his
college days; the dazzle of his millions; the promise of his young man-
hood; his wide notoriety, so nearly real fame; his romantic elopement
with the meteoric authoress whose sudden cascade of fiction had made
her so great a name so young, whose beauty and charm were so much
heralded; the frightful scandal of the breach-of-promise suit that followed; his bride's devotion through it all; their sudden quarrel after
it was all over; their divorce; the too much advertised announcement
of his approaching marriage to the plaintiff in the breach-of-promise
suit; his precipitate remarriage to his divorced bride; their second
quarrel and second divorce; his departure from his native land; his
advent in the Dark Continent. The sense of all this rushed over me
and I believe Van Rieten felt it, too, as he sat silent.

Then he asked, "Where is Werner?"

"Dead," said Etcham. "He died before I joined Stone."

"You were not with Stone above Luebo?"

"No," said Etcham, "I joined him at Stanley Falls."

"Who is with him?" Van Rieten asked.

"Only his Zanzibar servants and the bearers," Etcham replied.

"What sort of bearers?" Van Rieten demanded.

"Mang-Battu men," Etcham responded simply.

Now that impressed both Van Rieten and myself greatly. It bore out Stone's reputation as a notable leader of men. For up to that time no one had been able to use Mang-Battu as bearers outside of their own country, or to hold them for long or difficult expeditions.

"Were you long among the Mang-Battu?" was Van Rieten's next question.

"Some weeks," said Etcham. "Stone was interested in them and made up a fair-sized vocabulary of their words and phrases. He had a theory that they are an offshoot of the Balunda and he found much confirmation in their customs."

"What do you live on?" Van Rieten inquired.

"Game, mostly," Etcham lisped.

"How long has Stone been laid up?" Van Rieten next asked.

"More than a month," Etcham answered.

"And you have been hunting for the camp?" Van Rieten exclaimed.

Etcham's face, burnt and flayed as it was, showed a flush.

"I missed some easy shots," he admitted ruefully. "I've not felt ve'y fit myself."

"What's the matter with your chief?" Van Rieten enquired.

"Something like carbuncles," Etcham replied.

"He ought to get over a carbuncle or two," Van Rieten declared.

"They are not carbuncles," Etcham explained. "Nor one or two. He has had dozens, sometimes five at once. If they had been carbuncles he would have been dead long ago. But in some ways they are not so bad, though in others they are worse."

"How do you mean?" Van Rieten queried.

"Well," Etcham hesitated, "they do not seem to inflame so deep nor so wide as carbuncles, nor to be so painful, nor to cause so much fever. But then they seem to be part of a disease that affects his mind.

He let me help him dress the first, but the others he has hidden most carefully, from me and from the men. He keeps to his tent when they puff up, and will not let me change the dressings or be with him at all."

"Have you plenty of dressings?" Van Rieten asked.

"We have some," said Etcham doubtfully. "But he won't use them; he washes out the dressings and uses them over and over."

"How is he treating the swellings?" Van Rieten enquired.

"He slices them off clear down to flesh level, with his razor."

"What?" Van Rieten shouted.

Etcham made no answer but looked him steadily in the eyes.

"I beg pardon," Van Rieten hastened to say. "You startled me. They can't be carbuncles. He'd have been dead long ago."

"I thought I had said they are not carbuncles," Etcham lisped.

"But the man must be crazy!" Van Rieten exclaimed.

"Just so," said Etcham. "He is beyond my advice or control."

"How many has he treated that way?" Van Rieten demanded.

"Two, to my knowledge," Etcham said.

"Two?" Van Rieten queried.

Etcham flushed again.

"I saw him," he confessed, "through a crack in the hut. I felt impelled to keep a watch on him, as if he was not responsible."

"I should think not," Van Rieten agreed. "And you saw him do that twice?"

"I conjecture," said Etcham, "that he did the like with all the rest."

"How many has he had?" Van Rieten asked.

"Dozens," Etcham lisped.

"Does he eat?" Van Rieten enquired.

"Like a wolf," said Etcham. "More than any two bearers."

"Can he walk?" Van Rieten asked.

"He crawls a bit, groaning," said Etcham simply.

"Little fever, you say," Van Rieten ruminated.

"Enough and too much," Etcham declared.

"Has he been delirious?" Van Rieten asked.

"Only twice," Etcham replied; "once when the first swelling broke, and once later. He would not let anyone come near him then.

But we could hear him talking, talking steadily, and it scared the natives."

"Was he talking their patter in delirium?" Van Rieten demanded.

"No," said Etcham, "but he was talking some similar lingo. Hamed Burghash said he was talking Balunda. I know too little Balunda. I do not learn languages readily. Stone learned more Mang-Battu in a week than I could have learned in a year. But I seemed to hear words like Mang-Battu words. Anyhow the Mang-Battu bearers were scared."

"Scared?" Van Rieten repeated, questioningly.

"So were the Zanzibar men, even Hamed Burghash, and so was I," said Etcham, "only for a different reason. He talked in two voices."

"In two voices," Van Rieten reflected.

"Yes," said Etcham, more excitedly than he had yet spoken. "In two voices, like a conversation. One was his own, one a small, thin, bleaty voice like nothing I ever heard. I seemed to make out, among the sounds the deep voice made, something like Mang-Battu words I knew, as *nedru, metababa,* and *nedo,* their terms for 'head,' 'shoulder,' 'thigh,' and perhaps *kudra* and *nekere* ('speak' and 'whistle') ; and among the noises of the shrill voice *matomipa, angunzi,* and *kamomami* ('kill,' 'death,' and 'hate'). Hamed Burghash said he also heard those words. He knew Mang-Battu far better than I."

"What did the bearers say?" Van Rieten asked.

"They said, '*Lukundoo, Lukundoo!*' " Etcham replied. "I did not know that word; Hamed Burghash said it was Mang-Battu for 'leopard.' "

"It's Mang-Battu for 'witchcraft,' " said Van Rieten.

"I don't wonder they thought so," said Etcham. "It was enough to make one believe in sorcery to listen to those two voices."

"One voice answering the other?" Van Rieten asked perfunctorily.

Etcham's face went gray under his tan.

"Sometimes both at once," he answered huskily.

"Both at once!" Van Rieten ejaculated.

"It sounded that way to the men, too," said Etcham. "And that was not all."

He stopped and looked helplessly at us for a moment.

"Could a man talk and whistle at the same time?" he asked.

"How do you mean?" Van Rieten queried.

"We could hear Stone talking away, his big, deep-chested baritone rumbling along, and through it all we could hear a high, shrill whistle, the oddest, wheezy sound. You know, no matter how shrilly a grown man may whistle, the note has a different quality from the whistle of a boy or a woman or a little girl. They sound more treble, somehow. Well, if you can imagine the smallest girl who could whistle keeping it up tunelessly right along, that whistle was like that, only even more piercing, and it sounded right through Stone's bass tones."

"And you didn't go to him?" Van Rieten cried.

"He is not given to threats," Etcham disclaimed. "But he had threatened, not volubly, nor like a sick man, but quietly and firmly, that if any man of us (he lumped me in with the men), came near him while he was in his trouble, that man should die. And it was not so much his words as his manner. It was like a monarch commanding respected privacy for a deathbed. One simply could not transgress."

"I see," said Van Rieten shortly.

"He's ve'y seedy," Etcham repeated helplessly. "I thought perhaps . . ."

His absorbing affection for Stone, his real love for him, shone out through his envelope of conventional training. Worship of Stone was plainly his master passion.

Like many competent men, Van Rieten had a streak of hard selfishness in him. It came to the surface then. He said we carried our lives in our hands from day to day just as genuinely as Stone; that he did not forget the ties of blood and calling between any two explorers, but that there was no sense in imperiling one party for a very problematical benefit to a man probably beyond any help; that it was enough of a task to hunt for one party; that if two were united, providing food would be more than doubly difficult; that the risk of starvation was too great. Deflecting our march seven full days' journey (he complimented Etcham on his marching powers) might ruin our expedition entirely.

III

Van Rieten had logic on his side and he had a way with him. Etcham sat there apologetic and deferential, like a fourth-form schoolboy before a head master. Van Rieten wound up. "I am after Pygmies, at the risk of my life. After Pygmies I go." "Perhaps, then, these will interest you," said Etcham, very quietly.

He took two objects out of the sidepocket of his blouse, and handed them to Van Rieten. They were round, bigger than big plums, and smaller than small peaches, about the right size to enclose in an average hand. They were black, and at first I did not see what they were.

"Pygmies!" Van Rieten exclaimed. "Pygmies, indeed! Why, they wouldn't be two feet high! Do you mean to claim that these are adult heads?"

"I claim nothing," Etcham answered evenly. "You can see for yourself."

Van Rieten passed one of the heads to me. The sun was just setting and I examined it closely. A dried head it was, perfectly preserved, and the flesh as hard as Argentine jerked beef. A bit of a vertebra stuck out where the muscles of the vanished neck had shriveled into folds. The puny chin was sharp on a projecting jaw, the minute teeth white and even between the retracted lips, the tiny nose was flat, the little forehead retreating, there were inconsiderable clumps of stunted wool on the Lilliputian cranium. There was nothing babyish, childish or youthful about the head, rather it was mature to senility.

"Where did these come from?" Van Rieten inquired.

"I do not know," Etcham replied precisely. "I found them among Stone's effects while rummaging for medicines or drugs or anything that could help me to help him. I do not know where he got them. But I'll swear he did not have them when we entered this district."

"Are you sure?" Van Rieten queried, his eyes big and fixed on Etcham's.

"Ve'y sure," lisped Etcham.

"But how could he have come by them without your knowledge?"
Van Rieten demurred.

"Sometimes we were apart ten days at a time hunting," said
Etcham. "Stone is not a talking man. He gave me no account of his
doings and Hamed Burghash keeps a still tongue and a tight hold on
the men."

"You have examined these heads?" Van Rieten asked.

"Minutely," said Etcham.

Van Rieten took out his notebook. He was a methodical chap.
He tore out a leaf, folded it and divided it equally into three pieces.
He gave one to me and one to Etcham.

"Just for a test of my impressions," he said, "I want each of us
to write separately just what he is most reminded of by these heads.
Then I want to compare the writings."

I handed Etcham a pencil and he wrote. Then he handed the pencil back to me and I wrote.

"Read the three," said Van Rieten, handing me his piece.

Van Rieten had written, "An old Balunda witch doctor."

Etcham had written, "An old Mang-Battu fetish-man."

I had written, "An old Katongo magician."

"There!" Van Rieten exclaimed. "Look at that! There is nothing
Wagabi or Batwa or Wambuttu or Wabotu about these heads. Nor
anything Pygmy either."

"I thought as much," said Etcham.

"And you say he did not have them before?"

"To a certainty he did not," Etcham asserted.

"It is worth following up," said Van Rieten. "I'll go with you.
And first of all, I'll do my best to save Stone."

He put out his hand and Etcham clasped it silently. He was grateful all over.

IV

Nothing but Etcham's fever of solicitude could have taken him in
five days over the track. It took him eight days to retrace with full
knowledge of it and our party to help. We could not have done it in

seven, and Etcham urged us on, in a repressed fury of anxiety, no mere fever of duty to his chief, but a real ardor of devotion, a glow of personal adoration for Stone which blazed under his dry conventional exterior and showed in spite of him.

We found Stone well cared for. Etcham had seen to a good, high thorn *zareeba* round the camp, the huts were well built and thatched and Stone's was as good as their resources would permit. Hamed Burghash was not named after two Seyyids for nothing. He had in him the making of a sultan. He had kept the Mang-Battu together, not a man had slipped off, and he had kept them in order. Also he was a deft nurse and a faithful servant.

The two other Zanzibaris had done some creditable hunting. Though all were hungry, the camp was far from starvation.

Stone was on a canvas cot and there was a sort of collapsible camp-stool-table, like a Turkish tabouret, by the cot. It had a water-bottle and some vials on it and Stone's watch, also his razor in its case.

Stone was clean and not emaciated, but he was far gone; not unconscious, but in a daze; past commanding or resisting anyone. He did not seem to see us enter or to know we were there. I should have recognized him anywhere. His boyish dash and grace had vanished utterly, of course. But his head was even more leonine; his hair was still abundant, yellow and wavy; the close, crisped blond beard he had grown during his illness did not alter him. He was big and big-chested yet. His eyes were dull and he mumbled and babbled mere meaningless syllables, not words.

Etcham helped Van Rieten to uncover him and look him over. He was in good muscle for a man so long bedridden. There were no scars on him except about his knees, shoulders and chest. On each knee and above it he had a full score of roundish cicatrices, and a dozen or more on each shoulder, all in front. Two or three were open wounds and four or five barely healed. He had no fresh swellings, except two, one on each side, on his pectoral muscles, the one on the left being higher up and farther out than the other. They did not look like boils or carbuncles, but as if something blunt and hard were being pushed up through the fairly healthy flesh and skin, not much inflamed.

"I should not lance those," said Van Rieten, and Etcham assented. They made Stone as comfortable as they could, and just before sunset we looked in at him again. He was lying on his back, and his chest showed big and massive yet, but he lay as if in a stupor. We left Etcham with him and went into the next hut, which Etcham had resigned to us. The jungle noises were no different there than anywhere else for months past, and I was soon fast asleep.

V

Sometime in the pitch dark I found myself awake and listening. I could hear two voices, one Stone's, the other sibilant and wheezy. I knew Stone's voice after all the years that had passed since I heard it last. The other was like nothing I remembered. It had less volume than the wail of a newborn baby, yet there was an insistent carrying power to it, like the shrilling of an insect. As I listened I heard Van Rieten breathing near me in the dark, then he heard me and realized that I was listening, too. Like Etcham I knew little Balunda, but I could make out a word or two. The voices alternated with intervals of silence between.

Then suddenly both sounded at once and fast. Stone's baritone basso, full as if he were in perfect health, and that incredibly stridulous falsetto, both jabbering at once like the voices of two people quarreling and trying to talk each other down.

"I can't stand this," said Van Rieten. "Let's have a look at him."

He had one of those cylindrical electric night candles. He fumbled about for it, touched the button and beckoned me to come with him. Outside of the hut he motioned me to stand still, and instinctively turned off the light, as if seeing made listening difficult.

Except for a faint glow from the embers of the bearers' fire we were in complete darkness, little starlight struggled through the trees, the river made but a faint murmur. We could hear the two voices together and then suddenly the creaking voice changed into a razor-edged, slicing whistle, indescribably cutting, continuing right through Stone's grumbling torrent of croaking words.

"Good God!" exclaimed Van Rieten.

Abruptly he turned on the light.

We found Etcham utterly asleep, exhausted by his long anxiety and the exertions of his phenomenal march and relaxed completely now that the load was in a sense shifted from his shoulders to Van Rieten's. Even the light on his face did not wake him.

The whistle had ceased and the two voices now sounded together. Both came from Stone's cot, where the concentrated white ray showed him lying just as we had left him, except that he had tossed his arms above his head and had torn the coverings and bandages from his chest.

The swelling on his right breast had broken. Van Rieten aimed the center line of the light at it and we saw it plainly. From his flesh, grown out of it, there protruded a head, such a head as the dried specimens Etcham had shown us, as if it were a miniature of the head of a Balunda fetish-man. It was black, shining black as the blackest African skin; it rolled the whites of its wicked, wee eyes and showed its microscopic teeth between lips repulsively Negroid in their red fullness, even in so diminutive a face. It had crisp, fuzzy wool on its minikin skull, it turned malignantly from side to side and chittered incessantly in that inconceivable falsetto. Stone babbled brokenly against its patter.

Van Rieten turned from Stone and waked Etcham, with some difficulty. When he was awake and saw it all, Etcham stared and said not one word.

"You saw him slice off two swellings?" Van Rieten asked.

Etcham nodded, chokingly.

"Did he bleed much?" Van Rieten demanded.

"Ve'y little," Etcham replied.

"You hold his arms," said Van Rieten to Etcham.

He took up Stone's razor and handed me the light. Stone showed no sign of seeing the light or of knowing we were there. But the little head mewled and screeched at us.

Van Rieten's hand was steady, and the sweep of the razor even and true. Stone bled amazingly little and Van Rieten dressed the wound as if it had been a bruise or scrape.

Stone had stopped talking the instant the excrescent head was severed. Van Rieten did all that could be done for Stone and then fairly grabbed the light from me. Snatching up a gun he scanned the ground by the cot and brought the butt down once and twice, viciously.

We went back to our hut, but I doubt if I slept.

VI

Next day, near noon, in broad daylight, we heard the two voices from Stone's hut. We found Etcham dropped asleep by his charge. The swelling on the left had broken, and just such another head was there miauling and spluttering. Etcham woke up and the three of us stood there and glared. Stone interjected hoarse vocables into the tinkling gurgle of the portent's utterance.

Van Rieten stepped forward, took up Stone's razor and knelt down by the cot. The atomy of a head squealed a wheezy snarl at him.

Then suddenly Stone spoke English.

"Who are you with my razor?"

Van Rieten started back and stood up.

Stone's eyes were clear now and bright, they roved about the hut.

"The end," he said; "I recognize the end. I seem to see Etcham, as if in life. But Singleton! Ah, Singleton! Ghosts of my boyhood come to watch me pass! And you, strange specter with the black beard and my razor! Aroint ye all!"

"I'm no ghost, Stone," I managed to say. "I'm alive. So are Etcham and Van Rieten. We are here to help you."

"Van Rieten!" he exclaimed. "My work passes on to a better man. Luck go with you, Van Rieten."

Van Rieten went nearer to him.

"Just hold still a moment, old man," he said soothingly. "It will be only one twinge."

"I've held still for many such twinges," Stone answered quite distinctly. "Let me be. Let me die in my own way. The hydra was nothing to this. You can cut off ten, a hundred, a thousand heads, but the curse you can not cut off, or take off. What's soaked into the bone won't come out of the flesh, any more than what's bred there. Don't hack me any more. Promise!"

His voice had all the old commanding tone of his boyhood and it swayed Van Rieten as it always had swayed everybody.

"I promise," said Van Rieten.

Almost as he said the word Stone's eyes filmed again.

Then we three sat about Stone and watched that hideous, gibbering prodigy grow up out of Stone's flesh, till two horrid, spindling little black arms disengaged themselves. The infinitesimal nails were perfect to the barely perceptible moon at the quick, the pink spot on the palm was horridly natural. These arms gesticulated and the right plucked toward Stone's blond beard.

"I can't stand this," Van Rieten exclaimed and took up the razor again.

Instantly Stone's eyes opened, hard and glittering.

"Van Rieten break his word?" he enunciated slowly. "Never!"

"But we must help you," Van Rieten gasped.

"I am past all help and all hurting," said Stone. "This is my hour. This curse is not put on me; it grew out of me, like this horror here. Even now I go."

His eyes closed and we stood helpless, the adherent figure spouting shrill sentences.

In a moment Stone spoke again.

"You speak all tongues?" he asked quickly. And the emergent minikin replied in sudden English, "Yea, verily, all that you speak," putting out its microscopic tongue, writhing its lips and wagging its head from side to side. We could see the thready ribs on its exiguous flanks heave as if the thing breathed.

"Has she forgiven me?" Stone asked in a muffled strangle.

"Not while the moss hangs from the cypresses," the head squeaked. "Not while the stars shine on Lake Pontchartrain will she forgive."

And then Stone, all with one motion, wrenched himself over on his side. The next instant he was dead.

When Singleton's voice ceased the room was hushed for a space. We could hear each other breathing. Twombly, the tactless, broke the silence.

"I presume," he said, "you cut off the little minikin and brought it home in alcohol."

Singleton turned on him a stern countenance.

"We buried Stone," he said, "unmutilated as he died."

"But," said the unconscionable Twombly, "the whole thing is incredible."

Singleton stiffened.

"I did not expect you to believe it," he said; "I began by saying that although I heard and saw it, when I look back on it I cannot credit it myself."

```
┌─────────────────────────────────────────────┐
│                                             │
│   A WOMAN SELDOM FOUND                      │
│                                             │
│                      BY WILLIAM SANSOM      │
│                                             │
└─────────────────────────────────────────────┘
```

❡ ONCE a young man was on a visit to Rome.

It was his first visit; he came from the country but he was neither on the one hand so young nor on the other so simple as to imagine that a great and beautiful capital should hold out finer promises than any·· where else. He already knew that life was largely illusion, that though wonderful things could happen, nevertheless as many disappointments came in compensation: and he knew, too, that life could offer a quality even worse—the probability that nothing would happen at all. This was always more possible in a great city intent on its own business.

Thinking in this way, he stood on the Spanish steps and surveyed the momentous panorama stretched before him. He listened to the swelling hum of the evening traffic and watched as the lights went up against Rome's golden dusk. Shining automobiles slunk past the fountains and turned urgently into the bright Via Condotti, neon-red signs stabbed the shadows with invitation; the yellow windows of buses were packed with faces intent on going somewhere—everyone in the city seemed intent on the evening's purpose. He alone had nothing to do.

He felt himself the only person alone of everyone in the city. But searching for adventure never brought it—rather kept it away. Such a mood promised nothing. So the young man turned back up the steps, passed the lovely church, and went on up the cobbled hill toward his

From *A Contest of Ladies* by William Sansom. Reprinted by permission of the author. Reynal & Company, Inc., New York, and The Hogarth Press, London.

hotel. Wine bars and food shops jostled with growing movement in those narrow streets. But out on the broad pavements of the Vittorio Veneto, under the trees mounting to the Borghese Gardens, the high world of Rome would be filling the most elegant cafés in Europe to enjoy with apéritifs the twilight. That would be the loneliest of all! So the young man kept to the quieter, older streets on his solitary errand home.

In one such street, a pavementless alley between old yellow houses, a street that in Rome might suddenly blossom into a secret piazza of fountain and baroque church, a grave secluded treasure-place—he noticed that he was alone but for the single figure of a woman walking down the hill toward him.

As she drew nearer, he saw that she was dressed with taste, that in her carriage was a soft Latin fire, that she walked for respect. Her face was veiled, but it was impossible to imagine that she would not be beautiful. Isolated thus with her, passing so near to her, and she symbolizing the adventure of which the evening was so empty—a greater melancholy gripped him. He felt wretched as the gutter, small, sunk, pitiful. So that he rounded his shoulders and lowered his eyes—but not before casting one furtive glance into hers.

He was so shocked at what he saw that he paused, he stared, shocked, into her face. He had made no mistake. She was smiling. Also—she too had hesitated. He thought instantly: "Whore?" But no—it was not that kind of smile, though as well it was not without affection. And then amazingly she spoke.

"I—I know I shouldn't ask you . . . but it is such a beautiful evening—and perhaps you are alone, as alone as I am. . . ."

She was very beautiful. He could not speak. But a growing elation gave him the power to smile. So that she continued, still hesitant, in no sense soliciting.

"I thought . . . perhaps . . . we could take a walk, an apéritif. . . ."

At last the young man achieved himself.

"Nothing, *nothing* would please me more. And the Veneto is only a minute up there."

She smiled again.

"My home is just here. . . ."

They walked in silence a few paces down the street, to a turning the young man had already passed. This she indicated. They walked to where the first humble houses ended in a kind of recess. In the recess was set the wall of a garden, and behind it stood a large and elegant mansion. The woman, about whose face shone a curious pale glitter —something fused of the transparent pallor of fine skin, of gray but brilliant eyes, of dark eyebrows and hair of lucent black—inserted her key in the garden gate.

They were greeted by a servant in velvet livery. In a large and exquisite salon, under chandeliers of fine glass and before a moist green courtyard where water played, they were served with a frothy wine. They talked. The wine—iced in the warm Roman night—filled them with an inner warmth of exhilaration. But from time to time the young man looked at her curiously.

With her glances, with many subtle inflections of teeth and eyes she was inducing an intimacy that suggested much. He felt he must be careful. At length he thought the best thing might be to thank her —somehow thus to root out whatever obligation might be in store. But here she interrupted him, first with a smile, then with a look of some sadness. She begged him to spare himself any perturbation; she knew it was strange, that in such a situation he might suspect some second purpose; but the simple truth remained that she was lonely and—this with a certain deference—something perhaps in him, perhaps in that moment of dusk in the street, had proved to her inescapably attractive. She had not been able to help herself.

The possibility of a perfect encounter—a dream that years of disillusion will never quite kill—decided him. His elation rose beyond control. He believed her. And thereafter the perfections compounded. At her invitation they dined. Servants brought food of great delicacy; shellfish, fat bird flesh, soft fruits. And afterward they sat on a sofa near the courtyard, where it was cool. Liqueurs were brought. The servants retired. A hush fell upon the house. They embraced.

A little later, with no word, she took his arm and led him from the room. How deep a silence had fallen between them! The young man's heart beat fearfully—it might be heard, he felt, echoing in the hall whose marble they now crossed, sensed through his arm to hers. But such excitement rose now from certainty. Certainty that at such a moment, on such a charmed evening—nothing could go wrong. There was no need to speak. Together they mounted the great staircase.

In her bedroom, to the picture of her framed by the bed curtains and dimly naked in a silken shift, he poured out his love; a love that was to be eternal, to be always perfect, as fabulous as this their exquisite meeting.

Softly she spoke the return of his love. Nothing would ever go amiss, nothing would ever come between them. And very gently she drew back the bedclothes for him.

But suddenly, at the moment when at last he lay beside her, when his lips were almost upon hers—he hesitated.

Something was wrong. A flaw could be sensed. He listened, felt—and then saw the fault was his. Shaded, soft-shaded lights by the bed —but he had been so careless as to leave on the bright electric chandelier in the center of the ceiling. He remembered the switch was by the door. For a fraction, then, he hesitated. She raised her eyelids—saw his glance at the chandelier, understood.

Her eyes glittered. She murmured, "My beloved, don't worry—don't move. . . ."

And she reached out her hand. Her hand grew larger, her arm grew longer and longer, it stretched out through the bedcurtains, across the long carpet, huge and overshadowing the whole of the long room, until at last its giant fingers were at the door. With a terminal click, she switched out the light.

THE PERFECTIONIST

BY MARGARET ST. CLAIR

❦ I HAD nightmares about it for several years afterward—the kind where something is on your heels, and you make desperate efforts, each more futile than the last, to escape it—and always felt bad about them when I woke up. I never could decide whether I was justified in having bad dreams at all.

It began when I went to live with Aunt Muriel in 1933. I hadn't had a job for six months when I got the letter of invitation from her, and I hadn't eaten much at all for two weeks.

Aunt Muriel wasn't exactly my aunt, to begin with. She was a sort of great-aunt, once removed, on my mother's side, and I hadn't seen her since I was a beady-eyed kid in knee breeches.

The invitation might have surprised me—though she explained in the letter that she was an old woman, getting lonely, and felt the need of some kindred face near her—only I was too hungry to wonder.

There was a money order in the letter, and a ticket to Downie, where she lived. After I paid the back room rent with the money order and got myself a meal with double portions of everything, I had two dollars and thirteen cents left. I caught the afternoon train to Downie, and a little before noon the next day I was walking up the steps to Aunt Muriel's house.

Aunt Muriel herself met me at the door. She seemed glad to see me. She wrinkled up her mouth in a smile of welcome.

"So *good* of you to come, Charles!" she said. "I really can't thank you enough! So very *good* of you!" She ran to italics.

I was beginning to warm up to the old girl. She didn't look any older to me than she had fifteen years before. She'd been held together by whalebone and net collars then, and she still was. I put the more flattering portion of this idea into words.

"Oh, Charles," she chirped, "you *flatterer!*" She gave me another smile and then led me into the hall.

I followed her up the stairs to my room on the second floor front. It had a high ceiling and a tall four-poster bed which should have had curtains around it to cut off the draft. After she left, I put my imitation leather suitcase in the big closet and went into the bath next door to clean up.

Lunch was laid on the dining-room table when I came down, and a maid, who looked a good deal older than Aunt Muriel, was fluttering in and out with more dishes. With my aunt's encouragement, I ate enough to keep me comatose all afternoon, and then sat back with a cigarette and listened to her talk.

She began by doing a good deal of commiserating with herself on the subject of her age and loneliness, and a good deal of self-congratulation because she was going to have a young kinsman around from now on.

It developed that I was expected to make myself useful in small ways like walking the dog—an unpleasant Pomeranian named Teddy —and taking letters to the mailbox. This was perfectly all right with me, and I told her so.

There was a short hiatus in the conversation. Then, picking Teddy up off the floor where he'd been during the meal, she installed him in her lap and launched out on an account of what she called her *hobby.* In the last year or so she'd taken up drawing and it had become, from what she said, almost an obsession.

Holding Teddy under one arm, she rose and went to the walnut sideboard and returned with a portfolio of drawings for me to look at.

"I do almost all my drawing here in the dining room," she said, "because the light is so good. Tell me, what do you think of *these?*" She handed me fifty or sixty small sheets of drawing paper.

I spread the drawings out on the dining-room table, among the litter of dishes, and examined them carefully. They were all in pencil, though one or two had been touched up with blotches of water color, and they were all of the same subject, four apples in a low china bowl. They had been labored over; Aunt Muriel had erased and re-erased until the surface of the paper was gritty and miserable. I racked my brains for something nice to say about them.

"You—unh—you've really caught something of the essence of those apples," I forced out after a moment. "Very creditable."

My aunt smiled. "I'm *so* glad you like them," she replied. "Amy said—the maid, you know—that I was silly to work at them so much, but I couldn't stop, I couldn't *bear* to stop, until they were *perfect.*" She paused, then added, "Do you know, Charles, I had the biggest difficulty!"

"Yes?"

"The apples kept withering! It was dreadful. I put them in the icebox just as soon as I got through for the day, but still they went bad after two or three weeks. It wasn't until Amy thought of *dipping* them in melted wax that they lasted long enough."

"Good idea."

"Yes, wasn't it? But you know, Charles, I've gotten rather *tired* of apples lately. I'd like to try something else. . . . I've been thinking, that little tree out on the lawn would make a good subject."

She went over to the window to show me the tree she meant. I followed her. It was a young sapling, just coming into leaf. My aunt said it was a flowering peach.

"*Don't* you think that would be a good subject, Charles? I believe I'll try it this afternoon while you take Teddy for a little walk."

Amy helped bundle my aunt up in several layers of coats and mufflers, and I carried the stool, the easel, the box of pencils and the paper out into the garden for her.

She was rather fussy about the location of the various items, but I finally got them fixed to her satisfaction. Then, though I'd much rather have had an after-luncheon nap upstairs, I snapped the lead on Teddy's objectionable little collar and started out for a survey of the town of Downie.

I soon realized that Downie was the sort of town whose social life centers around the drugstore, but I managed to kill the next two hours by letting Teddy investigate the lamp posts which caught his fancy.

I expected to find Aunt Muriel on the lawn when I got back, hard at work on her drawing, but she had gone in and the easel and stool were gone, too. I looked around for her, but she wasn't in sight, so I let Teddy climb into his box in the dining room and went upstairs for that belated nap.

After all, I couldn't get to sleep. For some irrelevant reason I kept thinking of all those painstaking drawings of the bowl of apples, and I lay on the bed and counted the spots on the wall until dinner time.

The dinner was good, and plentiful. My aunt, however, was definitely snappish. After Amy had cleared away the dishes and my aunt had restored Teddy to his accustomed place on her lap, I found out what the reason was.

"My drawing went *badly*," she complained. "The wind kept whipping those leaves around until I couldn't get a *thing* done."

"I didn't notice much wind, Aunt Muriel," I said rather stupidly.

"You just don't notice things!" she flared. "Why, the leaves weren't still a single *minute*."

I hastened to make amends.

"I can see that a careful craftsman like yourself might be distracted," I placated her. "I'm sorry. I haven't been with artists much."

The reference to herself as an artist pleased my aunt.

"Oh, I'm sure you didn't mean to give offense," she said. "It's just that I can't work with anything unless it's *absolutely* still. That's why I stayed with the apples so long. But I *would* like to draw that tree. I wonder . . ." She went into a brown study which lasted until she had emptied two cups of coffee.

"Charles," she said finally, "I've been thinking. I want you to chop that tree down for me tomorrow and bring it into the house. I'll put it in one of those two-quart milk bottles. That way I can draw it without the wind bothering me."

"But it's such a nice little tree," I protested. "Besides, it won't last long after it's been cut down."

"Oh, it's only a tree," she replied. "I'll get another from the nursery. And about the withering, Amy is wonderful with flowers. She puts aspirin and sugar in the water, and they last forever. Of course, I'll have to work fast. But if I put in two or three hours in the morning and four or five after lunch, I ought to get something done."

As far as she was concerned, the matter was settled.

Immediately after breakfast next morning, Aunt Muriel led me to the tool shed in the rear of the house and gave me a rusty hatchet. She watched with ghoulish interest while I put an edge on the hatchet and then escorted me to the scene of the execution. Feeling like a murderer, I severed the little sapling from its trunk with a couple of chops and then carried it into the house.

I spent the rest of that day, and the next three or four days, working in the garden. I've always liked gardening, and there were some nice things in the place, though they'd been badly neglected. I divided some perennials and fertilized the earth around them with bone meal. Somebody had stocked up the shed with Red Arrow and nicotine sulphate, and I had a good time spraying for aphids and beetles.

Friday morning at breakfast I found a five-dollar bill folded up in my napkin. I raised my eyebrows toward Aunt Muriel. She nodded, yes, it was for me, while a faint flush washed up in her flabby cheeks.

I folded it neatly and put it in my pocket, feeling a warm glow of gratitude for the old girl. It really was extraordinarily decent of her to provide me with cigarette money. I resolved to go shopping for a little present for her that afternoon.

I found that the resources of Downie were limited. After hesitating between a China fawn and a bowl of fan-tailed goldfish, I decided that the goldfish had more verve. I went in after them, and discovered that Drake, the clerk who sold them to me, had been to California, too, and was practically a friend. I made a date with him for a gabfest the following night.

Aunt Muriel seemed genuinely delighted with the fish. She oohed and ahhed over the sinuosity and filminess of their tails and ended by installing the bowl on the little stand beside her easel.

We began to settle into a routine. In the mornings and early afternoons Aunt Muriel drew in the dining room while I worked in the garden. Later in the day I ran errands, walked Teddy, and undertook a bunch of small repairs around the house.

About the middle of my second week with Aunt Muriel, the peach tree withered beyond any hope. She told me at dinner time, with the tone of one announcing a major disaster, that she had had to throw it out. We held a post mortem on the batch of thirty-two drawings she had been able to complete before the catastrophe.

I picked out one of them as having more plastic value than the rest. She admitted it was her favorite, too, and everything was fine. I could see, though, that she was wondering what she could draw next. The next day she flitted restlessly through the house looking for something to draw. She kept popping out into the yard where I was transplanting antirrhinum seedlings, to ask my opinion of this or that as a subject for her pencil. I noticed, when I went in to lunch, that she kept watching the goldfish bowl speculatively, but I didn't make anything of it at the time.

That night when I returned from Drake's house she met me at the door and led me to the kitchen with an air of mysterious triumph.

"I was a little nervous about it," she said, with her hand on the handle of the refrigerator door. "But really, it came out ever so well!" She opened the refrigerator, fumbled in its depths a moment, and pulled out the goldfish bowl. Moisture began to condense on its surface. I stared at it stupidly.

"I *knew* the fish would never hold still, and yet I was just *aching* to draw them," she went on. "So I thought and I thought—and really, I *do* think it was a splendid idea, even if it was my own! I just turned the cold control way down, and put the bowl in, and came back in a couple of hours, and it was frozen solid!

"I was afraid the bowl would crack when it began to freeze, but it didn't. See, the ice is perfectly clear." She picked up a dish towel and rubbed the moisture away until I could see the two goldfish neatly incased in transparent ice. "And now I'll be able to draw them without any trouble. Isn't it *wonderful?*"

I said yes, it was wonderful and went upstairs as soon as I decently could. The incident left an unpleasant taste in my mouth. Not that I held any especial brief for the continued existence of the goldfish, but somehow . . .

She'd seemed to enjoy watching them swimming about so much, and I'd given them to her, and— Oh, hell!

I woke up the next morning feeling faintly unhappy before I could remember what was disturbing me. When I remembered, I decided that I was acting like a champion chump. To let the demise of two goggle-eyed fish upset me was tops in imbecility. Whistling, I went down to breakfast.

After the meal was over, Aunt Muriel got the bowl out of the refrigerator and set to work. I went out in the shed and messed around with the spray gun for a while.

Looking up at the scaling side of the house, I had an idea. Why not repaint it? I asked my aunt and she approved. Accordingly, after some calculation, I brought home a bucket of paint from the store and started sloshing it on.

The work proceeded slowly. Days went by and I got to be a familiar customer at the paint store. Aunt Muriel had finished her eighty-first study of the frozen goldfish before I'd given the big house its first coat, and the surface was so bad it was going to require at least two.

Spring drifted imperceptibly into early summer, and I was still painting the house and Aunt Muriel was still drawing the goldfish, both of us increasingly absorbed in our tasks.

I was having a pretty good time. Drake had introduced me to his sister, a vivid brunette with just the combination of honey and claws which attracts me most in a woman, and he'd got another girl for himself. We went out together several nights each week. My room in the city with the unpaid rent, the hopeless hunt for a job, and the hunger, seemed a long way off.

I got the painting on the house done the day before Aunt Muriel decided she had exhausted the goldfish. I felt like celebrating. So I mixed soapsuds and nicotine sulphate, stirred up a mess of Red Arrow, and puttered among the neglected plants to my heart's content.

Aunt Muriel handed me the last of the goldfish studies at dinner the next day and I went over the entire group with her. I was beginning to hate these inquests over the anatomy of whatever she'd been drawing, but I bore up under it as well as I could.

When we'd finished, she said, "Charles, I've been wondering. Do you suppose Teddy would be a good subject for me next?"

I looked down at the little animal where he was lying in her lap and said, yes, I thought he would, but would he hold still enough?

My aunt looked thoughtful.

"I don't know," she said. "I'll have to try to think of something. Perhaps I could give him his dinner right after breakfast. Or . . ." She went off into one of those periods of meditation of hers and, after a while, I left unobtrusively for my date with Virginia, Drake's sister. We sat in the porch swing in the dark and held hands while the breeze blew the smell of purple lilacs toward us. It was a sweet, sad, sentimental sort of date.

The next day was Saturday. After breakfast my aunt told me to take Teddy for a walk, and to get him thoroughly tired out. She was going to feed him when I got back and she hoped that the exercise, plus the food, might make him comatose enough to serve as a model.

Obediently, we started out. Teddy and I assessed every lamp post in Downie at least twice, and if he wasn't tired out when I brought him back, he should have been. My aunt took the lead from his collar and led him to the pantry where his food dish was waiting, piled high with hamburger.

Teddy ate like a little pig. When he had finished he lay down on the floor of the pantry with a resolute air. My aunt had to carry him into the dining room and deposit him in a sunny spot near her easel. He was asleep and snoring before I left the room.

We had lunch late that day, almost two-thirty in the afternoon, so Aunt Muriel would be able to take full advantage of Teddy's lethargy. I was hungry, and Amy had prepared a really snazzy meal, centering around fried chicken Southern style. As a result, it wasn't until I had finished with the fresh peach mousse that I paid much attention to my aunt. Then I saw that she was looking distracted and morose.

"Didn't the drawing go well this morning, Aunt Muriel?" I asked.

She shook her head until the pendants of her bright earrings jangled violently.

"No, Charles, it did not. Teddy—" She halted, looking very sad.

"What was the matter? Wouldn't he stay asleep?"

If my aunt had been a different type of woman she would have laughed sardonically. As it was, she gave a tiny, delicate snort.

"Oh, he *slept*," she replied. "Yes, he *slept*. But he kept twitching and jumping and panting in his sleep until—well, really, Charles, it was *quite* impossible. Like trying to draw an aspen in a high wind!"

"That's too bad. I guess you'll have to find another subject."

For a moment my aunt did not answer. Looking at her, I thought I caught the glint of tears in her eyes.

"Yes," she replied slowly, "I guess I will. . . . I think, Charles,

I'll go into town this afternoon and buy a few little things for Teddy."

For a moment something cold slid up and down my spine. Then it was gone, and I was thinking it was nice of the old girl, considering how much store she set by her drawing, not to be annoyed at the little dog. . . .

She came up to my room just before dinner and showed me what she'd bought for Teddy. There was a bright red collar with a little bell, a chocolate-flavored rubber bone, and a box of some weird confection called "Dog Treet," which, according to the label, was a wholesome sweetmeat for pets.

She put the collar on Teddy while I watched and then gave him two of the dark brown lozenges out of the "Dog Treet" box. He ate them with a flurry of little growls, and seemed to relish them. . . .

Sunday morning I sat around, nursing the old bones until my watch told me it was time to get going if I didn't want to be late for the all-day hike Drake and I had planned with the girls.

We had a fine time in the country. Drake wandered into a thicket of poison oak, and Virginia, giggling, dropped a woolly caterpillar down my neck.

It was quite dark when I returned to the house. Even before I got inside I noticed that all the lights were on and that there was a general air of confusion.

When I opened the door I found Aunt Muriel standing in the hallway, having what looked like a fit. Amy was standing before her waving a bottle of smelling salts.

"It's *Teddy!*" my aunt gasped when she saw me. "Oh, Charles, he's—"

I put my arm around her comfortingly, and my aunt dissolved into tears. They began to trickle over the coating of talcum powder on her cheeks and drop on the high net collar around her neck.

"It's Teddy," she whimpered. "Oh, Charles, he's dead!"

I'd been expecting it subconsciously, but all the same I jumped. "What happened?" I asked.

"I let him out in the yard for a little run about three hours ago. He was gone a *long* time, and at last I went out to look for him. I called and called and finally I found him out under the rhododendron. He was *awfully* sick. So I came right in and called the doctor, but when he got here, poor little Teddy—was—was gone. Somebody must have poisoned him." She began to cry again.

I stroked my aunt's shoulder and murmured reassuring words while my mind was busy. Some one of the neighbors? Teddy had been a quiet little beast, but he did bark once in a while, and some people just don't like dogs.

"Dr. Jones was ever so nice and *sympathetic* about it. He took poor little Teddy away in a bag. He's going to take him to a man he knows and have him *stuffed*."

Stuffed? I felt sweat break out along my shoulder blades and under my arms. Mechanically I pulled the handkerchief out of my hip pocket and handed it to my aunt.

She took it and began to blot her eyes. "It's such a *comfort* to me, anyway," she said, blowing her nose, "to think that he did—enjoy his —last day—on earth."

I took her up to her room and mixed her a bromide. I stood over her while she drank and talked to her soothingly and patted her hand. After a while I got her calm enough so I could go to my room.

I lay down on the bed and stared up at the spots on the ceiling for a while. My heart was beating hard and quick. Pretty soon I reached in my coat pocket for cigarettes and began to smoke.

I emptied the pack while I lay there, looking at the ceiling, not thinking about anything, keeping my mind back, with an effort that was barely conscious, from the edge of something I didn't want to explore. About twelve I undressed and went to bed.

I felt soggy the next day. I'd slept, but it hadn't done me any good. Aunt Muriel came in later after I'd pushed aside my toast. She was red-eyed. I said good morning and went out into the garden.

The day was muggy and overcast, and I didn't feel like doing much, anyhow. I disbudded peonies for a while and clipped off seed pods; then I decided to give the Oriental cherries a light going-over with the pruning shears. It ought to have been done earlier. When I'd finished, I went into the shed for some linseed oil and bordeaux to mix a poultice for their wounds.

Reaching for the can of bordeaux, an unfamiliar gleam in the corner behind it caught my eyes. It was a can of arsenate of lead. The label bore the usual skull and crossbones. I opened the can. About a quarter of an inch of the poison was gone.

It might have been in the shed before, of course; I wasn't sure it hadn't been. I held on to that idea: I wasn't sure.

I don't know what I did the rest of the day. I must have pottered around in the garden, trying not to think, until dinner time. Aunt Muriel came to the window once and asked me if I didn't want any lunch, and I said I wasn't hungry.

I guess she spent the day looking at Teddy's box in the living room.

Well, I got over it. Two or three days later, when Teddy came back from the taxidermist's, I'd pushed the whole thing back so far in my mind that my reaction had begun to seem slightly comic as well as inexplicable.

Even when Aunt Muriel got her pencils and started on an endless series of sketches of the little stuffed animal, it was all right with me. If anyone had asked me, I'd have said it was only natural for her to want to draw the pet of which she'd been so fond.

While she drew Teddy over and over again, I started re-roofing the house. It was a rough job because it was full of old-fashioned turrets and cupolas, and the summer was well along before I finished.

Aunt Muriel kept urging me to relax, but I just couldn't be quiet.

After the roof, I started a lath house in back for seedlings. Virginia and I were dating almost every night, and I told myself I was feeling fine. I did notice a slight, steady loss of weight, but I pretended it was due to my smoking too much.

One hot night toward the end of August, my aunt got out the packet of drawings she'd made of Teddy, and I went over them with her.

"I think I'll try a few more," she said when I'd laid the last sketch aside. "And then—well, I must get something else." She looked sad.

"Yes," I said noncommittally. The subject made me uneasy, somehow. But so thoroughly had I repressed my awareness, I had no idea why.

"Charles," she said after a minute. She was looking more depressed than ever. "You've made an old woman very happy. This Virginia you've been going around with so much—are you *fond* of her?"

"Why—unh—yes. Yes, I am."

"Well, I've been *thinking*. Would you like it, Charles, if—if I were to advance you the money to set up a little nursery business here in Downie? You seem to have a real *talent* for that sort of thing. I'd miss you, of course, but if you *wanted* to—I'm sure you'd be happy with Virginia, and—" She choked up and couldn't go on.

The old darling! I went around to her side of the table and gave her a hug and kiss. I managed to tell her how happy it would make me and how much I'd been wanting to do just what she suggested. A business of my own, and Virginia for a wife! She was better than a fairy godmother!

We sat up late discussing plans for the nursery—location, stock, advertising, policy—items that I found fascinating, and Aunt Muriel seemed to enjoy listening to.

When I went upstairs to bed, I was feeling so elated I didn't think I could ever get to bed. I whistled while I undressed. And, despite my expectations, I corked off almost as soon as my head hit the pillow.

I awoke about three in the morning, my mind filled with an unalterable conviction. It was as if what I'd only suspected, what I'd made myself forget, had added itself up and become, while I slept, an unyielding certainty.

I sat on the edge of the bed in my pajamas, shivering.

Aunt Muriel was going to kill me.

Lovingly, regretfully, she was going to put poison in my food or in my drink. Lovingly, regretfully, she was going to watch my agonies or smooth my pillow.

With tears in her eyes, she would delay calling the doctor until it was too late. She'd be most unhappy over the whole thing. And, after I was dead, she'd give me to the best mortician in Downie to embalm.

A week later, after drawing me for eighteen hours daily, she'd consign me to the earth, still regretfully, but with her regret a little alleviated by the knowledge that my last days on earth had been happy ones. The nursery business and the marriage with Virginia Drake were, you see, to be the equivalent for me of Teddy's red collar and chocolate-flavored bone.

I went over my chain of reasoning rapidly. It was flawless. But there was one thing more—I had to see for myself.

I drew on my bathrobe and tiptoed along the corridor and down the back stairs. When I got into the shed, I lighted matches and looked until I found the spot on the shelf behind the can of bordeaux where the arsenate of lead should have been. It wasn't there.

Back in my room, I dressed, threw things into my suitcase, and exited in the classical way. That is, I knotted sheets together, tied them to the four-poster bed, and slid down them to the ground. I caught the five-thirty train for the city at the station.

I never heard from Aunt Muriel again. After I got to L.A. I wrote a few cards to Virginia, without any address, just to let her know I hadn't forgotten her. After a while I got into private employment and met a nice girl. One thing led to another, and we got married.

But there's one thing I'd give a good deal to know. What did Aunt Muriel draw next?

THE PRICE OF THE HEAD

❦ THE POSSESSIONS of Christopher Alexander Pellett were these: his name, which he was always careful to retain intact; a suit of ducks, no longer intact, in which he lived and slept; a continuous thirst for liquor, and a set of red whiskers. Also he had a friend. Now no man can gain friendship, even among the gentle islands of Polynesia, except by virtue of some quality attaching to him. Strength, humor, villainy: he must show some trait by which the friend can catch and hold. How, then, explain the loving devotion lavished upon Christopher Alexander Pellett by Karaki, the company boat boy? This was the mystery at Fufuti.

There was no harm in Pellett. He never quarreled. He never raised his fist. Apparently he had never learned that a white man's foot, though it wabble ever so, is given him wherewith to kick natives out of the road. He never even cursed anyone except himself and the Chinese half-caste who sold him brandy: which was certainly allowable because the brandy was very bad.

On the other hand, there was no perceptible good in him. He had long lost the will to toil, and latterly even the skill to beg. He did not smile, nor dance, nor exhibit any of the amiable eccentricities that sometimes recommend the drunken to a certain toleration. In any other part of the world he must have passed without a struggle. But some chance had drifted him to the beaches where life is as easy as a song and his particular fate had given him a friend. And so he persisted. That was all. He persisted, a sodden lump of flesh preserved in alcohol. . . .

Copyright 1916 by John Russell.

47

Karaki, his friend, was a heathen from Bougainville, where some people are smoked and others eaten. Being a black, a Melanesian, he was as much an alien in brown Fufuti as any white. He was a serious, efficient little man with deeply sunken eyes, a great mop of kinky hair, and a complete absence of expression. His tastes were simple. He wore a red cotton kerchief belted around his waist and a brass curtain ring suspended from his nose.

Some powerful chief in his home island had sold Karaki into the service of the trading company for three years, annexing his salary of tobacco and beads in advance. When the time should be accomplished, Karaki would be shipped back to Bougainville, a matter of some eight hundred miles, where he would land no richer than before except in experience. This was the custom. Karaki may have had plans of his own.

It is seldom that one of the black races of the Pacific shows any of the virtues for which subject populations are admired. Fidelity and humility can be exacted from other colors between tan and chocolate. But the black remains the inscrutable savage. His secret heart is his own. Hence the astonishment of Fufuti, which knew the ways of black recruits, when Karaki took the worthless beachcomber to his bosom.

"Hy, you, Johnny," called Moy Jack, the Chinese half-caste. "Better you come catch this fella mahster b'long you. He fella plenty too much drunk, galow."

Karaki left the shade of the copra shed where he had been waiting an hour or more and came forward to receive the sagging bulk that was thrust out-of-doors. He took it scientifically by wrist and armpit and swung toward the beach. Moy Jack stood on his threshold watching with cynic interest.

"Hy, you," he said; "what name you make so much bobeley 'long that fella mahster? S'pose you bling me all them fella pearl; me pay you one dam fella good trade—my word!"

It annoyed Moy Jack that he had to provide the white man with a daily drunk in exchange for the little seed pearls with which Pellett was always flush. He knew where those pearls came from. Karaki did forbidden diving in the lagoon to get them. Moy Jack made a good thing of the traffic, but he could have made a much better thing by trading directly with Karaki for a few sticks of tobacco.

"What name you give that fella mahster all them fella pearl?" demanded Moy Jack offensively. "He plenty too much no good, galow. Close up he die altogether."

Karaki did not reply. He looked at Moy Jack once, and the half-caste trailed off into mutterings. For an instant there showed a strange light in Karaki's dull eyes, like the flat, green flicker of a turning shark glimpsed ten fathoms down. . . .

Karaki bore his charge down the beach to the little thatched shelter of pandanus leaves that was all his home. Tenderly he eased Pellett to a mat, pillowed his head, bathed him with cool water, brushed the filth from his hair and whiskers. Pellett's whiskers were true whiskers, the kind that sprout like the barbels of a catfish, and they were a glorious coppery, sun-gilt red. Karaki combed them out with a sandalwood comb. Later he sat by with a fan and kept the flies from the bloated face of the drunkard.

It was a little past midday when something brought him scurrying into the open. For weeks he had been studying every weather sign. He knew that the change was due when the southeast trade begins to harden through this flawed belt of calms and cross-winds. And now, as he watched, the sharp shadows began to blur along the sands and a film crept over the face of the sun.

All Fufuti was asleep. The house boys snored on the back veranda. Under his netting the agent dreamed happily of big copra shipments and bonuses. Moy Jack dozed among his bottles. Nobody would have been mad enough to stir abroad in the noon hour of repose: nobody but Karaki, the untamed black, who cared nothing for custom nor yet for dreams. The light pad of his steps was lost in the surf drone on the barrier reefs. He flitted to and fro like a wraith. And while Fufuti slept he applied himself to a job for which he had never been hired. . . .

Karaki had long ago ascertained two vital facts: where the key to the trade room was kept and where the rifles and ammunition were hidden. He opened the trade room and selected three bolts of turkey-red cloth, a few knives, two cases of tobacco, and a fine small ax. There was much else he might have taken as well. But Karaki was a man of simple tastes, and efficient.

With the ax he next forced the rifle chest and removed therefrom one Winchester and a big box of cartridges. With the ax again he broke into the boat sheds. Finally with the ax he smashed the bottoms out of the whaleboat and the two cutters so they would be of no use to anyone for many days to come. It was really a very handy little ax, a true tomahawk, ground to a shaving edge. Karaki took a workman's pleasure in its keen, deep strokes. It was almost his chief prize.

On the beach lay a big proa, a stout outrigger canoe of the kind Karaki's own people used at Bougainville, so high of prow and stern as to be nearly crescent shaped. The northwest monsoon of last season had washed it ashore at Fufuti and Karaki had repaired it, by the agent's own order. This proa he now launched in the lagoon, and aboard of it he stored his loot.

Of supplies he had to make a hasty selection. He took a bag of rice and another of sweet potatoes. He took as many coconuts as he could carry in a net in three trips. He took a cask of water and a box of biscuit. And here happened an odd thing.

In his search for the biscuit he came upon the agent's private store of liquor, a dozen bottles of rare Irish whisky. He glanced at them and passed them by. He knew what the stuff was, and he was a savage, a black man. But he passed it by. When Moy Jack heard of that later he remembered what he had seen in Karaki's eyes and ventured the surprising prediction that Karaki would never be taken alive.

When all was ready Karaki went back to his thatch and aroused Christopher Alexander Pellett.

"Hy, mahster, you come 'long me."

Mr. Pellett sat up and looked at him. That is to say, he looked. Whether he saw anything or not belongs among the obscurer questions of psychopathy.

"Too late," said Mr. Pellett profoundly. "This shop is closed. Copy boy! Give all those damned loafers good night. I'm—I'm goin' —bed!"

Whereupon he fell flat on his back.

"Wake up, mahster," insisted Karaki, shaking him. "You too much strong fella sleep. Hy-ah, mahster! Rum! You like'm rum? You catch'm rum any amount—my word! Plenty rum, mahster!"

But even this magic call, which never failed to rouse Pellett from his couch in the mornings, fell now on deaf ears. Pellett had had his skinful, and the fitness of things decreed that he should soak the clock around.

Karaki knelt beside him, pried him up until he could get a shoulder under his middle, and lifted him like a loose bag of meal. Pellett weighed one hundred and fifty pounds; Karaki not much more than a hundred. Yet in some deft coolie fashion of his own the little black man packed his burden, with the feet dragging behind, clear down to the beach. Moreover, he managed to get it aboard the proa. Pellett was half drowned and the proa half swamped. But Karaki managed.

No man saw their departure. Fufuti still dreamed on. Long before the agent awoke to wrath and ruin their queer crescent craft had slipped from the lagoon and faded away on the wings of the trade.

The first day Karaki had all he could do to keep the proa running straight before the wind. Big smoky seas came piling up out of the southeast and would have piled aboard if he had given them the least chance. He was only a heathen who did not know a compass from a degree of latitude. But his forefathers used to people these waters on cockleshell voyages that made the venture of Columbus look like a ride in a ferryboat. Karaki bailed with a tin pan and sailed with a mat and steered with a paddle: but he proceeded.

Along about sunrise Mr. Pellett stirred in the bilge and raised a pea-green face. He took one bewildered glance overside at the seething waste and collapsed with a groan. After a decent interval he tried again, but this was an illusion that would not pass, and he twisted around to Karaki sitting crouched and all aglisten with spray in the stern.

"Rum!" he demanded.

Karaki shook his head, and a haunted look crept into Pellett's eyes.

"Take—take away all that stuff," he begged pathetically, pointing at the ocean. . . .

Thereafter for two days he was very, very sick, and he learned how a small boat in any kind of a sea can move forty-seven different ways within one and the same minute. This was no trifling bit of knowledge, as those who have acquired it can tell. It was nearly fatal to Pellett.

On the third day he awoke with a mouth and a stomach of fumed leather and a great weakness, but otherwise in command of his few faculties. The gale had fallen and Karaki was quietly preparing fresh coconuts. Pellett quaffed two before he thought to miss the brandy with which his breakfast draught was always laced. But when he remembered the milk choked in his throat.

"Me like'm rum."

"No got'm rum."

Pellett looked forward and aft, to windward and to lee. There was a great deal of horizon in sight, but nothing else. For the first time he was aware of a strangeness in events.

"What name you come so far?" he asked.

"We catch'm one big fella wind," explained Karaki.

Pellett was in no condition to question his statement nor to observe from the careful stocking of the proa that they had not been blown to sea on a casual fishing trip. Pellett had other things to think of. Some of the things were pink and others purple and others were striped like the rainbow in most surprising designs, and all were highly novel and interesting. They came thronging up out of the vasty deep to entertain Christopher Alexander Pellett. Which they did.

You cannot cut off alcohol from a man who has been continuously pickled for two years without results more or less picturesque. These were days when the proa went shouting across the empty southern seas to madrigal and choric song. Tied hand and foot and lashed under a thwart, Pellett raved in the numbers of his innocent youth. It would have been singular hearing had there been any to hear, but there was only Karaki, who did not care for the lesser Cavalier poets and on whom whole pages of "Atalanta in Calydon" were quite wasted. Now and then he threw a dipperful of sea water over the white man, or spread a mat to keep the sun from him, or fed him with coconut milk by force. Karaki was a poor audience, but an excellent nurse. Also, he combed Pellett's whiskers twice every day.

They ran into calms. But the trade picked them up again more gently, so that Karaki ventured to make westing, and they fled under skies as bright as polished brass.

My heart is within me
As an ash in the fire;
Whosoever hath seen me
Without lute, without lyre,
Shall sing of me grievous things,
even things that were ill
to desire—

Thus chanted Christopher Alexander Pellett, whose face began to show a little more like flesh and a little less like rotten kelp. . . .

Whenever a fair chance offered, Karaki landed on the lee of some one of the tiny islets with which the Santa Cruz region is peppered, and would make shift to cook rice and potatoes in the tin dipper. This was risky, for one day the islet proved to be inhabited. Two white men in a cutter came out to stop them. Karaki could not hide his resemblance to a runaway nigger, and he did not try to. But when the cutter approached within fifty yards he suddenly announced himself as a runaway nigger with a gun. He left the cutter sinking and one of the men dead.

"There's a bullet hole alongside me here," said Pellett from under the thwart. "You'd better plug it."

Karaki plugged it and released his passenger, who sat up and began stretching himself with a certain naïve curiosity of his own body.

"So you're real," observed Pellett, staring hard at Karaki. "By George, you *are*, and that's comfort."

He was right. Karaki was very real.

"What side you take'm this fella canoe?"

"Balbi," said Karaki, using the native word for Bougainville.

Pellett whistled. An eight-hundred-mile evasion in an open boat was a considerable undertaking. It enlisted his respect. Moreover, he had just had emphatic proof of the efficiency of this little black man.

"Balbi all some home b'long you?"

"Yes."

"All right, commodore," said Pellett. "Lead on. I don't know why you shipped me for supercargo, but I'll see you through."

Strangely—or perhaps not so strangely—the whole Fufuti interval of his history had been fading from his brain while the poison was ebbing from his tissues. The Christopher Alexander Pellett that emerged was one from earlier years: pretty much of a wreck, it was true, and a feckless, indolent, paltry creature at best, but ordinarily human and rather more than ordinarily intelligent.

He was very feeble at first, but Karaki's diet of coconuts and sweet potatoes did wonders for him, and the time came when he could rejoice in the good salt taste of the spray on his lips and forget for hours together the crazy craving for stimulant. They made a strange crew, this pair—simple savage and convalescent drunkard—but there was never any question as to which was in command. That was well seen in the third week when their food began to fail and Pellett noticed that Karaki ate nothing for a whole day.

"See here, this won't do," he cried. "You've given me the last coconut and kept none for yourself."

"Me no like'm eat," said Karaki shortly.

Christopher Alexander Pellett pondered many matters in long, idle hours while the rush of foam under the proa and the creak and fling of her outriggers were the only sounds between sea and sky. Sometimes his brow was knotted with pain. It is not always pleasant to be wrenched back into level contact with one's memories. Thoughts are no sweeter company for having long been drowned. He had met the horrors of delirium. He had now to face the livelier devils of his past. He had fled them before.

But here was no escape of any kind. So he turned and grappled with them and laid them one by one.

When they had been at sea twenty-nine days they had nothing left of their provisions but a little water. Karaki doled it out by moistening a shred of coconut husk and giving Pellett the shred to suck. In spite of Pellett's petulant protest, he would take none himself. Again the heathen nursed the derelict, this time through the last stages of thirst, scraping the staves of the cask and feeding him the ultimate drop of moisture on the point of a knife.

On the thirty-sixth day from Fufuti they sighted Choiseul, a great green wall that built up slowly across the west.

Once fairly under its headlands, Karaki might have indulged a certain triumph. He had taken as his target the whole length of the Solomons, some six hundred miles. But to have fetched the broadside of them anywhere in such a craft as the proa through storm and current, without instrument or chart, was distinctly a feat of navigation. Karaki, however, did no celebrating. Instead, he stared long and anxiously over his shoulder into the east.

The wind had been fitful since morning. By noon it was dead calm on a restless, oily sea. A barometer would have told evil tales, but Karaki must have guessed them anyway, for he staggered forward and unstepped the little mast. Then he bound all his cargo securely under the thwarts and put all his remaining strength into the paddle, heading for a small outpost island where a line of white showed beach. They had been very lucky thus far, but they were still two miles offshore when the first rush of the hurricane caught them.

Karaki himself was reduced to a rattle of bones in a dried skin, and Pellett could scarce lift a hand. But Karaki fought for Pellett among the waves that leaped up like sheets of fire on the reef. Why or how they got through neither could have said. Perhaps because it was written that after drink, illness, madness, and starvation the white man should be saved by the black man again and a last time from ravening waters. When they came ashore on the islet they were both nearly flayed, but they were alive, and Karaki still gripped Pellett's shirt. . . .

For a week they stayed while Pellett fattened on unlimited coconut and Karaki tinkered with the proa. It had landed in a waterlogged tangle, but Karaki's treasures were safe. He got his bearings from a passing native fisherman, and then he knew that *all* his treasures were safe. His home island lay across Bougainville Strait, the stretch of water just beyond.

"Balbi over there?" asked Pellett.

"Yes," said Karaki.

"And a mighty good thing too," cried Pellett heartily. "This is the limit of British authority, old boy. Big fella mahster b'long Beretani stop'm here, no can go that side."

Karaki was quite aware of it. If he feared one thing in the world, he feared the Fiji High Court and its Resident Commissioner for the Southern Solomons, who did sure justice upon all who transgressed in its jurisdiction. Once beyond the strait he might still be liable for the stolen goods and the broken contract. But never—this was the point—never could he be punished for anything he might choose to do over there in Bougainville.

So Karaki was content.

And so was Christopher Alexander Pellett. His body had been wrung and swept and scoured, and he had downed his devils. Sweet air and sunshine were on his lips and in his heart. His bones were sweet in him. As his vigor returned he swam the lagoon or helped Karaki at the proa. He would spend hours hugging the warm sand or rejoicing in the delicate tracery of some tiny seashell, singing softly to himself, while the ground-swell hushed along the beach, savoring life as he never had done.

"Oh, this is good—good!" he said.

Karaki puzzled him. Not that he vexed himself, for a smiling wonder at everything, almost childlike, filled him these days. But he thought of this taciturn savage, how he had capped thankless service with rarest sacrifice. And now that he could consider soberly, the why of it eluded him. Why? Affection? Friendship? It must be so, and he warmed toward the silent little man with the sunken eyes and the expressionless face from which he could never raise a wink.

"Hy, you, Karaki, what name you no laugh all same me? What? You too much fright 'long that fella stuff you steal? Forget it, you old black scamp. If they ever trouble you, I'll square them somehow. By George, I'll say I stole it myself!"

Karaki only grunted and sat down to clean his Winchester with a bit of rag and some drops of oil he had crushed from a dried coconut.

"No, that don't reach him either," murmured Pellett, baffled. "I'd like to know what's going on under that topknot of yours, old chap.

You're like Kipling's cat, that walks by himself. God knows I'm not ungrateful. I wish I could show you—"

He sprang up.

"Karaki! He one big fella friend 'long you; savee? You one big fella friend 'long me; savee? We two dam' big fella friend, my word! ... What?"

"Yes," said Karaki. No other response. He looked at Pellett and he looked away toward Bougainville. "Yes," he said, "my word," and went on cleaning his gun—the black islander, inscrutable, incomprehensible, an enigma always, and to the end.

The end came two days later at Bougainville.

Under a gorgeous dawn they came into a bay that opened before their prow as with jeweled arms of welcome. The land lay lapped in bright garments like a sleeper half awakened, all flushed and smiling, sensuous, intimate, thrilling with life, breathing warm scents—

These were some of the foolish phrases Pellett babbled to himself as he leaped ashore and ran up on a rocky point to see and to feel and to draw all the charm of the place to himself.

Meanwhile Karaki, that simple and efficient little man, was proceeding methodically about his own affairs. He landed his bolts of cloth, his tobacco, his knives, and the other loot. He landed his box of cartridges and his rifle and his fine tomahawk. The goods were somewhat damaged by sea water, but the weapons had been carefully cleaned and polished. . . .

Pellett was declaiming poetry aloud to the alluring solitude when he was aware of a gentle footfall and turned, surprised, to find Karaki standing just behind him with the rifle at his hip and the ax in his hand.

"Well," said Pellett cheerfully, "what d'you want, old chappie?"

"Me like," said Karaki, while there gleamed in his eyes the strange light that Moy Jack had glimpsed there, like the flicker of a turning shark; "me like'm too much one fella head b'long you!"

"What? Head! Whose—my head?"

"Yes," said Karaki simply.

That was the way of it. That was all the mystery. The savage had fallen enamored of the head of the beachcomber, and Christopher Alexander Pellett had been betrayed by his fatal red whiskers. In Karaki's country a white man's head, well smoked, is a thing to be desired above wealth, above lands and chiefship's fame, and the love of women. In all Karaki's country was no head like the head of Pellett. Therefore Karaki had served to win it with the patience and single faith of a Jacob. For this he had schemed and waited, committed theft and murder, expended sweat and cunning, starved and denied himself, nursed, watched, tended, fed, and saved his man that he might bring the head alive and on the hoof—so to speak—to the spot where he could remove it at leisure and enjoy the fruits of his labor in safety.

Pellett saw all this at a flash, understood it so far as any white could understand it: the whole elemental and stupendous simplicity of it. And standing there in his new strength and sanity under the fair promise of the morning, he gave a laugh that pealed across the waters and started the sea birds from their cliffs, the deep-throated laugh of a man who fathoms and accepts the last great jest.

For finally, by corrected list, the possessions of Christopher Alexander Pellett were these: his name still intact; the ruins of some rusty ducks; his precious red whiskers—and a soul which had been neatly recovered, renewed, refurbished, reanimated, and restored to him by his good friend Karaki.

> *Thou shouldst die as he dies,*
> *For whom none sheddeth tears;*
> *Filling thine eyes*
> *And fulfilling thine ears*
> *With the brilliance . . . the bloom*
> *and the beauty . . .*

Thus chanted Christopher Alexander Pellett over the waters of the bay, and then whirled, throwing wide his arms.

"Shoot, damn you! It's cheap at the price!"

LOVE COMES TO MISS LUCY

BY Q. PATRICK

❡ THEY SAT around the breakfast table, their black coats hanging sleevelessly from their shoulders in the Mexican tourist fashion. They looked exactly what they were—three middle-aged ladies from the most respectable suburbs of Philadelphia.

"*Mas cafe*," demanded Miss Ellen Yarnell from a recalcitrant waitress. Miss Ellen had traveled before and knew how to get service in foreign countries.

"And *mas* hot—*caliente*," added Mrs. Vera Truegood who was the oldest of the three and found the mornings in Mexico City chilly.

Miss Lucy Bram didn't say anything. She looked at her watch to see if it was time for Mario to arrive.

The maid dumped a tin pot of lukewarm coffee on the table.

"Don't you think, Lucy," put in Ellen, "that it would be a good idea if we got Mario to come earlier in the morning? He could take us out somewhere so we could get a nice hot breakfast."

"Mario does quite enough for us already." Miss Lucy flushed slightly as she spoke of the young Mexican guide. She flushed because her friends had teased her about him, and because she had just been thinking of his strong, rather cruel Mexican legs as she had seen them yesterday when he rowed them through the floating gardens of Xochimilco.

Miss Lucy Bram had probably never thought about a man's legs (and certainly not at breakfast time) in all her fifty-two years of polite, Quakerish spinsterhood. This was another disturbing indication of the change which had taken place in her since her cautious arrival in Mexico a month before. The change, perhaps, had in fact happened earlier, when the death of an ailing father had left her suddenly and bewilderingly rich, both in terms of bonds and a release from bondage. But Miss Lucy had only grown aware of it later, here in Mexico—on the day when she had found Mario in Taxco.

It had been an eventful day for Miss Lucy. Perhaps the most eventful of all these new Mexican days. Her sense of freedom, which still faintly shocked her sedate soul, had awakened with her in her sunny hotel bedroom. It had hovered over her patio breakfast with her two companions (whose expenses she was discreetly paying). It had been quenched neither by Vera's complaints of the chill mountain air nor by Ellen's travel-snobbish remark that Taxco was sweet, of course, but nowhere near as picturesque as the hill towns of Tuscany.

To Miss Lucy, with only Philiadelphia and Bar Harbor behind her, Taxco's pink weathered roofs and pink, feathery-steepled churches was the impossible realization of a dream. "A rose-red city half as old as time. . . ."

The raffish delight of "foreignness," of being her own mistress, had reached a climax when she saw The Ring.

She saw it in one of the little silversmith shops below the leafy public square. It caught her attention while Vera and Ellen were haggling with the proprietor over a burro pin. It wasn't a valuable ring. To her Quaker eyes, severely trained against the ostentatious, it was almost vulgar. A large, flamboyant white sapphire on a slender band of silver. But there was something tempting in its brash sparkle. She slipped it on her finger and it flashed the sunlight back at her. It made her mother's prim engagement ring, which was worth certainly fifty times as much, fade out of the picture. Miss Lucy felt unaccountably gay, and then self-conscious. With a hurried glance at the stuffy black backs of Vera and Ellen, she tried to take it off her finger.

It would not come off. And while she was still struggling Vera and Ellen joined her, inspecting it with little cries of admiration.

"My, Lucy, it's darling."

"Pretty as an engagement ring."

Miss Lucy flushed. "Don't be foolish. It's much too young for me. I just tried it on. I don't seem to be able . . ."

She pulled at the ring again. The Mexican who owned the shop hovered at her side, purring compliments.

"Go on, Lucy," said Ellen daringly. "Buy it."

"Really, it's annoying. But since I can't seem to get it off, I suppose I'll have to. . . ."

Miss Lucy bought the white sapphire ring for a sum which was higher than its value, but which was still negligible to her. While Ellen who handled all the financial aspects of the trip because she was "so clever" at those things, settled with the proprietor, Miss Lucy said to Vera, "I'll get it off with soap and water back at the hotel."

But she didn't take it off. Somehow her new disturbing happiness had become centered in it.

In Taxco Miss Lucy's energy seemed boundless. That evening, before dinner, while Vera and Ellen were resting aching feet in their rooms, she decided upon a second trip to the Church of Santa Prisca which dominated the public square. Her first visit had been marred by the guidebook chatter of her companions. She wanted to be alone in that cool, tenebrous interior, to try to get the feeling of its atmosphere, so different from the homespun godliness of her own Quaker meeting-house at home.

As she stepped through the ornate wooden doors, the fantastic Churrigueresque altar of gold-leaf flowers and cherubs gleamed richly at her. An ancient peasant woman, sheathed in black, was offering a guttering candle to an image of the Virgin. A mongrel dog ran past her into the church, looked around and ran out again. The splendor and the small humanities of the scene had a curious effect upon Miss Lucy. This stood for all that was "popish" and alien and yet it seemed to call her. On an impulse which she less than half understood, she dropped to her knees, in imitation of the peasant woman, and crossed herself, the sapphire ring flashing with some of the exotic quality of the church itself.

Miss Lucy remained kneeling only a short time, but before she rose she was conscious of a presence close to her on the right. She glanced around and saw that a Mexican youth in a spotless white suit had entered the church and was kneeling a few yards away, the thick black hair shining on his reverently bent head. As she got up, his gaze met hers. It was only a momentary glance, but she retained a vivid impression of his face. Honey-brown skin and the eyes—particularly the eyes—dark and patient with a gentle, passive beauty. Somehow that brief contact gave her the sensation of seeing a little into the mind of this strange city of strange people. Remembering him, her spontaneous genuflection seemed somehow the right thing to have done. Not, of course, that she would ever speak of it to Vera and Ellen.

She left the church, happy and ready for dinner. The evening light had faded, and as she passed from the crowded Xocalo into the deserted street which led to the hotel, it was almost night. Her footsteps echoed unfamiliarly against the rough cobblestones. The sound seemed to emphasize her loneliness. A single male figure, staggering slightly, was coming up the hill now toward her. Miss Lucy was no coward, but with a tingle of alarm she realized that the oncomer was drunk. She looked around. There was no one else in sight. A weak impulse urged her to return to the Xocalo, but she suppressed it. After all, she was an American, she would not be harmed. She marched steadfastly on.

But the seeds of fear were there, and when she came abreast of the man, he peered at her and swung toward her. He was bearded and shabby and his breath reeked of tequila. He started a stream of Spanish which she couldn't understand. She knew he was begging and, trained to organized charities, Miss Lucy had no sympathy for street beggars. She shook her head firmly and tried to move on. But a dirty hand grabbed her sleeve, and the soft whining words continued. She freed her arm more violently than she intended. Anger glinted in the man's eyes. He raised his arm in an indignant gesture.

Although he was obviously not intending to strike her, Miss Lucy recoiled instinctively and as she did so, caught her high heel in the uneven cobbles and fell rather ungracefully on the ground. She lay there, her ankle twisted underneath her while the man stood threateningly, it seemed, over her.

For a moment, Miss Lucy felt panic—blind overwhelming terror completely unjustified by the almost farcical unpleasantness of the situation.

And then from the shadows, another man appeared. A slight man in a white suit. Miss Lucy could not see his face but she knew that it was the boy from the church. She was conscious of his white-sleeved arm flashing toward the beggar and pushing him away.

She saw the beggar reel backward and shuffle mutteringly off. Then she was aware of a young face close to her own, and a strong arm was helping her to rise. She could not understand all her rescuer said, but his voice was gentle and concerned.

"*Qué malo*," he said, grinning in the direction of the departing beggar. "*Malo Mexicano*." The teeth gleamed white in the moonlight. "Me Mario, from the church, yes? Me help the señora, no?"

He almost carried Miss Lucy, who had twisted her ankle painfully, back to the hotel and right into her room where she was turned over to the flustered administrations of Vera and Ellen.

As Mario hovered solicitously around, Ellen grabbed at her pocketbook with a whispered: "How much, Lucy?"

But here Miss Lucy showed a will of her own. "No. Money would be an insult."

And Mario, who seemed to understand, said "*Gracias, Señora*." And after several sentences, in which Miss Lucy understood only the word "*madre*," he picked up Miss Lucy's left hand—the one with the new sapphire ring—kissed it and then bowed himself smilingly out.

That was how Mario had come into their lives. And having come in, it was apparent that he intended to stay. Next morning he came to the hotel to inquire for Miss Lucy and she saw him squarely for the first time. He was not really handsome. His long-lashed eyes were perhaps a shade too close together. His slight mustache above the full-lipped mouth was perhaps too long. But his figure, though slight, was powerful, and there was something about him that inspired both affection and confidence.

He was, he explained, a student anxious to make a little money on vacation. He wanted to be a guide to the Señoras, and since Miss Lucy could not walk with her twisted ankle, he suggested that he hire a car and act as their chauffeur. The fee he requested was astonishingly small and he stubbornly refused to accept more.

The next day he hired a car at a low price which more than satisfied even the parsimonious Miss Ellen and from then on he drove the ladies around to points of interest with as much care and consideration as if they had been his three "*madres*."

His daily appearances, always in spotless white, were a constant delight to Miss Lucy—indeed, to all three of them. He was full of plans for their entertainment. One day he drove them around the base of Mount Popocatepetl and for several hours they were able to rhapsodize over what is certainly one of the most beautiful and mysterious mountains in the world. And for a moment when they happened to be alone together, staring at the dazzling whiteness of the mountain's magnificent summit, Miss Lucy felt her hand taken in Mario's firm brown one and softly squeezed.

It was, of course, his way of telling her, despite the difficulties of language, that they were sharing a great Mexican experience and he was glad they were sharing it together. Under his touch the large sapphire in the ring pressed into her finger painfully, but another feeling, different from pain, stirred in her.

After the Popocatepetl trip, Miss Lucy decided that it was time to leave Taxco and take up their quarters in Mexico City.

She instructed Ellen to dismiss Mario—to give him an extra hundred pesos and to let him know politely yet firmly that his services were terminated. But Ellen might as well have tried to dispel Popocatepetl or bid it remove itself into the sea. Mario just laughed at her, waved away the hundred pesos, and referred himself directly to Miss Lucy. There were bad Mexicans in Mexico City. He threw out his strong, honey-gold hands. He would take care of them. No, of no importance was the money of Señora Ellen (the other two women were always Señora to him, Miss Lucy alone was Señorita). The important thing was that he should show them everything. Here the strong arms waved to embrace the sun, the sky, the mountains, all of Mexico. And the dark eyes with the two thick lashes embraced Miss Lucy too.

And Miss Lucy, against some deeply rooted instinct, yielded. Mario went with them to Mexico City.

It was the second week of their stay in Mexico City and they had decided upon a trip to the pyramids at Teotihuacan. As usual Miss Lucy sat in front with Mario. He was an excellent driver and she loved to watch his profile as he concentrated on the road; loved his occasional murmurs to himself when something pleased or displeased him. She liked it less when he turned to her, flashing his dark eyes caressingly on her face and lowering them to her breast.

His gaze embarrassed her and today something prompted her to say to him in English, "Mario, you are what in America we call a flirt. I imagine you are very popular with the girls here in Mexico."

For a moment he did not seem to understand her remark. Then he burst out, "Girls—*muchachas. Para me, no.*" His hand went into his breast pocket and he brought out a small battered photograph. "*Mi muchacha.* My girl, *mi unica muchacha . . . Una sola . . .*"

Miss Lucy took the photograph. It was of a woman older than herself with gray hair and large sad eyes. There were lines of worry and illness in her face.

"Your mother?" said Miss Lucy gently. "Tell me about her."

Mario rattled on, not in the slow careful Spanish which he generally reserved for the ladies, but in a rapid monologue of which Miss Lucy understood but part. She gathered that Mario's mother was terribly poor, that she had devoted her life in a tiny Guerreros village to raising fatherless children, and was a saint on earth. It was obvious that Mario felt the almost idolatrous love for his mother that is so frequent in young Mexican males.

While he talked excitedly, Miss Lucy reached a decision. Somehow, before her vacation was over, she'd get from Mario his mother's address and she'd write and send her money, enough money to finance Mario at college. A mother surely would accept it even though her son might be too proud to yield to persuasion.

"Is that one of the pyramids?" It was Ellen's disappointed voice that broke the chain of Miss Lucy's thought. "Why, it's nothing compared to the pyramids in Egypt!"

Miss Lucy was thrilled, however, by the Pyramids of the Sun and the Moon. And as she gazed at their somber, ancient magnificence, she felt that strange inner elation which she had felt on the morning when she had genuflected and crossed herself in the church at Taxco.

"I'm not going to climb up all those crumbly steps," said Ellen peevishly. "I'm too old and it's too hot."

And Vera, though never too hot, was far too old. She stood at the foot of the pyramid, her coat hanging sleevelessly over her shoulders, the inevitable cigarette held in her clawlike hand. "You go, Lucy—you're young and active."

Lucy went.

With Mario's help she climbed to the very top of the Pyramid of the Sun and she was hardly out of breath when she reached the summit, so great was her sense of mystic exaltation.

They sat alone and close together on the summit, this cultivated woman past fifty with a degree from Bryn Mawr, and this almost ignorant boy from an adobe hut in the hinterland of Guerreros. They looked over the vast design of the square where the ancient village had been with its Temple of Quetzalcoatl of the Plumed Serpents, gazing down at the Road of the Dead which led from the Temple to the Pyramid of the Moon.

Mario started to tell her of the sacrificial rites of the feast of Toxcatl which, in ancient days, took place once a year.

As he talked, Miss Lucy half-closed her eyes and visualized the scene: the assembled public hushed in the huge square beneath them; the priests, each in his appointed place on the steps of the Pyramid; the spotless youth who was, of course, Mario.

And because it was Mario who was being sacrificed in her mind, sacrificed to the futility of life and beauty, she felt a warm human pity for him and instinctively her hand went out—the hand with the cheap sapphire ring that would not come off—and it found his, and was held fast in his warm brown fingers.

Miss Lucy was hardly aware of it when Mario's arm slipped round her, and his dark head dropped against her breast. It was not until she became conscious of a smell like warm brown sugar, which was his skin, and a smell of flowery oil which he used on his hair, that all Philadelphia came rushing back. She jumped up hastily—jumping out of the centuries to this practical moment when two friends would be waiting at the base of the pyramid, hungry for lunch—and there were a great many steps to descend.

On the way home Miss Lucy decided that she and Vera would take the back seat, so Ellen sat in front and argued with the sulky Mario.

When they reached the pension, Miss Lucy said quickly, "It's a Sunday tomorrow, Mario. You'd better take a holiday."

He began to protest. When Lucy repeated, "No, not tomorrow, Mario," his face fell like a disappointed child's. Then his expression changed, and his dark eyes looked squarely, challengingly into hers.

As she turned into the house, Miss Lucy felt her heart pounding. The intimacy of that glance had brought into the open the thing which she had not dared to contemplate before. She was quite certain of it now.

Somehow—for some reason that she did not understand and in some way that her simple mind had never dreamed of—Mario desired her.

He desired her physically.

That night, before she went to bed, Miss Lucy did something she had never done in her life before. She stood in her plain cotton nightgown for several minutes before the long Venetian mirror in the sumptuous room and took stock of herself as a woman.

She saw nothing new or startling—nothing external to balance the startling changes which were going on inside her. Her face was not beautiful. It never had been, even in youth, and now it was uncompromisingly middle-aged. Her hair was almost white but not white enough. It was soft and plentiful and sat rather prettily on her forehead. Her eyes were clear and pleasing in themselves, but surrounded by the lines and shadows natural to her age. Her breasts were firm beneath the cotton nightgown but her figure was in no way remarkable. In fact, there was nothing externally desirable either about her face or her body. And yet she was desired. She knew it. For some reason a handsome Mexican youth found her desirable.

Miss Lucy was sure of that.

There was no nonsense about Miss Lucy and she knew that young men often make up to rich older women in the hopes of eventually obtaining money from them. But Mario, apart from the fact that he'd refused all financial offers, did not even know that Miss Lucy was by far the richest of the three ladies. Only a Philadelphia lawyer or a member of their old Quaker family could possibly know how rich Miss Lucy really was. No, if Mario had wanted money, he would have concentrated on Ellen who held the purse strings and never for a moment let it be known to anyone that it was Miss Lucy's money she was dispensing.

There was nothing about Miss Lucy, drab, black-clad Miss Lucy, to suggest wealth. True, her mother's engagement ring had a rather valuable diamond in it. But only an expert jeweler would recognize that. As for the flashy white sapphire ring, that wasn't worth anyone's time or energy and Miss Lucy would have gladly given it to Mario out of gratitude if only she could have got it off her finger.

No, there were thousands of other women in Mexico City with far more obvious signs of wealth. There were young, beautiful women and any one of them might have been pleased and proud to have Mario as an escort and—yes, Miss Lucy faced it uncompromisingly—as something else.

And yet . . . suddenly Miss Lucy became frightened at the illogicality of it all.

Some virginal instinct stirred in her and warned her of—danger.

And because there was no nonsense about Miss Lucy, she decided that she must do something final about it. Lying there quietly beneath the sheets, she came to her great resolution.

Miss Lucy and Vera were waiting at the bus station. Both of them hugged their coats around them as if cold. Vera was always cold, of course. But today Miss Lucy was cold, too, despite the splendid warmth of the spring sunshine. Her eyes—and her nose—were red.

They were waiting for Ellen who had been left behind to deliver the final *coup de grâce* to Mario. The bus for Patzcuaro was leaving in twenty minutes.

At last Ellen appeared. Her nose was red too.

"You shouldn't have done it, Lucy," she snapped. "It was cruel." She thrust two one-hundred-peso bills into Lucy's hands. "I thought he was going to hit me when I gave him these." She sniffed. "And he burst into tears like a child when he read your letter."

Miss Lucy did not speak. In fact, she spoke very little during the entire length of the tiring bus journey to Patzcuaro.

The three women had been sitting since dinner around their table on the veranda overlooking the serene expanse of Lake Patzcuaro. Ellen, restlessly voluble, was discussing possible plans for the next day. Miss Lucy was, apparently, paying no attention. Her eyes studied the evening gray-green waters of the lake with its clustering islands and its obscene bald-headed vultures that squawked and fought greedily over scraps of carrion on the lake shore.

After a short time she rose, saying, "It's getting a bit cold. I think I'll go up to my room. Good night."

Miss Lucy's room, with its small veranda, commanded a view of the lake from another angle. Below her, in the growing darkness, the fishermen were pottering with their boats, talking in low, sibilant voices or singing snatches of Michoacan songs.

Miss Lucy sat watching them. She was thinking of Mario, missing him with an intensity that was almost painful. She had thought of him constantly since she left Mexico City and now was appalled at her harshness in dismissing him by proxy through Ellen. She should have spoken to him herself. She would hate to have him think . . . The thoughts went on with a goading persistence. She had done him a wrong, hurt him. . . .

At some indeterminate stage of her reverie she became conscious of a white-clad figure moving among the fishermen below. Miss Lucy's gaze rested on him and then her heart turned over. She strained forward and peered into the darkness. Surely, surely, there was something familiar about those light, graceful movements—that small, compact form.

But it couldn't be Mario! She had left him hundreds of miles away in Mexico City, and Ellen had been particularly instructed not to tell him where they were going.

The figure in white moved away from the lake shore toward her window. He passed through a shaft of light from an open door. There was no doubt about it now.

It was Mario.

She bent over the balcony, her heart fluttering like a foolish bird. He was only about fifteen feet below her.

"Oh, Miss Lucy, I have found you." He spoke in the slow careful Spanish which he reserved for her. "I knew I would find you."

"But, Mario, how . . . ?"

"The bus company told me you had come here. I got a ride and I have been waiting."

She saw his teeth gleaming as he smiled at her. "Miss Lucy, why did you go away without saying *adios*?"

She did not answer.

"But I am back now to take care of you. And tomorrow you and I—we will go on the lake. Before the other two ladies are up. You and I alone together. There will be a moon and then the sunrise."

"Yes . . ."

"At five o'clock in the morning I come. I will have a boat. Before even the birds awake I will be waiting here."

"Yes, yes . . ."

"Good night, *carissima*."

Miss Lucy went back into her room. Her hands were trembling as she undid her dress and slipped into bed.

And she was still trembling when—in the middle of the night, it seemed—a low whistle beneath her window told her that Mario had come for her.

She dressed swiftly, patted her soft gray hair into place, threw a coat over her shoulders and hurried downstairs. The hotel was very quiet. No one saw her as she made her way through the deserted lobby and no one saw her as she went down the slope to where Mario was waiting for her with the boat.

He took her hand and pressed it to his lips. Then he drew her gently toward the boat.

She did not resist. It was as though he were Destiny leading her onward toward the inevitable.

Mario had been right. There was a moon—full and lemon-white, it shed a weird light on the opaque waters of the lake.

Miss Lucy was in the bottom of the boat, lying on her coat. It was cold, but she did not seem to notice it. She was watching Mario as he stood up in the boat, guiding it skillfully past the other craft into the deep waters of the lake. He had rolled his trousers up beyond his knees and his legs looked strong and somehow cruel in the moonlight. He was singing.

Miss Lucy had not realized before what a beautiful voice he had. The song seemed sweet and ineffably sad. Mario's eyes caressed her as his gaze traveled downward from her face and rested on her hands which lay impassive on her lap. The cheap sapphire sparkled in the moonlight.

Miss Lucy was not conscious of time or place as the boat moved slowly toward the secret heart of the lake with its myriad islets. She was not conscious of the dimming stars and the moon paling before the dawn. She felt only a deep, utter tranquillity, as though this gentle almost imperceptible motion must go on forever. She started at the sound of Mario's voice.

"Listen, the birds."

She heard them in the cluster of small islands that were all around her, but she could see only the vultures that hovered silently overhead.

Mario rested from his rowing and produced a parcel. It contained *tortas*, butter, and goat cheese. He also brought out a bottle of red Mexican wine.

He spread butter on a *torta* with his large clasp knife and handed it to Miss Lucy. Suddenly she realized that she was very hungry. She ate wolfishly and drank from the bottle of the sweet Mexican wine. It went to her head and made her feel girlish and happy. She laughed at everything Mario said and he laughed too while his eyes still caressed her.

And so they breakfasted like honeymoon lovers, as a sunrise splashed red gold over the lake, miles away now from anyone, with only the visible vultures and the invisible songsters to witness them.

When the last *torta* was eaten and the bottle drained, Mario took up his paddle again and propelled the boat deeper into the heart of the lake, on and on without speaking.

As soon as she saw the island, Miss Lucy knew it was the one Mario had chosen. It looked more solitary, more aloof than the rest of them, and there was a fringe of high reeds around its edges.

He steered the boat carefully through the reeds which were so tall that they were completely hidden in a little world of their own. When they reached the shore, he took her hand and raised her gently with the one word, "Come."

She followed him like a child. He found a dry spot and spread out her coat for her. Then, as she lay down, he sat with her head in his lap. She could see his face above hers very close; could see those dark eyes set a little too close together; could feel the warm breath, wine-scented, that came from his lips.

She closed her eyes knowing that this was the moment to which everything had been leading—ever since the day in the church of Santa Prisca when she had first met Mario. She could feel his hands caressing her hair, her face, gently, gently. She felt him take her hand, felt him touch the sapphire ring.

The moment he touched the ring, she knew. She could feel it in his fingers, an outflowing, obsessive desire. The whole pattern which had seemed so complex was plain.

His hands moved upward. His fingers, still gentle, reached her throat. She didn't scream. She wasn't even frightened.

As his hands tightened their grasp, the full mouth came down upon hers, and their lips met in their first and only kiss.

Mario threw the bloodstained knife away. He hated the sight of blood and it had disgusted him that he had had to cut off a finger to get the ring.

He hadn't even bothered about the engagement ring that had belonged to Miss Lucy's mother. It was a plain, cheap affair, and for weeks now the great beauty of the sapphire had blinded him to anything else.

He spread the coat carefully over Miss Lucy's body. For a moment he considered putting it in the reeds, but it might float away and be discovered by the fishermen.

Here, on the island, it could be years before anyone came, and by that time—he glanced up at the vultures hovering eternally overhead. . . .

Without looking back Mario went to the boat and rowed toward the deserted mainland shore. There he landed, overturned the boat, and pushed it free so that it would drift into deep water.

An American woman had gone out in a boat on the lake with an inexperienced boatman. They had both been drowned. The officials would never drag so big a lake to find the bodies.

Mario made his way in the direction of the railroad track. He could board a freight car and tomorrow perhaps he would be in Guerreros.

He was sure his mother would like the ring.

SREDNI VASHTAR

BY "SAKI" (H. H. MUNRO)

℃ CONRADIN was ten years old, and the doctor had pronounced his professional opinion that the boy would not live another five years. The doctor was silky and effete, and counted for little, but his opinon was endorsed by Mrs. de Ropp, who counted for nearly everything. Mrs. de Ropp was Conradin's cousin and guardian, and in his eyes she represented those three-fifths of the world that are necessary and disagreeable and real; the other two-fifths, in perpetual antagonism to the foregoing, were summed up in himself and his imagination. One of these days Conradin supposed he would succumb to the mastering pressure of wearisome necessary things—such as illnesses and coddling restrictions and drawn-out dullness. Without his imagination, which was rampant under the spur of loneliness, he would have succumbed long ago.

Mrs. de Ropp would never, in her honestest moments, have confessed to herself that she disliked Conradin, though she might have been dimly aware that thwarting him "for his good" was a duty which she did not find particularly irksome. Conradin hated her with a desperate sincerity which he was perfectly able to mask. Such few pleasures as he could contrive for himself gained an added relish from the likelihood that they would be displeasing to his guardian, and from the realm of his imagination she was locked out—an unclean thing, which should find no entrance.

In the dull, cheerless garden, overlooked by so many windows that were ready to open with a message not to do this or that, or a

From *The Short Stories of Saki* (H. H. Munro), copyright 1930 by The Viking Press, Inc.; used by permission of The Viking Press and Brandt & Brandt.

reminder that medicines were due, he found little attraction. The few fruit trees that it contained were set jealously apart from his plucking, as though they were rare specimens of their kind blooming in an arid waste; it would probably have been difficult to find a market-gardener who would have offered ten shillings for their entire yearly produce. In a forgotten corner, however, almost hidden behind a dismal shrubbery, was a disused toolshed of respectable proportions, and within its walls Conradin found a haven, something that took on the varying aspects of a playroom and a cathedral. He had peopled it with a legion of familiar phantoms, evoked partly from fragments of history and partly from his own brain, but it also boasted two inmates of flesh and blood. In one corner lived a ragged-plumaged Houdan hen, on which the boy lavished an affection that had scarcely another outlet. Further back in the gloom stood a large hutch, divided into two compartments, one of which was fronted with close iron bars. This was the abode of a large polecat-ferret, which a friendly butcher-boy had once smuggled, cage and all, into its present quarters, in exchange for a long-secreted hoard of small silver. Conradin was dreadfully afraid of the lithe, sharp-fanged beast, but it was his most treasured possession. Its very presence in the toolshed was a secret and fearful joy, to be kept scrupulously from the knowledge of the Woman, as he privately dubbed his cousin. And one day, out of Heaven knows what material, he spun the beast a wonderful name, and from that moment it grew into a god and a religion. The Woman indulged in religion once a week at a church nearby, and took Conradin with her, but to him the church service was an alien rite in the House of Rimmon. Every Thursday, in the dim and musty silence of the toolshed, he worshiped with mystic and elaborate ceremonial before the wooden hutch where dwelt Sredni Vashtar, the great ferret. Red flowers in their season and scarlet berries in the wintertime were offered at his shrine, for he was a god who laid some special stress on the fierce impatient side of things, as opposed to the Woman's religion, which, as far as Conradin could observe, went to great lengths in the contrary direction. And on great festivals powdered nutmeg was strewn in front of his hutch, an important feature of the offering being that the nutmeg had to be stolen. These festivals were of irregular occurrence, and were chiefly appointed to celebrate some passing event. On one occasion, when Mrs. de Ropp suffered from acute toothache for three days, Conradin kept up the festival during the entire three days, and almost succeeded in persuading himself that Sredni Vashtar was personally responsible for the toothache. If the malady had lasted for another day the supply of nutmeg would have given out.

The Houdan hen was never drawn into the cult of Sredni Vashtar. Conradin had long ago settled that she was an Anabaptist. He did not pretend to have the remotest knowledge as to what an Anabaptist was, but he privately hoped that it was dashing and not very respectable. Mrs. de Ropp was the ground plan on which he based and detested all respectability.

After a while Conradin's absorption in the toolshed began to attract the notice of his guardian. "It is not good for him to be pottering down there in all weathers," she promptly decided, and at breakfast one morning she announced that the Houdan hen had been sold and taken away overnight. With her shortsighted eyes she peered at Conradin, waiting for an outbreak of rage and sorrow, which she was ready to rebuke with a flow of excellent precepts and reasoning. But Conradin said nothing: there was nothing to be said. Something perhaps in his white set face gave her a momentary qualm, for at tea that afternoon there was toast on the table, a delicacy which she usually banned on the ground that it was bad for him; also because the making of it "gave trouble," a deadly offense in the middle-class feminine eye.

"I thought you liked toast," she exclaimed, with an injured air, observing that he did not touch it.

"Sometimes," said Conradin.

In the shed that evening there was an innovation in the worship of the hutch-god. Conradin had been wont to chant his praises, tonight he asked a boon.

"Do one thing for me, Sredni Vashtar."

The thing was not specified. As Sredni Vashtar was a god he must be supposed to know. And choking back a sob as he looked at that other empty corner, Conradin went back to the world he so hated.

And every night, in the welcome darkness of his bedroom, and every evening in the dusk of the toolshed, Conradin's bitter litany went up: "Do one thing for me, Sredni Vashtar."

Mrs. de Ropp noticed that the visits to the shed did not cease, and one day she made a further journey of inspection.

"What are you keeping in that locked hutch?" she asked. "I believe it's guinea pigs. I'll have them all cleared away."

Conradin shut his lips tight, but the Woman ransacked his bedroom till she found the carefully hidden key, and forthwith marched down to the shed to complete her discovery. It was a cold afternoon, and Conradin had been bidden to keep to the house. From the furthest window of the dining room the door of the shed could just be seen beyond the corner of the shrubbery, and there Conradin stationed himself. He saw the Woman enter, and then he imagined her opening the door of the sacred hutch and peering down with her shortsighted eyes into the thick straw bed where his god lay hidden. Perhaps she would prod at the straw in her clumsy impatience. And Conradin fervently breathed his prayer for the last time. But he knew as he prayed that he did not believe. He knew that the Woman would come out presently with that pursed smile he loathed so well on her face, and that in an hour or two the gardener would carry away his wonderful god, a god no longer, but a simple brown ferret in a hutch. And he knew that the Woman would triumph always as she triumphed now, and that he would grow ever more sickly under her pestering and domineering and superior wisdom, till one day nothing would matter much more with him, and the doctor would be proved right. And in the sting and misery of his defeat, he began to chant loudly and defiantly the hymn of his threatened idol:

> *Sredni Vashtar went forth,*
> *His thoughts were red thoughts and his teeth were white.*
> *His enemies called for peace, but he brought them death.*
> *Sredni Vashtar the Beautiful.*

And then of a sudden he stopped his chanting and drew closer to the windowpane. The door of the shed still stood ajar as it had been left, and the minutes were slipping by. They were long minutes, but they slipped by nevertheless. He watched the starlings running and flying in little parties across the lawn; he counted them over and over again, with one eye always on that swinging door. A sour-faced maid came in to lay the table for tea, and still Conradin stood and waited and watched. Hope had crept by inches into his heart, and now a look of triumph began to blaze in his eyes that had only known the wistful patience of defeat. Under his breath, with a furtive exultation, he began once again the paean of victory and devastation. And presently his eyes were rewarded: out through that doorway came a long, low, yellow-and-brown beast, with eyes a-blink at the waning daylight, and dark wet stains around the fur of jaws and throat. Conradin dropped on his knees. The great polecat-ferret made its way down to a small brook at the foot of the garden, drank for a moment, then crossed a little plank bridge and was lost to sight in the bushes. Such was the passing of Sredni Vashtar.

"Tea is ready," said the sour-faced maid; "where is the mistress?"

"She went down to the shed some time ago," said Conradin.

And while the maid went to summon her mistress to tea, Conradin fished a toasting fork out of the sideboard drawer and proceeded to toast himself a piece of bread. And during the toasting of it and the buttering of it with much butter and the slow enjoyment of eating it, Conradin listened to the noises and silences which fell in quick spasms beyond the dining-room door. The loud foolish screaming of the maid, the answering chorus of wondering ejaculations from the kitchen region, the scuttering footsteps and hurried embassies for outside help, and then, after a lull, the sacred sobbings and the shuffling tread of those who bore a heavy burden into the house.

"Whoever will break it to the poor child? I couldn't for the life of me!" exclaimed a shrill voice. And while they debated the matter among themselves, Conradin made himself another piece of toast.

LOVE LIES BLEEDING

BY PHILIP MacDONALD

❡ CYPRIAN didn't like rushing over dinner, so they had eaten early. And now, at eight o'clock, he was alone with coffee in Astrid's living room while Astrid herself was in the bedroom out of sight and sound, changing into some frock suitable for the rather tedious party they were going to together.

It was very quiet in Astrid's apartment, very comfortable. The maid had gone as soon as they had finished eating, so there weren't even sounds of movements from dining room and kitchen to disturb the peace. And there was plenty of time. Plenty. Because they needn't arrive at the Ballards' before nine-thirty at the earliest.

Cyprian stretched luxuriously. He picked his coffee cup from the mantel and drained it and set it down again, his fingers momentarily caressing the delicate texture of the thin china.

He strolled about the room, thinking how well Astrid had done with it, taking pleasure in the blendings and contrasts of color under the soft lights, the balance and position of furniture, the choice and subject of the few paintings.

He went back to the mantel, and took the fragile, thistle-shaped liqueur glass from beside his empty coffee cup. He couldn't remember what was in it, and sniffed at it, his thin sensitive nostrils quivering a little as the sharp, bitter-orange aroma stung them pleasantly. He smiled; he should have known that Astrid wouldn't make mistakes.

He sipped slowly, letting the hot stringency slide over his tongue.

He turned his back to the room and faced himself in the big mirror over the mantel and was pleased by what he saw. He could find this evening nothing at variance with the appearance of Cyprian Morse as he wished it to be. With absorbed interest he studied Cyprian—the graceful, high-shouldered slenderness so well set off by the dinner jacket of midnight blue; the fine-textured pallor of the odd, high-cheekboned face with its heavy-lidded eyes and chiseled mouth which seemed to lift at one corner in satire perpetual but never overstressed; the long slim fingers of the hand which twitched with languid dexterity at the tie which so properly enhanced the silken snowy richness of the shirt and its collar.

The blue gleam of the carved lapis lazuli in his signet ring made him think of Charles, and the time when Charles had given it to him. He turned away from the mirror and sipped at the liqueur again and wished Charles were here and wondered how long it would be before Charles returned from Venezuela. He was looking forward to Charles and Astrid meeting, though he wasn't too sure what Charles's initial reaction would be. Astrid would be all right, of course—and, after all, Charles would very soon find out what she was like, just an awfully nice girl, and a great, an inspired designer. He toyed with visions of making Charles work too. With Astrid doing the sets, and Charles letting himself go on weird, macabre decor, Cyprian Morse's *Abanazar* could well be the most sensational production ever seen in the theater.

Cyprian finished the liqueur, and set down the glass. Still musing on the possibilities of *Abanazar*, he dropped into a big low chair, and found himself—his eyes almost level with a coffee table— looking straight at a photograph of Astrid he hadn't seen before. It was an excellent portrait, oddly and interestingly lighted, and the camera had caught and registered that somehow astringent little smile which some people said spoiled her looks, but which had always been for Cyprian a sort of epitome of why he liked her. He went on looking at it now, and thought, as he had thought many times looking at her in life, how necessary a smile it was. Without it there would be no way of knowing that the full-blown and almost aggressive femininity of Astrid's structure was merely an accident in design; no way of telling that in fact she had no nonsense about her but was simply the best of designers and—he was beginning to believe more and more as their association developed—the best of friends.

He stretched again and relaxed in the chair. He was in the after-dinner mood which he liked best, and which only seemed to come when he had had exactly the right amount of a-little-too-much-to-drink. All his senses, all his perceptions, were sharpened to a fine edge beneath a placid sheath of contentment. There was a magazine lying on the table near the photograph, and he reached out a lazy arm and picked it up. It was last month's *Manhattan,* and it fell open in his hands to the theatrical page and the beginning of Burn Heyward's long glowing review of *The Square Triangle.* He knew it nearly by heart, but nevertheless began to read and savor it afresh, starting with the headline, *CYPRIAN MORSE DOES IT AGAIN,* and going through its delicious paeans to the shiny super-plum of the very last paragraph, ". . . *There is no doubt left that, despite his youth and (in this instance at least) his dubious choice of subject, Morse is one of the really important playwrights of the day, certainly the most significant in America. . . ."*

He heard the door open behind him, and let the magazine fall shut on his knee and said, "Ready?" without turning around.

"*Cyprian!*" said Astrid's voice.

There was something strange about the sound, a quality which inexplicably, as if it had been some dreadful psychic emanation, seemed to change the shape of his every thought and sensation, so that where he had been relaxed and warmly content, he was now tense and chill with formless apprehension.

"*Cyprian!*" said the voice again, and he came to his feet in a single spasmodic movement, turning to face Astrid as he rose.

He stared at her in stunned amazement and a useless hope of disbelief. His flesh crept, and he seemed to feel the hairs on his neck rising like the hackles on a dog.

She came toward him, slowly—and he backed away. She mustn't touch him, she mustn't touch him.

She drew inexorably closer. She held out her arms to him. He didn't know he was still moving away until the edge of the mantelshelf came hard against his shoulders. He could feel sweat clammy cold on his forehead, his upper lip, his neck. Desperately, his mind struggled for mastery over his body. His mind knew that, in reality, this was merely a distressing incident hardly removed from the commonplace. His mind knew that a few simple words, a curl of the lip, a lift of the shoulders—any or all of these would free him not only now but forever. But the words had to be uttered, the gestures made —and his body refused the tasks.

She was close now. Very close. She was going to touch him.

She said, in the same thick voice, "Cyprian! Don't look at me like that." And she said, "I love you, Cyprian, you must know that . . ."

There was a ringing in his ears, and the tight grip of nausea in his stomach. His throat worked as he tried to speak, but no words came from his mouth.

She touched him. She was close against him. His body could feel the dreadful soft warmness of her. There was a mist over his eyes and he could hardly see her through it.

And then her arms were around his neck, soft but implacably strong. His mind screamed something, but the arms tightened their hold. She was speaking, but he couldn't hear through the roaring in his head. Somehow, he tore himself free. Forgetting, he tried to retreat, and thudded against the brick of the mantel. With a scrabbling lunge, he went sideways—and almost fell.

He clutched wildly. His left hand caught the edge of the mantelshelf and checked his fall. His right hand, swinging, struck against something metallic and closed around it.

"Cyprian—" said the voice. "*Cyprian!*"

She was going to touch him again. Through the haze he could see her, the arms reaching.

There was a clatter of metal as the rest of the fire-irons fell, and his right hand, still grasping the logpick it had closed around, raised itself above his head and swung downward, with more than all his force.

Through the rushing in his ears, through the red-flecked haze over his eyes, he heard the sick dull crushing of the first blow, saw the slender shape crumple and collapse. . . .

The haze and the roaring faded, and he found himself standing half-crouched over the thing on the floor—striking down at it again and again. It was as if some outside power had taken charge of him, so that the blows came without his conscious volition—thudding with the broadside of the heavy bar, then thrusting, slashing, tearing with the sharp point of the spike. . . .

Then, piercing the haze and thrusting him back into knowledge of himself, there was a sharp pain in his shoulder as a muscle twisted and cramped.

The logpick fell from his hands, thudding onto the thick carpet. He looked down at what he had done—and then, an arm flung across his eyes, he turned and ran, stumbling and wavering, for the outer door of the apartment.

He smashed into it—scrabbled with shaking hands for the latch —tore it open—plunged out into the corridor—and, sightless, witless, came into heavy collision with a man and a woman just passing the door.

The woman lurched against the opposite wall. Cursing, the man snarled at Cyprian and caught him by the shoulder and straightened his slim bent body and thrust him back against the door jamb. The woman took one horrified look at Cyprian and screamed. The man stared and said, "What in the name of—"

Cyprian swayed. Everything—the figures facing him, the walls and doors, the lights overhead, the pattern of the corridor carpet— all swung crazily together before his eyes; swung and tilted so that he reeled, and clutched vainly for support—and slid down against the jamb to sit sprawled and ungainly on the floor, clutching at his whirling head.

The woman said, "Look at him. *Look* at him!" in a shaking voice. "That's *blood!*" And the man said heavily, "What goes on around here?"

Cyprian moaned—and began to vomit. Above him the man said, "I'm going to take a look in there," and moved through the open doorway.

The woman went after him, and there glowed in Cyprian's mind the first sudden and frightful awareness of his danger. Even as another spasm shook him, a tiny self-preservatory spark was born, and when the woman began to scream just inside the door, he was already mumbling to himself, "... *there was a man ... he went through the window ...*"

And then the beginning of the long nightmare.

The man and woman rushing out of the apartment. Shouting. Doors opening. People. More screaming. Trying to get to his feet and failing. More men, one in shirt sleeves, another in a robe, standing over him like guards. Sirens wailing outside. Whistles. Noise. Voices. Elevator doors clanging and heavy feet tramping down the corridor. New voices, harsh and different. Men in uniform. The other faces going, the new faces staring down at him, looming behind the harsh voices. A hand as ruthless as God's pulling him to his feet....

He wanted help. He craved succor. "... *there was a man ... he went through the window ...*"

He wanted a friend. He wanted Charles. Charles would know what to do. Charles would deal with these bullying louts.

"... *there was a man ... he went through the window ...*"

And Charles was thousands of miles away.

The nightmare went on. The questions. First in the room where men—not in uniform now—worked over the horror on the floor, muttering to each other, measuring, flashing lights, pointing cameras, scribbling in notebooks.

Then in another room, after a hellish, siren-screaming journey in a crowded car. Questions, questions. All framed with the certainty, the *knowledge*, that he had done what he must not admit having done.

Questions. And the white light aching in his eyes. His throat stiff and his lips unmanageable. His whole body shaking, shaking. The inside of his head shaking too.

—Why did you kill her?

—What time did you kill her?

—What did you kill her for? What had she done?

—How long after ya killed her before you run out?

—*I didn't. I didn't ... there was a man ... he went through the window ...*

—All right—so there was a man. An' he went outa the window. Whaddud he do? Jump? Fly?

—You don't expect us to swallow that, do you?

—Yeah. How d'ya figure this sorta hooey's goin' to help?

—*I tell you there was a man . . . he went through the window . . . Down the fire escape . . .*

—He did? Leavin' your prints all over the poker?

—Yeah. An' splashin' her blood all over ya?

—Now, listen, Mr. Morse; it's completely certain that you killed this woman. The evidence is overwhelming. Can't you realize that you're doing yourself no good by your attitude?

—*I'm telling the truth. There was a man. I—I was in the bathroom. I heard a noise. I ran in. I saw Astrid. There was a man. He climbed out of the window. I'm telling the truth.*

—Very well. So you're telling the truth. Which window did this man go out?

—Yeah? And how come he locked it behind him?

—Never mind that, Mr. Morse. Answer the other question. Which window?

—*I—I don't know . . . The window in the—the end wall . . . Next the fire escape . . .*

—Which window? The right as you face? Or the left?

—Yeah. Which? One of 'em was locked, bud. Which?

Questions. And the light. Questions all around him. Questions from faces. Coarse, brutal faces. Sharp fox-faces. They began to associate themselves with the voices.

And another face with wise gray eyes that watched him always. A face with no voice. A face in the corner. A face more to be feared than all the faces with voices.

Questions. And the light. Time standing still, immobilized. He had always been here. He would always be here. "*. . . there was a man . . . he went through the window . . .*"

It was a pattern, diabolic and infinite: Fear—questions—fear fear—light—fear fear fear—fatigue.

Fatigue. First a dull dead core of exhaustion, but now beginning to reach out all around itself, encroaching more and more on all other feeling.

Until even fear was going . . . going . . . almost gone—

—Why don't we wind this up, Morse?

—Yes. We know you killed her, and you know we know. Why not get it over with?

—Yeah. How's about it, fella? Why doncha come clean, so's we can let up on ya?

Fear flickering again, momentarily reborn.

—*I didn't I didn't I didn't . . . There was a man. When I ran in, he was climbing out of the window . . .*

For an instant a picture forming behind his eyes. An image of Charles—tall, tough, elegant, dangerous, one shoulder lifting higher than the other, a cigarette jutting from the corner of his long mouth, his creased face creasing more in a mastering smile. Charles coming through the door, being suddenly framed in the doorway, standing and looking down at the faces, the stupid crafty animal faces—

Then his eyes closing. His head falling forward. Then nothing. Except the hard scratched feeling of the table-top against his cheek. And a ghost smell of soap and pencils and agony.

A rough hand biting into his shoulder. Shaking. His head lolling, jerking back and forward like a marionette's—

Then a new voice, quiet, sharp, charged with authority.

—That's enough. Let him alone. Schraff, you go find Dr. Innes. This isn't any Bowery bum you're handling.

His head resting on the table again. The voices muttering all around him, not thrusting at him now.

Consciousness of someone standing over him. Not touching him. Just standing.

Opening his eyes. Forcing muscles to roll up the ton-weight lids. Seeing the wise gray eyes looking down at him, contemplating him, understanding everything.

Staring dully up into the gray eyes for a moment, dully wondering. Then letting the heavy lids fold down over his own eyes again.

The door opening, and brisk footsteps. And quick impersonal hands upon him. Doctor's hands. Feeling at his temples, his wrist. Tilting back his unbearably heavy head, with a deft thumb rolling back those eyelids.

Then muttering above his head. His coat being eased off, shirt sleeve rolled up.

Indefinite pause—and then the fingers on his arm, and the sting of the needle . . .

When he waked it was to grayness. A gray blanket over him; gray walls; a door of gray bars; gray light filtering through a small grilled window.

For some timeless interval the drug held memory in check. But at last, with a sick gray emptiness in his stomach, recollection came. And fear again, all the worse because its edges were dulled now and instead of it being so intense that there was no room in him for other emotions, it was now entangled and heightened by remorse and shame and horror.

He threw off the blanket and swung his feet to the floor and propped his elbows on his knees and dropped his face into his hands.

There was a clanging sound, and he started convulsively and raised his head and saw a uniformed guard coming into the cell. The man was carrying a big suitcase which he put down as he closed the barred door. On the side of the case were the initials C.M., and Cyprian saw with dull surprise that it was his own, the one Charles had given him in London. He heard himself saying, "Where did you get that?" and the fellow looked at him and said, "Came from y'r apartment. There's clothes an' shaving tack an' setra." He had a strange manner, at once meaning and noncommittal, official and yet faintly sycophantic.

He came closer to Cyprian and looked down at him. He said, "Mr. Friar fixed it. An' about sendin' out for what you want."

A little faint glow of warmth came to life somewhere in Cyprian's coldness. Trust John Friar, he thought.

The guard said, "You like anything now? Breakfast? Or just coffee?"

Cyprian went on staring at him: it was as if his mind was so full that he didn't hear words until long after they had been spoken.

"Coffee," he said at last. "Just coffee."

The man nodded, and went to the door and opened it again, and paused. "Like to see the papers?" he said over his shoulder.

This time the words penetrated fast. Cyprian recoiled from them as if they were blows. "No!" he said. "No—no!"

He closed his eyes and held them screwed shut until he had heard the door open and clang shut, and then receding footsteps echoing. A shudder shook him at the thought of newspapers, and once more he covered his face with his hands. Headlines—as if on an endless ticker-tape—began to unroll behind his eyes, running the gamut from the sober through the sensational to the nadir of the tabloid—

—*FAMOUS PLAYWRIGHT HELD ON MURDER CHARGE. DESIGNER SLAIN . . .*

—*CYPRIAN MORSE ARRAIGNED FOR MURDER. GIRL ASSOCIATE BRUTALLY BATTERED TO DEATH . . .*

—*PARK AVENUE LOVE-FIEND MURDER. FAMOUS THEATER BEAUTY SLASHED. MORSE, BROADWAY FIG-URE, JAILED . . .*

He groaned and twisted his body this way and that and desperately pressed the heels of his palms against his eyes until a spark-shot red mist seemed to swim under the lids. But the tape went on unrolling—a ceaseless stream of words.

He jumped up and began to pad about the cell—and then mercifully heard footsteps in the corridor again and mastered himself and was sitting on the edge of the gray cot when the guard reappeared with a tray.

He mumbled thanks and reached for the coffeepot. But his hand trembled so badly that, without speaking, the man filled a cup for him.

He drank greedily, and felt strength coming back to him. He looked up and said, "Can I—would—is it allowed to send a cablegram?"

"Could be. With an okay from the Warden's office." The fellow reached into a pocket, produced a little memo pad and a stump of pencil. "Want to write it down?"

Cyprian took the things. Once more he mumbled thanks. He didn't look at the man; he didn't like his eyes. He began to write, not having to think, letting the pencil print the words—

—*Charles de Lastro Hotel Castilia Venezuela In terrible trouble need you desperately please come Reply care John Friar Cyprian.*

He handed the pad and pencil back, and watched while what he had written was read. He said, "Well—?" and met the eyes again as they flickered over him.

"Seems like this'll be okay." The guard turned a blue-clad back and went to the door. "I'll look after it."

Once more the clanging, the footsteps dying away—and Cyprian was alone again. His hand steadier now, he poured himself more coffee. Anything, any action, to keep him from thought.

He drained the cup. He picked up the suitcase and set it on the cot and opened it. Forcing himself to activity, he washed and shaved and put on the clothes he found packed. A suit of dark blue flannel— a white silk shirt—a plain maroon tie.

He felt a little better. It was easier to believe that this was Cyprian Morse—and he gave silent thanks to John Friar.

But there was nothing to do now—and if he weren't careful he might have to start thinking. He lit a cigarette from the box in the suitcase and began to pace the cell. There were five steps one way and six the other. . . .

So this was Cyprian Morse. Perhaps he did feel better after all. Perhaps—

Footsteps in the corridor again. One, two, three sets.

John Friar himself, with another man and the guard. Who opened the door, and stood aside to let the visitors in, and clanged the door shut again and stood outside, his back to it.

John Friar took Cyprian's hand in both of his and gripped hard. He was white-faced, strained. He looked less like a successful producer than ever, and more like a truncated and careworn Abe Lincoln. The man with him towered over him, a lank, loose-limbed, stooping giant with a thatch of white hair and a seamed, unlikely face which was neither saint's nor gargoyle's but something of both.

John Friar said, "Cyprian!" in a voice which wasn't quite steady. He made a gesture including the third man. He said, "Julius, meet Cyprian Morse . . . Cyprian, this is Julius Magnussen."

Again Cyprian's hand was taken, and enveloped in a vast paw which gripped firmly but with surprising gentleness. And Cyprian found himself looking up, tall though he was, into dark unreadable eyes which seemed jet black under the shaggy white brows.

John Friar said, "Julius is taking on your def—your case, Cyprian. And you know what that means!"

"I most definitely do!" Cyprian hoped they wouldn't hear the trembling in his throat. "Is there anyone in America who doesn't?"

Magnussen grunted. He turned away and folded his length in the middle and sat on the edge of the gray bed. He looked at Cyprian and said, "Better tell me about it," then moved a little and added, "Sit down here."

Cyprian found himself obeying. But he couldn't keep on meeting the dark eyes, and gave up trying to. He looked up at John Friar and essayed a smile. He said, "Of course," in Magnussen's direction—and then, faintly, all the fear and horror of memory breaking loose in his head again, "Where—where—d'you want me to start?" . . .

"At the beginning, Mr. Morse," Magnussen said, and Cyprian drew a deep breath to still the quaking inside him.

But it wouldn't be stilled. It spread from his body to his mind. He was being thrust into nightmare again—

—I can't . . . I can't . . .

—Would it be easier if I asked you questions?

Questions. The pattern returning. Fear—questions—fear fear—fatigue. But worse now. Hiding from friends not enemies.

—I have to ask you this: did you kill this woman Astrid Halmar?

—No—no—no! . . . *There was a man . . . he went through the window . . .*

—You know of no enemies Miss Halmar might have had?

—No. How should I? I—

—So you think the murderer was a stranger, a prowler?

—How—how do I know what he was! Or who! I don't know anything . . .

Questions. Questions. Fear. Thinking furiously before each answer without letting the pause be evident. Trying to screen the vortex of his mind with caution. Time standing still again. He had always been here. He would always be here.

—So you were in the bathroom for more than an hour?

—Yes—yes. I went there just after dinner. Just as—just after the maid left the apartment.

—Were you feeling unwell? Is that why you stayed so long? Had something you ate upset your stomach?

A straw. A solid straw. Snatch it!

—Yes. That's right. I was sick . . . It was the oysters . . .

More questions. More fear. Feeling the dark eyes always on his face. Not meeting them.

—And you were just about to come out of the bathroom when you heard a cry. Am I right?

Another straw. Snatch it!

—Yes. Yes. Astrid screamed . . .

—And you ran out, and along the passage to the living room?

—Yes.

—While you were running along the passage, did you happen to notice Miss Halmar's robe, lying on the floor?

—Robe? What—no, I don't think—

—Her robe was found by the door to the living room. The killer —however he gained entry to the apartment—must have struggled with her, snatched at her, in the passageway there, pulling off the robe as she fled into the living room. I am wondering—did you notice it?

A straw?

—I think I did. There was something—soft on the floor. It caught my shoe . . .

—Now, Mr. Morse, as you entered the living room, you saw the figure of a man just disappearing out of the window?

—Yes. Yes.

—And you saw Miss Halmar's body on the floor and ran to it?

—Yes. Of course I did. I—I had to try and help her . . .

—Naturally. Now, as your fingerprints are on the logpick, Mr. Morse, you must have handled it? Maybe you touched it—picked it up—when you went to her? It was in your way, was it?

A sudden lightening. As if some frightful pressure were easing. Fear actually receding. Knowing now that these were no accidental straws, but material for a raft. A life raft.

—Yes. That was it. I remember now. It—it was lying across her body. I—I picked it up and—threw it down, away from her.

—And in your shock and horror, when you found she was dead,

you forgot the telephone and ran blindly out to seek help, and then collapsed?

—Yes. Yes. That's it—exactly.

Questions. Questions. But not minding them now. Being eager for them. And being able to meet the dark eyes, keeping his own eyes on them.

The pattern had changed. Fear was there, as a permanent lowering background, but in front of it was hope. . . .

The hope persisted, even when he was alone once more. It seemed to widen the cell, and raise its roof. It set the blood flowing through his head again, so that his brain worked fast and clear and he started to elaborate on the structure Julius Magnussen had begun to build for him.

This work—and work it was—carried him through the dragging days and weeks with a surprising minimum of anguish. It even fortified him to some extent against the shock of the answering cablegram from Charles, which didn't arrive until several days after he had expected it.

The cable ran: *Hospitalized bad kickup malaria   Flying back immediately released maybe two weeks   Hang on   Charles.*

And that was bad news. Bad from two angles—that he would have to wait before Charles could get to him, that poor Charles was sick.

But whereas, before the first meeting with Julius Magnussen, Cyprian would have been crushed almost to extinction by these twin misfortunes, now they seemed merely to serve as a spur to his fortitude and his hope and his labor. So that he clenched his teeth and redoubled his efforts to produce appropriate "memories"—until he reached the point of being sure that at least Friar and Magnussen believed him, that he almost believed himself.

But it was as well for him that he wasn't present at any of the several meetings between Julius Magnussen and John Friar alone, or he would have heard talk which would have turned his hope-lightened purgatory into hopeless hell.

—A bad case, John. Don't hide it from yourself. We'll need a miracle.

—Good God, Julius, d'you mean you yourself don't believe—

—Stop. That's not a question I want to be asked. Or answer. Leave it at what I said. A bad case. No case at all.

—But the evidence against him's all circumstantial!

—And therefore the best, in spite of what they say in novels.

—But surely it's all open to two interpretations! Like—like his fingerprints on that poker.

—*And* the splashes of blood on him and his clothing? Have you thought of that, John? *Splashes.* Not smears, which are what should be there from raising her, examining her, trying to help her . . .

—But the boy's *gentle*, Julius! There's no violence in him. He couldn't even kill a fly that was pestering him.

—Maybe not. And don't think that's not going to be used. For more than all it's worth. For God's sake, it's practically all we have! You know the young man, John: tell me, how would he react to the suggestion of an alternative plea?

—You mean "not guilty, or guilty by reason of insanity"!—that gag! Good God, Julius—he wouldn't go for that if you tortured him.

—H'mm. I was afraid that would be the answer.

—Look now, what is all this? What are you trying to do—tell me you won't take the case after all? Is that it?

—Cool off, John. I'm trying to save your prodigy's life, that's all.

—I don't get this! Julius Magnussen, of all people, scared of a setup like this! . . . Remember that police photograph you showed me? Well, think of it. Not the head wounds, the others. Think of 'em! Cyprian could not have been responsible for that frightful *sort* of brutality. Think of what was done to that girl, man! . . . Can't you see—can't you?

—Oh, yes, John, I can see. A great many things. . . .

But Cyprian knew nothing of such conversations, and it seemed to him, every time he saw his counsel, that more and more confidence radiated from that towering, loose-limbed figure; that the penetrating dark eyes looked always more cheerful.

So he rode out the rest of the dragging days and nights and came in good enough order to the morning when the trial was to open. It was a Thursday, and he liked that because he had had a fancy, since an episode in his boyhood, that Thor's was his lucky day. Further, a bright autumnal sun was glittering over New York and even—a rare occurrence in the weeks he had been there—pushing rays through the bars of the small window high up in the wall of the cell.

He dressed with great, almost finicking care. He drank a whole pot of coffee and then sent for more. He even ate a little of his breakfast.

He was ready and waiting a full half-hour before they came for him. He spent it pacing the cell, smoking too much and too fast, glancing occasionally toward the pile of letters which he hadn't read and had no more intention of ever reading than he had of looking in court at any of the reporters' faces. He didn't think of what was before him today. He daren't think of that, in the same way—only infinitely multiplied—that he never thought about what was coming on a first night.

So he considered, with furious intensity, anything and everything except what was coming. The sure hope at the back of his mind must be kept inviolate.

He came naturally to thoughts of Charles. Every day he had been sure this must be the day when he would hear again—and every day he had been disappointed. He had wired again, and he had written—just a note which John Friar had air-mailed for him. But still no answer. Charles must be very ill indeed. Or—a wonderful idea which he dare not dwell upon for more than one delicious instant— Charles was well again and had arrived in New York, and was on his way here.

The third alternative he shuddered away from. The thought of Charles dead was so black, so bleak, so dreadful, that it would have driven him back in escape to thoughts of the immediate future if he hadn't been saved by the arrival of his guard.

For once he was glad to see the fellow. He said, "Do we start now?" and moved toward the door.

But the man shook his head. "They ain't here yet," he said. "Take it easy." He drew a folded yellow envelope from a pocket and held it out to Cyprian. "Sent over from Friar's," he said. "He reckoned you might like to have it right away."

Cyprian almost snatched it from the outstretched hand. His heart was pounding, and sudden color had tinged his pallid face. With fingers which he didn't know were shaking, he fumbled at the flimsy envelope, ripped it open at last, and unfolded the sheet it contained.

And read: *Better   Out next Wednesday will fly arriving Thursday   Charles.*

The new color deepened in Cyprian's face. He read the cable again—and again. Here was the best of all possible omens. Almost as good as his wild daydream of a few moments before—that perhaps Charles would arrive in person. On second thought, perhaps better. Because now he was supremely confident, and he would so far prefer to have all this ugliness behind him when Charles returned; out of sight and wrapped up and put away, to be disinterred and examined, if ever, at a safe distance in time and then only for personal historic interest.

He moved his shoulders unconsciously, as if in reflex to the removal of a heavy weight. He folded the strip of paper carefully, and stowed it away in his breast pocket. And then looked at the guard and smiled, and said softly, "Thank you. Thank you very much. . . ."

There was a tramping of feet in the corridor—and two uniformed men he had never seen before. One of them pushed the cell door wide and looked at him with no expression and said, "All set?"

Cyprian smiled at this man too, and walked out into the corridor quickly, lightly, almost jauntily. . . .

But there was no lightness in him when he came back eight hours later, and no square of sunshine from the barred window. There was only night outside and here the hard cold light of the single bulb overhead.

His face was lined and wax-white. His shoulders sagged and his body seemed not to fill his clothes. He lurched on his feet while they opened the door of the cell, and one of the men gripped his arm and said, "Take it easy."

They put him inside and he dropped on the edge of his cot and sat there limp and head-hanging, his eyes wide and staring at the floor and not seeing it.

The escort went away and his own guard came, and sometime

later the doctor. He couldn't get food down, and they put him to bed and gave him a sedative. He slept almost at once, and they left him.

He lay like a log for three hours, until the deadly numbness of fatigue had gone and the drug had eased its grip. And then he began to murmur and thrash around on the cot—and in a moment gave a harsh choked cry and sat upright, awake.

He remembered. He tried not to, he fought, but he couldn't stop memory from working. He remembered everything—at first in jumbled pictures, then in echoing phrases; at last, concentrated upon the gray-haired, gray-eyed figure of the District Attorney, he recalled the whole of the clear and ruthlessly dispassionate Opening for the Prosecution. The speech which, period by period, point by careful point, had not only stripped Cyprian Morse of all cover but had shattered all remnant of hope in him.

What had happened after the speech didn't matter. The irreparable damage to Cyprian Morse, the conviction of Cyprian Morse, had been brought about; those witnesses, the silly endless procession of them who answered silly endless questions, they were just so many more nails in his coffin. After the speech, which showed such complete, such eerie knowledge and understanding, as if the speaker had not only seen everything that had happened but had seen it with Cyprian's mind and Cyprian's eyes—after that, all else seemed time-prolonging and sadistic anticlimactic . . .

He didn't move. He sat as he was, and stared into the abyss. . . .

Morning came, and daylight, and people he heard and saw as if from a long distance. He moved then but was almost unconscious of moving. It was as if his body were an automaton and his mind a separate entity outside it, which had no concern with the robot movements.

The automaton clothed itself, and ate and drank, and went with his mind and the uniformed men and sat in the crowded courtroom in the same place as his undivided self had sat the day before.

The automaton sat still and went through motions—of listening to friends and Counsel, of answering them when necessary, of looking attentive to the gabber-jab of the unending witnesses, of considering thoughtfully the closing speech for the Prosecution, of hearing the crabbed Judge rule that the Court, this being Friday, should recess until the morning of Monday. . . .

But his mind, his actual self, was in hell without a permit. For sixty-two hours the automaton made all the foolish gestures of living; for uncountable stages of distorted time his mind gazed into the pit.

The Monday came, and the automaton moved accordingly. But the clean-cut edges of the schism between body and mind began to waver before the two parts of him left the cell, as if something had happened which demanded they should be joined again. Resisting the pull, his mind began to wonder what had caused it. His refusal to see John Friar or Magnussen during the recess? The odd, almost excited manner of his guard on bringing a newspaper to the cell and trying to insist on the automaton reading it? The looks which both his escorts cast at the automaton in the car on the way to court?

He didn't want the union. He would break, he felt, if he couldn't keep up the separation. But the pull grew stronger with every foot of the way, and almost irresistible as he entered the courtroom itself, and his mind felt a difference—a strange, disturbing, agitated alteration—in the other minds behind the faces staring at him.

And then, with a shivering, nauseating shock, his resistance went and he was swept back into his body once more, so that he was stripped and next to the world again with no transparent armor between.

It was the face of Magnussen's wizened clerk which brought it about, a face which always before had been harassed and grave and filled with foreboding, but which now was gay and eager and irradiated by a tremendous gnomelike smile. As Cyprian was about to take his seat, this smile was turned full on him, and his hand was surreptitiously taken and earnestly squeezed, and through the smile a voice came whispering something which couldn't be distinguished but all the same was pregnant with the most extreme importance.

Cyprian sat down, weakly. Once again, he had no strength. He looked up into the little clerk's face and muttered something—he wasn't sure of the words himself.

An astonished change came over the puckered visage. "Mr. Morse!" The voice cracked in amazement. "Do you mean to say you haven't *heard!*"

Dumbly Cyprian shook his head, the small movement leaving him exhausted.

"Not about the—the other killings! . . . Mr. Morse! There have been two more murders of unfortunate girls! In every respect the same as Miss Halmar's—even the—the mutilations identical. . . . On Saturday night the first victim was found; and another discovered in the early hours of this morning!"

Cyprian went on staring up into the excited, agitated face.

"D-don't you realize what this m-means!" The voice was stammering now. "All three deaths must be linked. *You* couldn't have caused the others! They're the work of a maniac—a Jack the Ripper!" Fluttering hands produced a newspaper, unfolded it, waved it. "Look here, Mr. Morse!"

There were black heavy headlines. They wavered in front of Cyprian's eyes, then focused sharply and made him catch at his breath.

POLICE CLUELESS IN NEW FIEND SLAYINGS! MORSE RELEASE DEMANDED BY PUBLIC!

"Oh," said Cyprian, his lips barely moving. "Oh, I see . . ." His whole body began to tingle, as if circulation had been withheld from it until now. He said, a little louder, "What—what will happen?"

The clerk sat down beside him. His hoarse whispering was as clear now as a shout in Cyprian's ears. "What will happen? I'll tell you, Mr. Morse. I'll tell you exactly. The D.A. will withdraw—and not long after Mr. Magnussen's opened. He'll withdraw, Mr. Morse, you mark my words!"

The words coincided with a stentorian bellow from the back of the courtroom, followed by a stamping rustle as everyone stood up—and Justice swept to its throne in a dusty black robe. . . .

And Cyprian, life welling up in him, found himself caught in a whirling timeless jumble of fact and feeling and emotion, a maelstrom which was in effect the precise opposite of the long nightmare succeeding his arrest—

Julius Magnussen towering on his feet, speaking of Cyprian Morse's innocence with an almost contemptuous certainty. Julius Magnussen examining detectives on the witness stand, forcing them to prove all three killings had been identical. Julius Magnussen calling more witnesses, then looking around haughtily at the Prosecution when the Court was asked to hear a statement. The District Attorney himself, gray eyes not understanding now but puzzled and confused, muttering that the state withdrew its case against Cyprian Morse. The Judge speaking, bestowing commiseration on Cyprian Morse, laudation on Julius Magnussen, censure upon their opponents—

Then bedlam breaking loose, himself the center. Friends. Strangers. Acquaintances. Reporters. All crowding, jabbering, laughing. Women weeping. Flashbulbs exploding. John Friar pumping both his hands. Magnussen clapping him on the shoulder. Himself the center of a wedge of policemen, struggling for the exit. An odd little instant of comparative quiet in the hallway, and hearing Magnussen say to John Friar behind him, "An apology, John, you were right."

Then John's big car, and the soft cushioned seat supporting him. And quietness, with the tires singing on the road and time to draw breath—and taste freedom. . . .

All horror was behind him and it was Wednesday evening and Charles was coming home. From John Friar's house in Westchester, in John Friar's car, driven by John Friar's chauffeur.

It was deepening dusk when they pulled into the parking lot behind the apartment house. Cyprian peered, and saw no sign of any human being and was pleased. He got out and smiled at the chauffeur and said warmly, "Thank you, Maurice. Thank you very much . . ." and thrust a lavish tip into the man's gloved hand and waved a cheerful salute and walked off toward the rear entrance of the building. His footsteps rang crisply on the concrete, and a faint, wreathlike mist from his breathing hung on the autumn air. He suppressed an impulse to stop and crane his neck to look up to the penthouse and see the warm lights glowing out from it. He knew they were there, because he had heard John Friar telephoning to his servant, telling him when Mr. Morse was to be expected.

Good old John, he thought. Thoughtful John! And then forgot John completely as he entered the service door, and still met no one and found one of the service elevators empty and waiting.

He forgot John. He forgot everyone and everything—except Charles.

And Charles would be here tomorrow. That was why Cyprian had insisted upon coming home tonight—so that he could supervise preparation.

He hurried the elevator with his mind, and when it reached the rear hallway of his penthouse, threw open the gate—and was faced, not by light and an open door and Walter's white-smiling black face, but by cold unwelcoming darkness.

He stepped out of the elevator and groped for the light switch and pressed it and blinked at the sudden glare. Frowning, he tried the door to the kitchen. It wasn't locked, but when he opened it there was more darkness. And no sound. No sound at all.

A chill settled on his mind. The warm excited glow which had been growing inside him evaporated with unnerving suddenness. He switched on more lights and went quickly through the bright-tiled neatness and threw open an inner door and called, "Walter! Walter, where are you?" into more darkness still.

Not such absolute darkness this time, but the more disturbing for that. The curtains across the big windows at the west side of the living room had not been drawn and there was still a sort of gray luminosity in the air.

Cyprian took two or three paces into the room. He called, "Walter!" again, and heard his own voice go up too high at the end of the word.

And another voice spoke from behind him—a cracked and casual voice.

"I sent him out for an hour or two," it said. "Hope you don't mind."

Cyprian started violently. He gasped, "*Charles!*" and wheeled around and saw a tall figure looming in the grayness. His heart pounded in his ears and he felt a swaying in his head.

There was no answering sound—and he said, "Charles!" again and moved toward a table near the figure and reached out for the lamp he knew was on it.

But his shoulder was caught in a grip which checked him completely. Long fingers strong as steel bit into his flesh, and Charles's voice said, "Take it easy. We don't need light just yet."

Cyprian felt cold. His head still whirled. He couldn't understand,

and the grip on his shoulder seemed to be paralyzing him and he was afraid with that worst of all fears which hasn't any shape.

He said wildly, "Charles, I don't understand—I—" and couldn't get out any more words. He contorted all the muscles in his face in a useless attempt to see Charles's face.

"You will," said Charles's voice. "Do you remember once telling me you'd never lie to me again?"

"Yes," Cyprian whispered—and then, his mouth drying with fear, "Let me go. You're hurting me . . ."

"Did you mean it?" The hand didn't relax its grip.

"Of course . . . And I never have lied to you since! I don't understand—"

"You will." The grip tightened and Cyprian caught his breath. "I want a truthful answer to one question. Will you give it?"

"Yes. Yes. Of course I will . . ."

"Did you kill that Halmar woman?"

"No—no—*there was a man . . . he went through the window . . .*"

"I thought you weren't going to lie to me. Did you kill her?"

"*No!* I—" The steel fingers bit deeper and Cyprian sobbed.

"Did you kill her? Don't lie to me."

"Yes! *Yes!*" Cyprian's face was writhing. His eyes stung with tears and his lips were trembling. "Yes, I killed her! I killed her—*I killed her! . . .*"

The grip eased. The hand lifted from his shoulder. He tottered on uncertain feet, and the lamp on the table jumped suddenly into life and through the mist over his eyes he saw Charles for the first time —and then heard Charles's voice say, easily and softly and with the old-time chuckle hidden somewhere in it, "Well, that's that. Just so long as we know . . . I'd like a drink." He turned away from Cyprian and crossed with his lounging walk to the bar—the lounging walk which always reminded Cyprian of the stalking of a cat—

And suddenly Cyprian knew.

He knew, and in the same moment that understanding flooded his mind, he thought—for the first time actively thought—of those other two deaths which had saved him from death.

A scream came to his throat and froze there. He shrank into himself as he stood there—and Charles turned, glass in hand, and looked at him.

His eyes burned in his head. He couldn't move their gaze from Charles's face. He said, "You did it. You killed those two women. You weren't ill. You got someone else to send those cables. You heard about Astrid and you flew back without anyone knowing. And you plotted and planned and stalked—and did that. As if they were animals. You did that!"

His voice died in his throat. All strength went out of him and he tottered to a chair and doubled up in it and sat crumpled.

"Don't fret, my dear Cyprian." Charles drank, looking at him over the rim of the glass. "We sit tight—and live happily ever after...."

Cyprian dropped his head into his hands.

"Oh, my God!" he said. "Oh, my God!"

THE DANCING PARTNER

BY JEROME K. JEROME

❡ "THIS STORY," commenced MacShaugnassy, "comes from Furtwangen, a small town in the Black Forest. There lived there a very wonderful old fellow named Nicholas Geibel. His business was the making of mechanical toys, at which work he had acquired an almost European reputation. He made rabbits that would emerge from the heart of a cabbage, flop their ears, smooth their whiskers, and disappear again; cats that would wash their faces, and mew so naturally that dogs would mistake them for real cats, and fly at them; dolls, with phonographs concealed within them, that would raise their hats and say, 'Good morning; how do you do?' and some that would even sing a song.

"But he was something more than a mere mechanic; he was an artist. His work was with him a hobby, almost a passion. His shop was filled with all manner of strange things that never would, or could, be sold—things he had made for the pure love of making them. He had contrived a mechanical donkey that would trot for two hours by means of stored electricity, and trot, too, much faster than the live article, and with less need for exertion on the part of the driver; a bird that would shoot up into the air, fly round and round in a circle, and drop to earth at the exact spot from where it started; a skeleton that, supported by an upright iron bar, would dance a hornpipe; a life-sized lady doll that could play the fiddle; and a gentleman with a hollow inside who could smoke a pipe and drink more lager beer than any three average German students put together, which is saying much.

Reprinted by permission of the executrix, Miss Rowena Jerome.

"Indeed, it was the belief of the town that old Geibel could make a man capable of doing everything that a respectable man need want to do. One day he made a man who did too much, and it came about in this way:

"Young Doctor Follen had a baby, and the baby had a birthday. Its first birthday put Doctor Follen's household into somewhat of a flurry, but on the occasion of its second birthday, Mrs. Doctor Follen gave a ball in honor of the event. Old Geibel and his daughter Olga were among the guests.

"During the afternoon of the next day some three or four of Olga's bosom friends, who had also been present at the ball, dropped in to have a chat about it. They naturally fell to discussing the men, and to criticizing their dancing. Old Geibel was in the room, but he appeared to be absorbed in his newspaper, and the girls took no notice of him.

" 'There seem to be fewer men who can dance at every ball you go to,' said one of the girls.

" 'Yes, and don't the ones who can give themselves airs,' said another; 'they make quite a favor of asking you.'

" 'And how stupidly they talk,' added a third. 'They always say exactly the same things: "How charming you are looking tonight." "Do you often go to Vienna? Oh, you should, it's delightful." "What a charming dress you have on." "What a warm day it has been." "Do you like Wagner?" I do wish they'd think of something new.'

" 'Oh, I never mind how they talk,' said a fourth. 'If a man dances well he may be a fool for all I care.'

" 'He generally is,' slipped in a thin girl, rather spitefully.

" 'I go to a ball to dance,' continued the previous speaker, not noticing the interruption. 'All I ask of a partner is that he shall hold me firmly, take me round steadily, and not get tired before I do.'

" 'A clockwork figure would be the thing for you,' said the girl who had interrupted.

" 'Bravo!' cried one of the others, clapping her hands, 'what a capital idea!'

" 'What's a capital idea?' they asked.

" 'Why, a clockwork dancer, or, better still, one that would go by electricity and never run down.'

"The girls took up the idea with enthusiasm.

" 'Oh, what a lovely partner he would make,' said one; 'he would never kick you, or tread on your toes.'

" 'Or tear your dress,' said another.

" 'Or get out of step.'

" 'Or get giddy and lean on you.'

" 'And he would never want to mop his face with his handker-chief. I do hate to see a man do that after every dance.'

" 'And wouldn't want to spend the whole evening in the supper room.'

" 'Why, with a phonograph inside him to grind out all the stock remarks, you would not be able to tell him from a real man,' said the girl who had first suggested the idea.

" 'Oh, yes, you would,' said the thin girl, 'he would be so much nicer.'

"Old Geibel had laid down his paper, and was listening with both his ears. On one of the girls glancing in his direction, however, he hurriedly hid himself again behind it.

"After the girls were gone, he went into his workshop, where Olga heard him walking up and down, and every now and then chuckling to himself; and that night he talked to her a good deal about dancing and dancing men—asked what they usually said and did—what dances were most popular—what steps were gone through, with many other questions bearing on the subject.

"Then for a couple of weeks he kept much to his factory, and was very thoughtful and busy, though prone at unexpected moments to break into a quiet low laugh, as if enjoying a joke that nobody else knew of.

"A month later another ball took place in Furtwangen. On this occasion it was given by old Wenzel, the wealthy timber merchant, to celebrate his niece's betrothal, and Geibel and his daughter were again among the invited.

"When the hour arrived to set out, Olga sought her father. Not finding him in the house, she tapped at the door of his workshop. He appeared in his shirt sleeves, looking hot but radiant.

" 'Don't wait for me,' he said, 'you go on, I'll follow you. I've got something to finish.'

"As she turned to obey he called after her, 'Tell them I'm going to bring a young man with me—such a nice young man, and an excellent dancer. All the girls will like him.' Then he laughed and closed the door.

"Her father generally kept his doings secret from everybody, but she had a pretty shrewd suspicion of what he had been planning, and so, to a certain extent, was able to prepare the guests for what was coming. Anticipation ran high, and the arrival of the famous mechanist was eagerly awaited.

"At length the sound of wheels was heard outside, followed by a great commotion in the passage, and old Wenzel himself, his jolly face red with excitement and suppressed laughter, burst into the room and announced in stentorian tones:

" 'Herr Geibel—and a friend.'

"Herr Geibel and his 'friend' entered, greeted with shouts of laughter and applause, and advanced to the center of the room.

" 'Allow me, ladies and gentlemen,' said Herr Geibel, 'to introduce you to my friend, Lieutenant Fritz. Fritz, my dear fellow, bow to the ladies and gentlemen.'

"Geibel placed his hand encouragingly on Fritz's shoulder, and the lieutenant bowed low, accompanying the action with a harsh clicking noise in his throat, unpleasantly suggestive of a death rattle. But that was only a detail.

" 'He walks a little stiffly' (old Geibel took his arm and walked him forward a few steps. He certainly did walk stiffly.) 'but then, walking is not his forte. He is essentially a dancing man. I have only been able to teach him the waltz as yet, but at that he is faultless. Come, which of you ladies may I introduce him to as a partner? He keeps perfect time; he never gets tired; he won't kick you or tread on your dress; he will hold you as firmly as you like, and go as quickly or as slowly as you please; he never gets giddy; and he is full of conversation. Come, speak up for yourself, my boy.'

"The old gentleman twisted one of the buttons at the back of his coat, and immediately Fritz opened his mouth, and in thin tones that appeared to proceed from the back of his head, remarked suddenly, 'May I have the pleasure?' and then shut his mouth again with a snap.

"That Lieutenant Fritz had made a strong impression on the company was undoubted, yet none of the girls seemed inclined to dance with him. They looked askance at his waxen face, with his staring eyes and fixed smile, and shuddered. At last old Geibel came to the girl who had conceived the idea.

" 'It is your own suggestion, carried out to the letter,' said Geibel, 'an electric dancer. You owe it to the gentleman to give him a trial.'

"She was a bright, saucy little girl, fond of a frolic. Her host added his entreaties, and she consented.

"Herr Geibel fixed the figure to her. Its right arm was screwed round her waist, and held her firmly; its delicately jointed left hand was made to fasten itself upon her right. The old toymaker showed her how to regulate its speed, and how to stop it and release herself.

" 'It will take you round in a complete circle,' he explained; 'be careful that no one knocks against you, and alters its course.'

"The music struck up. Old Geibel put the current in motion, and Annette and her strange partner began to dance.

"For a while everyone stood watching them. The figure performed its purpose admirably. Keeping perfect time and step, and holding its little partner tight clasped in an unyielding embrace, it revolved steadily, pouring forth at the same time a constant flow of squeaky conversation, broken by brief intervals of grinding silence.

" 'How charming you are looking tonight,' it remarked in its thin, faraway voice. 'What a lovely day it has been. Do you like dancing? How well our steps agree. You will give me another, won't you? Oh, don't be so cruel. What a charming gown you have on. Isn't waltzing delightful? I could go on dancing forever—with you. Have you had supper?'

"As she grew more familiar with the uncanny creature, the girl's nervousness wore off, and she entered into the fun of the thing.

" 'Oh, he's just lovely,' she cried, laughing. 'I could go on dancing with him all my life.'

"Couple after couple now joined them, and soon all the dancers in the room were whirling round behind them. Nicholas Geibel stood looking on, beaming with childish delight at his success.

"Old Wenzel approached him, and whispered something in his

ear. Geibel laughed and nodded, and the two worked their way quietly toward the door.

" 'This is the young people's house tonight,' said Wenzel, so soon as they were outside; 'you and I will have a quiet pipe and a glass of hock, over in the counting house.'

"Meanwhile the dancing grew more fast and furious. Little Annette loosened the screw regulating her partner's rate of progress, and the figure flew round with her swifter and swifter. Couple after couple dropped out exhausted, but they only went the faster, till at length they remained dancing alone.

"Madder and madder became the waltz. The music lagged behind: the musicians, unable to keep the pace, ceased, and sat staring. The younger guests applauded, but the older faces began to grow anxious.

" 'Hadn't you better stop, dear,' said one of the women, 'you'll make yourself so tired.'

"But Annette did not answer.

" 'I believe she's fainted,' cried out a girl who had caught sight of her face as it was swept by.

"One of the men sprang forward and clutched at the figure, but its impetus threw him down onto the floor, where its steel-cased feet laid bare his cheek. The thing evidently did not intend to part with its prize easily.

"Had anyone retained a cool head, the figure, one cannot help thinking, might easily have been stopped. Two or three men acting in concert might have lifted it bodily off the floor, or have jammed it into a corner. But few human heads are capable of remaining cool under excitement. Those who are not present think how stupid must have been those who were; those who are reflect afterward how simple it would have been to do this, that, or the other, if only they had thought of it at the time.

"The women grew hysterical. The men shouted contradictory directions to one another. Two of them made a bungling rush at the figure, which had the result of forcing it out of its orbit in the center of the room, and sending it crashing against the walls and furniture. A stream of blood showed itself down the girl's white frock, and followed her along the floor. The affair was becoming horrible. The women rushed screaming from the room. The men followed them.

"One sensible suggestion was made: 'Find Geibel—fetch Geibel.'

"No one had noticed him leave the room, no one knew where he was. A party went in search of him. The others, too unnerved to go back into the ballroom, crowded outside the door and listened. They could hear the steady whir of the wheels upon the polished floor as the thing spun round and round; the dull thud as every now and again it dashed itself and its burden against some opposing object and ricocheted off in a new direction.

"And everlastingly it talked in that thin ghostly voice, repeating over and over the same formula: 'How charming you are looking tonight. What a lovely day it has been. Oh, don't be so cruel. I could go on dancing forever—with you. Have you had supper?'

"Of course they sought for Geibel everywhere but where he was. They looked in every room in the house, then rushed off in a body to his own place, and spent precious minutes in waking up his deaf old housekeeper. At last it occurred to one of the party that Wenzel was missing also, and then the idea of the counting house across the yard presented itself to them, and there they found him.

"He rose up, very pale, and followed them; and he and old Wenzel forced their way through the crowd of guests gathered outside, and entered the room and locked the door behind them.

"From within there came the muffled sound of low voices and quick steps, followed by a confused scuffling noise, the silence, then the low voices again.

"After a time the door opened, and those near it pressed forward to enter, but old Wenzel's broad shoulders barred the way.

" 'I want you—and you, Bekler,' he said, addressing a couple of the elder men. His voice was calm, but his face was deadly white. 'The rest of you, please go—get the women away as quickly as you can.'

"From that day old Nicholas Geibel confined himself to the making of mechanical rabbits, and cats that mewed and washed their faces."

CASTING THE RUNES

BY M. R. JAMES

April 15th, 190–

❡ DEAR SIR,—I am requested by the Council of the ——— Association to return to you the draft of a paper on *The Truth of Alchemy*, which you have been good enough to offer to read at our forthcoming meeting, and to inform you that the Council do not see their way to including it in the program.

I am,
Yours faithfully,
——— *Secretary*

April 18th

DEAR SIR,—I am sorry to say that my engagements do not permit of my affording you an interview on the subject of your proposed paper. Nor do our laws allow of your discussing the matter with a Committee of our Council, as you suggest. Please allow me to assure you that the fullest consideration was given to the draft which you submitted, and that it was not declined without having been referred to the judgment of a most competent authority. No personal question (it can hardly be necessary for me to add) can have had the slightest influence on the decision of the Council.

Believe me (*ut supra*)

April 20th

The Secretary of the ——— Association begs respectfully to inform Mr. Karswell that it is impossible for him to communicate

From *The Collected Ghost Stories of M. R. James*. Reprinted by permission of the publisher, Edward Arnold, Ltd., London.

the name of any person or persons to whom the draft of Mr. Karswell's paper may have been submitted; and further desires to intimate that he cannot undertake to reply to any further letters on this subject.

"And who *is* Mr. Karswell?" inquired the Secretary's wife. She had called at his office, and (perhaps unwarrantably) had picked up the last of these three letters, which the typist had just brought in.

"Why, my dear, just at present Mr. Karswell is a very angry man. But I don't know much about him otherwise, except that he is a person of wealth, his address is Lufford Abbey, Warwickshire, and he's an alchemist, apparently, and wants to tell us all about it; and that's about all—except that I don't want to meet him for the next week or two. Now, if you're ready to leave this place, I am."

"What have you been doing to make him angry?" asked Mrs. Secretary.

"The usual thing, my dear, the usual thing: he sent in a draft of a paper he wanted to read at the next meeting, and we referred it to Edward Dunning—almost the only man in England who knows about these things—and he said it was perfectly hopeless, so we declined it. So Karswell has been pelting me with letters ever since. The last thing he wanted was the name of the man we referred his nonsense to; you saw my answer to that. But don't you say anything about it, for goodness' sake."

"I should think not, indeed. Did I ever do such a thing? I do hope, though, he won't get to know that it was poor Mr. Dunning."

"Poor Mr. Dunning? I don't know why you call him that; he's a very happy man, is Dunning. Lots of hobbies and a comfortable home, and all his time to himself."

"I only meant I should be sorry for him if this man got hold of his name, and came and bothered him."

"Oh, ah! yes. I dare say he would be poor Mr. Dunning then."

The Secretary and his wife were lunching out, and the friends to whose house they were bound were Warwickshire people. So Mrs. Secretary had already settled it in her own mind that she would question them judiciously about Mr. Karswell. But she was saved the trouble of leading up to the subject, for the hostess said to the host, before many minutes had passed, "I saw the Abbot of Lufford this morning." The host whistled. "*Did* you? What in the world brings him up to town?" "Goodness knows; he was coming out of the British Museum gate as I drcve past." It was not unnatural that Mrs. Secretary should inquire whether this was a real Abbot who was being spoken of. "Oh no, my dear: only a neighbor of ours in the country who bought Lufford Abbey a few years ago. His real name is Karswell." "Is he a friend of yours?" asked Mr. Secretary, with a private wink to his wife. The question let loose a torrent of declamation. There was really nothing to be said for Mr. Karswell. Nobody knew what he did with himself; his servants were a horrible set of people; he had invented a new religion for himself, and practised no one could tell what appalling rites; he was very easily offended, and never forgave anybody; he had a dreadful face (so the lady insisted, her husband somewhat demurring); he never did a kind action, and whatever influence he did exert was mischievous. "Do the poor man justice, dear," the husband interrupted. "You forget the treat he gave the school children." "Forget it, indeed! But I'm glad you mentioned it, because it gives an idea of the man. Now, Florence, listen to this. The first winter he was at Lufford this delightful neighbor of ours wrote to the clergyman of his parish (he's not ours, but we know him very well) and offered to show the school children some magic-lantern slides. He said he had some new kinds, which he thought would interest them. Well, the clergyman was rather surprised, because Mr. Karswell had shown himself inclined to be unpleasant to the children—complaining of their trespassing, or something of the sort; but of course he accepted, and the evening was fixed, and our friend went himself to see that everything went right. He said he never had been so thankful for anything as that his own children were all prevented from being there: they were at a children's party at our house, as a matter of fact. Because this Mr. Karswell had evidently set out with the intention of frightening these poor village children out of their wits, and I do believe, if he had been allowed to go on, he would actually have done so. He began with some comparatively mild things. Red Riding Hood was one, and even then, Mr. Farrer said, the wolf was so dreadful that several of the smaller children had to be taken out; and he said Mr. Karswell began the story by producing a noise like a wolf howling in the distance, which was the most gruesome thing he had ever heard. All the slides he showed, Mr. Farrer said, were most clever; they were absolutely realistic, and where he had got them or how he worked them he could not imagine. Well, the show went on, and the stories kept on becoming a little more terrifying each time, and the children were mesmerized into complete silence. At last he produced a series which represented a little boy passing through his own park—Lufford, I mean—in the evening. Every child in the room could recognize the place from the pictures. And this poor boy was followed, and at last pursued and overtaken, and either torn in pieces or somehow made away with, by a horrible hopping creature in white, which you saw first dodging about among the trees, and gradually it appeared more and more plainly. Mr. Farrer said it gave him one of the worst nightmares he ever remembered, and what it must have meant to the children doesn't bear thinking of. Of course this was too much, and he spoke very sharply indeed to Mr. Karswell, and said it couldn't go on. All *he* said was, 'Oh, you think it's time to bring our little show to an end and send them home to their beds? *Very* well!' And then, if you please, he switched on another slide, which showed a great mass of snakes, centipedes, and disgusting creatures with wings, and somehow or other he made it seem as if they were climbing out of the picture and getting in amongst the audience; and this was accompanied by a sort of dry rustling noise which sent the children nearly mad, and of course they stampeded. A good many of them were rather hurt in getting out of the room, and I don't suppose one of them closed an eye that night. There was the most dreadful trouble in the village afterward. Of course the mothers threw a good part of the blame on poor Mr. Farrer, and, if they could have got past the gates, I believe the fathers would have broken every window in the Abbey. Well, now, that's Mr. Karswell; that's the Abbot of Lufford, my dear, and you can imagine how we covet *his* society."

"Yes, I think he has all the possibilities of a distinguished criminal, has Karswell," said the host. "I should be sorry for anyone who got into his bad books."

"Is he the man, or am I mixing him up with someone else?" asked the Secretary (who for some minutes had been wearing the frown of the man who is trying to recollect something). "Is he the man who brought out a *History of Witchcraft* some time back—ten years or more?"

"That's the man; do you remember the reviews of it?"

"Certainly I do; and what's equally to the point, I knew the author of the most incisive of the lot. So did you: you must remember John Harrington; he was at John's in our time."

"Oh, very well indeed, though I don't think I saw or heard anything of him between the time I went down and the day I read the account of the inquest on him."

"Inquest?" said one of the ladies. "What happened to him?"

"Why, what happened was that he fell out of a tree and broke his neck. But the puzzle was, what could have induced him to get up there. It was a mysterious business, I must say. Here was this man— not an athletic fellow, was he? and with no eccentric twist about him that was ever noticed—walking home along a country road late in the evening—no tramps about—well known and liked in the place— and he suddenly begins to run like mad, loses his hat and stick, and finally shins up a tree—quite a difficult tree—growing in the hedge-row; a dead branch gives way, and he comes down with it and breaks his neck, and there he's found next morning with the most dreadful face of fear on him that could be imagined. It was pretty evident, of course, that he had been chased by something, and people talked of savage dogs, and beasts escaped out of menageries; but there was nothing to be made of that. That was in '89, and I believe his brother Henry (whom I remember as well at Cambridge, but *you* probably don't) has been trying to get on the track of an explanation ever since. He, of course, insists there was malice in it, but I don't know. It's difficult to see how it could have come in."

After a time the talk reverted to the *History of Witchcraft*. "Did you ever look into it?" asked the host.

"Yes, I did," said the Secretary. "I went so far as to read it."

"Was it as bad as it was made out to be?"

"Oh, in point of style and form, quite hopeless. It deserved all the pulverizing it got. But, besides that, it was an evil book. The man believed every word of what he was saying, and I'm very much mistaken if he hadn't tried the greater part of his receipts."

"Well, I only remember Harrington's review of it, and I must say if I'd been the author it would have quenched my literary ambition for good. I should never have held up my head again."

"It hasn't had that effect in the present case. But come, it's half-past three; I must be off."

On the way home the Secretary's wife said, "I do hope that horrible man won't find out that Mr. Dunning had anything to do with the rejection of his paper." "I don't think there's much chance of that," said the Secretary. "Dunning won't mention it himself, for these matters are confidential, and none of us will for the same reason. Karswell won't know his name, for Dunning hasn't published anything on the same subject yet. The only danger is that Karswell might find out, if he was to ask the British Museum people who was in the habit of consulting alchemical manuscripts: I can't very well tell them not to mention Dunning, can I? It would set them talking at once. Let's hope it won't occur to him."

However, Mr. Karswell was an astute man.

This much is in the way of prologue. On an evening rather later in the same week, Mr. Edward Dunning was returning from the British Museum, where he had been engaged in research, to the comfortable house in a suburb where he lived alone, tended by two excellent women who had been long with him. There is nothing to be added by way of description of him to what we have heard already. Let us follow him as he takes his sober course homeward.

A train took him to within a mile or two of his house, and an electric tram a stage farther. The line ended at a point some three hundred yards from his front door. He had had enough of reading when he got into the car, and indeed the light was not such as to allow him to do more than study the advertisements on the panes of glass that faced him as he sat. As was not unnatural, the advertisements in this particular line of cars were objects of his frequent contemplation, and, with the possible exception of the brilliant and convincing dialogue between Mr. Lamplough and an eminent K.C. on the subject of Pyretic Saline, none of them afforded much scope to his imagination. I am wrong: there was one at the corner of the car farthest from him which did not seem familiar. It was in blue letters

CASTING THE RUNES   115

on a yellow ground, and all that he could read of it was a name—John Harrington—and something like a date. It could be of no interest to him to know more; but for all that, as the car emptied, he was just curious enough to move along the seat until he could read it well. He felt to a slight extent repaid for his trouble; the advertisement was *not* of the usual type. It ran thus: "In memory of John Harrington, F.S.A., of The Laurels, Ashbrooke. Died Sept. 18th, 1889. Three months were allowed."

The car stopped. Mr. Dunning, still contemplating the blue letters on the yellow ground, had to be stimulated to rise by a word from the conductor. "I beg your pardon," he said, "I was looking at that advertisement; it's a very odd one, isn't it?" The conductor read it slowly. "Well, my word," he said, "I never see that one before. Well, that is a cure, ain't it? Someone bin up to their jokes 'ere, I should think." He got out a duster and applied it, not without saliva, to the pane and then to the outside. "No," he said, returning, "that ain't no transfer; seems to me as if it was reg'lar *in* the glass, what I mean in the substance, as you may say. Don't you think so, sir?" Mr. Dunning examined it and rubbed it with his glove, and agreed. "Who looks after these advertisements, and gives leave for them to be put up? I wish you would inquire. I will just take a note of the words." At this moment there came a call from the driver: "Look alive, George, time's up." "All right, all right; there's somethink else what's up at this end. You come and look at this 'ere glass." "What's gorn with the glass?" said the driver, approaching. "Well, and oo's 'Arrington? What's it all about?" "I was just asking who was responsible for putting the advertisements up in your cars, and saying it would be as well to make some inquiry about this one." "Well, sir, that's all done at the Company's orfice, that work is: it's our Mr. Timms, I believe, looks into that. When we put up tonight I'll leave word, and per'aps I'll be able to tell you tomorrer if you 'appen to be coming this way."

This was all that passed that evening. Mr. Dunning did just go to the trouble of looking up Ashbrooke, and found that it was in Warwickshire.

Next day he went to town again. The car (it was the same car) was too full in the morning to allow of his getting a word with the conductor; he could only be sure that the curious advertisement had been made away with. The close of the day brought a further element of mystery into the transaction. He had missed the tram, or else preferred walking home, but at a rather late hour, while he was at work in his study, one of the maids came to say that two men from the tramways was very anxious to speak to him. This was a reminder of the advertisement, which he had, he says, nearly forgotten. He had the men in—they were the conductor and driver of the car—and when the matter of refreshment had been attended to, asked what Mr. Timms had had to say about the advertisement. "Well, sir, that's what we took the liberty to step round about," said the conductor. "Mr. Timms 'e give William 'ere the rough side of his tongue about that; 'cordin' to 'im there warn't no advertisement of that description sent in, nor ordered, nor paid for, nor put up, nor nothink, let alone not bein' there, and we was playing the fool takin' up his time. 'Well,' I says, 'if that's the case, all I ask of you, Mr. Timms,' I says, 'is to take and look at it for yourself,' I says. 'Of course if it ain't there,' I says, 'you may take and call me what you like.' 'Right,' he says, 'I will'; and we went straight off. Now, I leave it to you, sir, if that ad, as we term 'em, with 'Arrington on it warn't as plain as ever you see anythink—blue letters on yeller glass, and as I says at the time, and you borne me out, reg'lar *in* the glass, because, if you remember, you recollect of me swabbing it with my duster." "To be sure I do, quite clearly—well?" "You may say well, I don't think. Mr. Timms he gets in that car with a light—no, he telled William to 'old the light outside. 'Now,' he says, 'where's your precious ad what we've 'eard so much about?' ' 'Ere it is,' I says, 'Mr. Timms,' and I laid my 'and on it." The conductor paused.

"Well," said Mr. Dunning, "it was gone, I suppose. Broken?"

"Broke!—not it. There warn't, if you'll believe me, no more trace of them letters—blue letters they was—on that piece o' glass, than—well, it's no good *me* talkin'. *I* never see such a thing. I leave it to William here if—but there, as I says, where's the benefit in me going on about it?"

"And what did Mr. Timms say?"

"Why 'e did what I give 'im leave to—called us pretty much anythink he liked, and I don't know as I blame him so much neither.

But what we thought, William and me did, was as we seen you take down a bit of a note about that—well, that letterin'—"

"I certainly did that, and I have it now. Did you wish me to speak to Mr. Timms myself, and show it to him? Was that what you came in about?"

"There, didn't I say as much?" said William. "Deal with a gent if you can get on the track of one, that's my word. Now perhaps, George, you'll allow as I ain't took you very far wrong tonight."

"Very well, William, very well; no need for you to go on as if you'd 'ad to frog's-march me 'ere. I come quiet, didn't I? All the same for that, we 'adn't ought to take up your time this way, sir; but if it so 'appened you could find time to step round to the Company's orfice in the morning and tell Mr. Timms what you seen for yourself, we should lay under a very 'igh obligation to you for the trouble. You see it ain't bein' called—well, one thing and another, as we mind, but if they got it into their 'ead at the orfice as we seen things as warn't there, why, one thing leads to another, and where we should be a twelvemunce 'ence—well, you can understand what I mean."

Amid further elucidations of the proposition, George, conducted by William, left the room.

The incredulity of Mr. Timms (who had a nodding acquaintance with Mr. Dunning) was greatly modified on the following day by what the latter could tell and show him; and any bad mark that might have been attached to the names of William and George was not suffered to remain on the Company's books; but explanation there was none.

Mr. Dunning's interest in the matter was kept alive by an incident of the following afternoon. He was walking from his club to the train, and he noticed some way ahead a man with a handful of leaflets such as are distributed to passers-by by agents of enterprising firms. This agent had not chosen a very crowded street for his operations: in fact, Mr. Dunning did not see him get rid of a single leaflet before he himself reached the spot. One was thrust into his hand as he passed: the hand that gave it touched his, and he experienced a sort of little shock as it did so. It seemed unnaturally rough and hot. He looked in passing at the giver, but the impression he got was so unclear that, however much he tried to reckon it up subsequently, nothing would come. He was walking quickly, and as he went on glanced at the paper. It was a blue one. The name of Harrington in large capitals caught his eye. He stopped, startled, and felt for his glasses. The next instant the leaflet was twitched out of his hand by a man who hurried past, and was irrecoverably gone. He ran back a few paces, but where was the passer-by? and where the distributor?

It was in a somewhat pensive frame of mind that Mr. Dunning passed on the following day into the Select Manuscript Room of the British Museum, and filled out tickets for Harley 3586, and some other volumes. After a few minutes they were brought to him, and he was settling the one he wanted first upon the desk, when he thought he heard his own name whispered behind him. He turned round hastily, and in doing so, brushed his little portfolio of loose papers onto the floor. He saw no one he recognized except one of the staff in charge of the room, who nodded to him, and he proceeded to pick up his papers. He thought he had them all and was turning to begin work, when a stout gentleman at the table behind him, who was just rising to leave, and had collected his own belongings, touched him on the shoulder, saying, "May I give you this? I think it should be yours," and handed him a missing quire. "It is mine, thank you," said Mr. Dunning. In another moment the man had left the room. Upon finishing his work for the afternoon, Mr. Dunning had some conversation with the assistant in charge, and took occasion to ask who the stout gentleman was. "Oh, he's a man named Karswell," said the assistant; "he was asking me a week ago who were the great authorities on alchemy, and of course I told him you were the only one in the country. I'll see if I can't catch him; he'd like to meet you, I'm sure."

"For heaven's sake, don't dream of it!" said Mr. Dunning, "I'm particularly anxious to avoid him."

"Oh! very well," said the assistant, "he doesn't come here often; I dare say you won't meet him."

More than once on the way home that day Mr. Dunning confessed to himself that he did not look forward with his usual cheerfulness to a solitary evening. It seemed to him that something ill defined and impalpable had stepped in between him and his fellow-men—had taken him in charge, as it were. He wanted to sit close up to his neighbors in the train and in the tram, but as luck would have it both train and car were markedly empty. The conductor George was thoughtful, and appeared to be absorbed in calculations as to the number of passengers. On arriving at his house he found Dr. Watson, his medical man, on his doorstep. "I've had to upset your household arrangements, I'm sorry to say, Dunning. Both your servants *hors de combat*. In fact, I've had to send them to the Nursing Home."

"Good heavens! what's the matter?"

"It's something like ptomaine poisoning, I should think; you've not suffered yourself, I can see, or you wouldn't be walking about. I think they'll pull through all right."

"Dear, dear! Have you any idea what brought it on?"

"Well, they tell me they bought some shellfish from a hawker at their dinnertime. It's odd. I've made inquiries, but I can't find that any hawker has been to other houses in the street. I couldn't send word to you; they won't be back for a bit yet. You come and dine with me tonight, anyhow, and we can make arrangements for going on. Eight o'clock. Don't be too anxious."

The solitary evening was thus obviated; at the expense of some distress and inconvenience, it is true. Mr. Dunning spent the time pleasantly enough with the doctor (a rather recent settler), and returned to his lonely home at about 11:30. The night he passed is not one on which he looks back with any satisfaction. He was in bed and the light was out. He was wondering if the charwoman would come early enough to get him hot water next morning, when he heard the unmistakable sound of his study door opening. No step followed it on the passage floor, but the sound must mean mischief, for he knew that he had shut the door that evening after putting his papers away in his desk. It was rather shame than courage that induced him to slip out into the passage and lean over the banister in his nightgown, listening. No light was visible; no further sound came; only a gust of warm, or even hot air played for an instant round his shins. He went back and decided to lock himself into his room. There was more unpleasantness, however. Either an economical suburban company had decided that their light would not be required in the small hours, and had stopped working, or else something was wrong with the meter; the effect was in any case that the electric light was off. The obvious course was to find a match, and also to consult his watch; he might as well know how many hours of discomfort awaited him. So he put his hand into the well-known nook under the pillow; only, it did not get so far. What he touched was, according to his account, a mouth, with teeth, and with hair about it, and, he declares, not the mouth of a human being. I do not think it is any use to guess what he said or did; but he was in a spare room with the door locked and his ear to it before he was clearly conscious again. And there he spent the rest of a most miserable night, looking every moment for some fumbling at the door; but nothing came.

The venturing back to his own room in the morning was attended with many listenings and quiverings. The door stood open, fortunately, and the blinds were up (the servants had been out of the house before the hour of drawing them down); there was, to be short, no trace of an inhabitant. The watch, too, was in its usual place; nothing was disturbed, only the wardrobe door had swung open, in accordance with its confirmed habit. A ring at the back door now announced the charwoman, who had been ordered the night before, and nerved Mr. Dunning, after letting her in, to continue his search in other parts of the house. It was equally fruitless.

The day thus begun went on dismally enough. He dared not go to the Museum; in spite of what the assistant had said, Karswell might turn up there, and Dunning felt he could not cope with a probably hostile stranger. His own house was odious; he hated sponging on the doctor. He spent some little time in a call at the Nursing Home, where he was slightly cheered by a good report of his housekeeper and maid. Toward lunch time he betook himself to his club, again experiencing a gleam of satisfaction at seeing the Secretary of the Association. At luncheon Dunning told his friend the more material of his woes, but could not bring himself to speak of those that weighed most heavily on his spirits. "My poor dear man," said the Secretary, "what an upset! Look here; we're alone at home, absolutely. You must put up with us. Yes! no excuse; send your things in this afternoon." Dunning was unable to stand out; he was, in truth, becoming acutely anxious, as the hours went on, as to what that night might have waiting for him. He was almost happy as he hurried home to pack up.

His friends, when they had time to take stock of him, were rather shocked at his lorn appearance, and did their best to keep him up to the mark. Not altogether without success; but, when the two men were smoking alone later, Dunning became dull again. Suddenly he said, "Gayton, I believe that alchemist man knows it was I who got his paper rejected." Gayton whistled. "What makes you think that?" he said. Dunning told of his conversation with the Museum assistant, and Gayton could only agree that the guess seemed likely to be correct. "Not that I care much," Dunning went on, "only it might be a nuisance if we were to meet. He's a bad-tempered party, I imagine." Conversation dropped again; Gayton became more and more strongly impressed with the desolateness that came over Dunning's face and bearing, and finally—though with a considerable effort—he asked him point-blank whether something serious was not bothering him. Dunning gave an exclamation of relief. "I was perishing to get it off my mind," he said. "Do you know anything about a man named John Harrington?" Gayton was thoroughly startled, and at the moment could only ask why. Then the complete story of Dunning's experiences came out—what had happened in the tramcar, in his own house, and in the street, the troubling of spirit that had crept over him, and still held him; and he ended with the question he had begun with. Gayton was at a loss how to answer him. To tell the story of Harrington's end would perhaps be right; only, Dunning was in a nervous state, the story was a grim one, and he could not help asking himself whether there were not a connecting link between these two cases, in the person of Karswell. It was a difficult concession for a scientific man, but it could be eased by the phrase "hypnotic suggestion." In the end he decided that his answer tonight should be guarded; he would talk the situation over with his wife. So he said that he had known Harrington at Cambridge, and believed he had died suddenly in 1889, adding a few details about the man and his published work. He did talk over the matter with Mrs. Gayton, and, as he had anticipated, she leaped at once to the conclusion which had been hovering before him. It was she who reminded him of the surviving brother, Henry Harrington, and she also who suggested that he might be got hold of by means of their hosts of the day before. "He might be a hopeless crank," objected Gayton.

"That could be ascertained from the Bennetts, who knew him," Mrs. Gayton retorted; and she undertook to see the Bennetts the very next day.

It is not necessary to tell in further detail the steps by which Henry Harrington and Dunning were brought together.

The next scene that does require to be narrated is a conversation that took place between the two. Dunning had told Harrington of the strange ways in which the dead man's name had been brought before him, and had said something, besides, of his own subsequent experiences. Then he had asked if Harrington was disposed, in return, to recall any of the circumstances connected with his brother's death. Harrington's surprise at what he heard can be imagined: but his reply was readily given.

"John," he said, "was in a very odd state, undeniably, from time to time, during some weeks before, though not immediately before, the catastrophe. There were several things; the principal notion he had was that he thought he was being followed. No doubt he was an impressionable man, but he never had had such fancies as this before. I cannot get it out of my mind that there was ill will at work, and what you tell me about yourself reminds me very much of my brother. Can you think of any possible connecting link?"

"There is just one that has been taking shape vaguely in my mind. I've been told that your brother reviewed a book very severely not long before he died, and just lately I have happened to cross the path of the man who wrote that book in a way he would resent."

"Don't tell me the man was called Karswell."

"Why not? that is exactly his name."

Henry Harrington leaned back. "That is final to my mind. Now I must explain further. From something he said, I feel sure that my brother John was beginning to believe—very much against his will—that Karswell was at the bottom of his trouble. I want to tell you what seems to me to have a bearing on the situation. My brother was a great musician, and used to run up to concerts in town. He came back, three months before he died, from one of these, and gave me his program to look at—an analytical program: he always kept them. 'I nearly missed this one,' he said. 'I suppose I must have dropped it;

anyhow, I was looking for it under my seat and in my pockets and so on, and my neighbor offered me his; said "might he give it me, he had no further use for it," and he went away just afterward. I don't know who he was—a stout, clean-shaven man. I should have been sorry to miss it; of course I could have bought another, but this cost me nothing.' At another time he told me that he had been very uncomfortable both on the way to his hotel and during the night. I piece things together now in thinking it over. Then, not very long after, he was going over these programs, putting them in order to have them bound up, and in this particular one (which by the way I had hardly glanced at), he found quite near the beginning a strip of paper with some very odd writing on it in red and black—most carefully done—it looked to me more like Runic letters than anything else. 'Why,' he said, 'this must belong to my fat neighbor. It looks as if it might be worth returning to him; it may be a copy of something; evidently someone has taken trouble over it. How can I find his address?' We talked it over for a little and agreed that it wasn't worth advertising about, and that my brother had better look out for the man at the next concert, to which he was going very soon. The paper was lying on the book and we were both by the fire; it was a cold, windy summer evening. I suppose the door blew open, though I didn't notice it; at any rate a gust—a warm gust it was—came quite suddenly between us, took the paper and blew it straight into the fire; it was light, thin paper, and flared and went up the chimney in a single ash. 'Well,' I said, 'you can't give it back now.' He said nothing for a minute; then rather crossly, 'No, I can't; but why you should keep on saying so I don't know.' I remarked that I didn't say it more than once. 'Not more than four times, you mean,' was all he said. I remember all that very clearly, without any good reason; and now to come to the point. I don't know if you looked at that book of Karswell's which my unfortunate brother reviewed. It's not likely that you should; but I did, both before his death and after it. The first time we made game of it together. It was written in no style at all—split infinitives, and every sort of thing that makes an Oxford gorge rise. Then there was nothing that the man didn't swallow: mixing up classical myths, and stories out of the *Golden Legend* with reports of savage customs of today—all very proper, no doubt, if you know how to use them, but he didn't; he seemed to put the *Golden Legend* and the *Golden Bough* exactly on a par, and to believe both: a pitiable exhibition, in short. Well, after the misfortune, I looked over the book again. It was no better than before, but the impression which it left this time on my mind was different. I suspected—as I told you— that Karswell had borne ill will to my brother, even that he was in some way responsible for what had happened; and now his book seemed to me to be a very sinister performance indeed. One chapter in particular struck me, in which he spoke of 'casting the Runes' on people, either for the purpose of gaining their affection or of getting them out of the way—perhaps more especially the latter; he spoke of all this in a way that really seemed to me to imply actual knowledge. I've not time to go into details, but the upshot is that I am pretty sure from information received that the civil man at the concert was Karswell; I suspect—I more than suspect—that the paper was of importance; and I do believe that if my brother had been able to give it back, he might have been alive now. Therefore, it occurs to me to ask you whether you have anything to put beside what I have told you."

By way of answer, Dunning had the episode in the Manuscript Room at the British Museum to relate. "Then he did actually hand you some papers; have you examined them? No? Because we must, if you'll allow it, look at them at once, and very carefully."

They went to the still empty house—empty, for the two servants were not yet able to return to work. Dunning's portfolio of papers was gathering dust on the writing table. In it were the quires of small-sized scribbling paper which he used for his transcripts; and from one of these, as he took it up, there slipped and fluttered out into the room with uncanny quickness, a strip of thin light paper. The window was open, but Harrington slammed it to, just in time to intercept the paper, which he caught. "I thought so," he said; "it might be the identical thing that was given to my brother. You'll have to look out, Dunning; this may mean something quite serious for you."

A long consultation took place. The paper was narrowly examined. As Harrington had said, the characters on it were more like Runes than anything else, but not decipherable by either man, and both hesitated to copy them, for fear, as they confessed, of perpetuating whatever evil purpose they might conceal. So it has remained impossible (if I may anticipate a little) to ascertain what was conveyed in this curious message or commission. Both Dunning and Harrrington are firmly convinced that it had the effect of bringing its possessors into very undesirable company. That it must be returned to the source whence it came they were agreed, and further, that the only safe and certain way was that of personal service; and here contrivance would be necessary, for Dunning was known by sight to Karswell. He must, for one thing, alter his appearance by shaving his beard. But then might not the blow fall first? Harrington thought they could time it. He knew the date of the concert at which the "black spot" had been put on his brother: it was June 18. The death had followed on September 18. Dunning reminded him that three months had been mentioned in the inscription on the car window. "Perhaps," he added, with a cheerless laugh, "mine may be a bill at three months too. I believe I can fix it by my diary. Yes, April 23 was the day at the Museum; that brings us to July 23. Now, you know, it becomes extremely important to me to know anything you will tell me about the progress of your brother's trouble, if it is possible for you to speak of it." "Of course. Well, the sense of being watched whenever he was alone was the most distressing thing to him. After a time I took to sleeping in his room, and he was the better for that; still, he talked a great deal in his sleep. What about? Is it wise to dwell on that, at least before things are straightened out? I think not, but I can tell you this: two things came for him by post during those weeks, both with a London postmark, and addressed in a commercial hand. One was a woodcut of Bewick's, roughly torn out of the page: one which shows a moonlit road and a man walking along it, followed by an awful demon creature. Under it were written the lines out of *The Ancient Mariner* (which I suppose the cut illustrates) about one who, having once looked round—

> *walks on,*
> *And turns no more his head;*
> *Because he knows a frightful fiend*
> *Doth close behind him tread.*

The other was a calendar, such as tradesmen often send. My brother paid no attention to this, but I looked at it after his death, and found that everything after September 18 had been torn out. You may be surprised at his having gone out alone the evening he was killed, but the fact is that during the last ten days or so of his life he had been quite free from the sense of being followed or watched."

The end of the consultation was this. Harrington, who knew a neighbor of Karswell's, thought he saw a way of keeping a watch on his movements. It would be Dunning's part to be in readiness to try to cross Karswell's path at any moment, to keep the paper safe and in a place of ready access.

They parted. The next weeks were no doubt a severe strain upon Dunning's nerves; the intangible barrier which had seemed to rise about him on the day when he received the paper, gradually developed into a brooding blackness that cut him off from the means of escape to which one might have thought he might resort. No one was at hand who was likely to suggest them to him, and he seemed robbed of all initiative. He waited with inexpressible anxiety as May, June, and early July passed on, for a mandate from Harrington. But all this time Karswell remained immovable at Lufford.

At last, less than a week before the date he had come to look upon as the end of his earthly activities, came a telegram: "LEAVES VICTORIA BY BOAT TRAIN THURSDAY NIGHT. DO NOT MISS. I COME TO YOU TONIGHT. HARRINGTON."

He arrived accordingly, and they concocted plans. The train left Victoria at nine and its last stop before Dover was Croydon West. Harrington would mark down Karswell at Victoria, and look out for Dunning at Croydon, calling to him if need were by a name agreed upon. Dunning, disguised as far as might be, was to have no label or initials on any hand luggage, and must at all costs have the paper with him.

Dunning's suspense as he waited on the Croydon platform I need not attempt to describe. His sense of danger during the last days had only been sharpened by the fact that the cloud about him had perceptibly been lighter; but relief was an ominous symptom, and, if Karswell eluded him now, hope was gone; and there were so many chances of that. The rumor of the journey might be itself a device. The twenty minutes in which he paced the platform and persecuted every porter with inquiries as to the boat train were as bitter as any he had spent. Still, the train came, and Harrington was at the window. It was important, of course, that there should be no recognition; so Dunning got in at the farther end of the corridor carriage, and only gradually made his way to the compartment where Harrington and Karswell were. He was pleased, on the whole, to see that the train was far from full.

Karswell was on the alert, but gave no sign of recognition. Dunning took the seat not immediately facing him, and attempted, vainly at first, then with increasing command of his faculties, to reckon the possibilities of making the desired transfer. Opposite to Karswell, and next to Dunning, was a heap of Karswell's coats on the seat. It would be of no use to slip the paper into these—he would not be safe, or would not feel so, unless in some way it could be proffered by him and accepted by the other. There was a handbag open, and with papers in it. Could he manage to conceal this (so that perhaps Karswell might leave the carriage without it), and then find and give it to him? This was the plan that suggested itself. If he could only have counseled with Harrington! but that could not be. The minutes went on. More than once Karswell rose and went out into the corridor. The second time Dunning was on the point of attempting to make the bag fall off the seat, but he caught Harrington's eye, and read in it a warning. Karswell, from the corridor, was watching; probably to see if the two men recognized each other. He returned, but was evidently restless; and, when he rose the third time, hope dawned, for something did slip off his seat and fall with hardly a sound to the floor. Karswell went out once more, and passed out of range of the corridor window. Dunning picked up what had fallen, and saw that the key was in his hands in the form of one of Cook's ticket cases, with tickets in it. These cases have a pocket in the cover, and within very few seconds the paper of which we have heard was in the pocket of this one. To make the operation more secure, Harrington stood in the doorway of the compartment and fiddled with the blind. It was done, and done at the right time, for the train was now slowing down toward Dover.

In a moment more Karswell re-entered the compartment. As he

did so, Dunning, managing, he knew not how, to suppress the tremble in his voice, handed him the ticket case, saying, "May I give you this, sir? I believe it is yours." After a brief glance at the ticket inside, Karswell uttered the hoped-for response, "Yes, it is; much obliged to you, sir," and he placed it in his breast pocket.

Even in the few moments that remained—moments of tense anxiety, for they knew not to what a premature finding of the paper might lead—both men noticed that the carriage seemed to darken about them and to grow warmer; that Karswell was fidgety and oppressed; that he drew the heap of loose coats near to him and cast it back as if it repelled him; and that he then sat upright and glanced anxiously at both. They, with sickening anxiety, busied themselves in collecting their belongings; but they both thought that Karswell was on the point of speaking when the train stopped at Dover Town. It was natural that in the short space between town and pier they should both go into the corridor.

At the pier they got out, but so empty was the train that they were forced to linger on the platform until Karswell should have passed ahead of them with his porter on the way to the boat, and only then was it safe for them to exchange a pressure of the hand and a word of concentrated congratulation. The effect upon Dunning was to make him almost faint. Harrington made him lean up against the wall, while he himself went forward a few yards within sight of the gangway to the boat, at which Karswell had now arrived. The man at the head of it examined his ticket, and, laden with coats, he passed down into the boat. Suddenly the official called after him, "You, sir, beg pardon, did the other gentleman show his ticket?" "What the devil do you mean by the other gentleman?" Karswell's snarling voice called back from the deck. The man bent over and looked at him. "The devil? Well, I don't know, I'm sure," Harrington heard him say to himself, and then aloud, "My mistake, sir; must have been your rugs! ask your pardon." And then, to a subordinate near him, " 'Ad he got a dog with him, or what? Funny thing; I could 'a' swore 'e wasn't alone. Well, whatever it was, they'll 'ave to see to it aboard. She's off now. Another week and we shall be gettin' the 'oliday customers." In five minutes more there was nothing but the lessening lights of the boat, the long line of the Dover lamps, the night breeze, and the moon.

Long and long the two sat in their room at the Lord Warden. In spite of the removal of their greatest anxiety, they were oppressed with a doubt, not of the lightest. Had they been justified in sending a man to his death, as they believed they had? Ought they not to warn him, at least? "No," said Harrington; "if he is the murderer I think him, we have done no more than is just. Still, if you think it better—but how and where can you warn him?" "He was booked to Abbeville only," said Dunning. "I saw that. If I wired to the hotels there in Joanne's Guide, 'Examine your ticket case, Dunning,' I should feel happier. This is the twenty-first; he will have a day. But I am afraid he has gone into the dark." So telegrams were left at the hotel office.

It is not clear whether these reached their destination, or whether, if they did, they were understood. All that is known is that, on the afternoon of the twenty-third, an English traveler, examining the front of St. Wulfram's Church at Abbeville, then under extensive repair, was struck on the head and instantly killed by a stone falling from the scaffold erected round the northwestern tower, there being, as was clearly proved, no workman on the scaffold at that moment; and the traveler's papers identified him as Mr. Karswell.

Only one detail shall be added. At Karswell's sale a set of Bewick, sold with all faults, was acquired by Harrington. The page with the woodcut of the traveler and the demon was, as he had expected, mutilated. Also, after a judicious interval, Harrington repeated to Dunning something of what he had heard his brother say in his sleep; but it was not long before Dunning stopped him.

THE VOICE IN THE NIGHT

BY WILLIAM HOPE HODGSON

❡ IT WAS a dark, starless night. We were becalmed in the Northern Pacific. Our exact position I do not know; for the sun had been hidden during the course of a weary, breathless week, by a thin haze which had seemed to float above us, about the height of our mastheads, at whiles descending and shrouding the surrounding sea.

With there being no wind, we had steadied the tiller, and I was the only man on deck. The crew, consisting of two men and a boy, were sleeping forward in their den; while Will—my friend, and the master of our little craft—was aft in his bunk on the port side of the little cabin.

Suddenly, from out of the surrounding darkness, there came a hail: "Schooner, ahoy!"

The cry was so unexpected that I gave no immediate answer, because of my surprise.

It came again—a voice curiously throaty and inhuman, calling from somewhere upon the dark sea away on our port broadside.

"Schooner, ahoy!"

"Hullo!" I sang out, having gathered my wits somewhat. "What are you? What do you want?"

"You need not be afraid," answered the queer voice, having probably noticed some trace of confusion in my tone. "I am only an old—man."

The pause sounded oddly; but it was only afterward that it came back to me with any significance.

"Why don't you come alongside, then?" I queried somewhat

Reprinted by permission of Miss Lissie S. Hodgson.

snappishly; for I liked not his hinting at my having been a trifle shaken.

"I—I—can't. It wouldn't be safe. I—" The voice broke off, and there was silence.

"What do you mean?" I asked, growing more and more astonished. "What not safe? Where are you?"

I listened for a moment; but there came no answer. And then, a sudden indefinite suspicion, of I knew not what, coming to me, I stepped swiftly to the binnacle, and took out the lighted lamp. At the same time, I knocked on the deck with my heel to waken Will. Then I was back at the side, throwing the yellow funnel of light out into the silent immensity beyond our rail. As I did so, I heard a slight, muffled cry, and then the sound of a splash as though someone had dipped oars abruptly. Yet I cannot say that I saw anything with certainty; save, it seemed to me, that the first flash of the light, there had been something upon the waters, where now there was nothing.

"Hullo, there!" I called. "What foolery is this!"

But there came only the indistinct sounds of a boat being pulled away into the night.

Then I heard Will's voice, from the direction of the after scuttle.

"What's up, George?"

"Come here, Will!" I said.

"What is it?" he asked, coming across the deck.

I told him the queer thing which had happened. He put several questions; then, after a moment's silence, he raised his hands to his lips, and hailed, "Boat, ahoy!"

From a long distance away there came back to us a faint reply, and my companion repeated his call. Presently, after a short period of silence, there grew on our hearing the muffled sound of oars; at which Will hailed again.

This time there was a reply.

"Put away the light."

"I'm damned if I will," I muttered; but Will told me to do as the voice bade, and I shoved it down under the bulwarks.

"Come nearer," he said, and the oar strokes continued. Then, when apparently some half-dozen fathoms distant, they again ceased.

"Come alongside," exclaimed Will. "There's nothing to be frightened of aboard here!"

"Promise that you will not show the light?"

"What's to do with you," I burst out, "that you're so infernally afraid of the light?"

"Because—" began the voice, and stopped short.

"Because what?" I asked quickly.

Will put his hand on my shoulder.

"Shut up a minute, old man," he said in a low voice. "Let me tackle him."

He leaned more over the rail.

"See here, mister," he said, "this is a pretty queer business, you coming upon us like this, right out in the middle of the blessed Pacific. How are we to know what sort of a hanky-panky trick you're up to? You say there's only one of you. How are we to know, unless we get a squint at you—eh? What's your objection to the light, anyway?"

As he finished, I heard the noise of the oars again, and then the voice came; but now from a greater distance, and sounding extremely hopeless and pathetic.

"I am sorry—sorry! I would not have troubled you, only I am hungry, and—so is she."

The voice died away, and the sound of the oars, dipping irregularly, was borne to us.

"Stop!" sung out Will. "I don't want to drive you away. Come back! We'll keep the light hidden, if you don't like it."

He turned to me.

"It's a damned queer rig, this; but I think there's nothing to be afraid of?"

There was a question in his tone, and I replied.

"No, I think the poor devil's been wrecked around here, and gone crazy."

The sound of the oars drew nearer.

"Shove that lamp back in the binnacle," said Will; then he leaned over the rail and listened. I replaced the lamp, and came back to his side. The dipping of the oars ceased some dozen yards distant.

"Won't you come alongside now?" asked Will in an even voice. "I have had the lamp put back in the binnacle."

"I—I cannot," replied the voice. "I dare not come nearer. I dare not even pay you for the—the provisions."

"That's all right," said Will, and hesitated. "You're welcome to as much grub as you can take—" Again he hesitated.

"You are very good," exclaimed the voice. "May God, Who understands everything, reward you—" It broke off huskily.

"The—the lady?" said Will abruptly. "Is she—"

"I have left her behind upon the island," came the voice.

"What island?" I cut in.

"I know not its name," returned the voice. "I would to God—!" it began, and checked itself as suddenly.

"Could we not send a boat for her?" asked Will at this point.

"No!" said the voice, with extraordinary emphasis. "My God! No!" There was a moment's pause; then it added, in a tone which seemed a merited reproach, "It was because of our want I ventured—because her agony tortured me."

"I am a forgetful brute," exclaimed Will. "Just wait a minute, whoever you are, and I will bring you up something at once."

In a couple of minutes he was back again, and his arms were full of various edibles. He paused at the rail.

"Can't you come alongside for them?" he asked.

"No—I *dare not*," replied the voice, and it seemed to me that in its tones I detected a note of stifled craving—as though the owner hushed a mortal desire. It came to me then in a flash that the poor old creature out there in the darkness was *suffering* for actual need of that which Will held in his arms; and yet, because of some unintelligible dread, refraining from dashing to the side of our schooner, and receiving it. And with the lightning-like conviction, there came the knowledge that the Invisible was not mad; but sanely facing some intolerable horror.

"Damn it, Will!" I said, full of many feelings, over which predominated a vast sympathy. "Get a box. We must float off the stuff to him in it."

This we did—propelling it away from the vessel, out into the darkness, by means of a boathook. In a minute, a slight cry from the Invisible came to us, and we knew that he had secured the box.

A little later, he called out a farewell to us, and so heartful a blessing that I am sure we were the better for it. Then, without more ado, we heard the ply of oars across the darkness.

"Pretty soon off," remarked Will, with perhaps just a little sense of injury.

"Wait," I replied. "I think somehow he'll come back. He must have been badly needing that food."

"And the lady," said Will. For a moment he was silent; then he continued, "It's the queerest thing ever I've tumbled across, since I've been fishing."

"Yes," I said, and fell to pondering.

And so the time slipped away—an hour, another, and still Will stayed with me; for the queer adventure had knocked all desire for sleep out of him.

The third hour was three parts through, when we heard again the sound of oars across the silent ocean.

"Listen!" said Will, a low note of excitement in his voice.

"He's coming, just as I thought," I muttered.

The dipping of the oars grew nearer, and I noted that the strokes were firmer and longer. The food had been needed.

They came to a stop a little distance off the broadside, and the queer voice came again to us through the darkness.

"Schooner, ahoy!"

"That you?" asked Will.

"Yes," replied the voice. "I left you suddenly; but—but there was great need."

"The lady?" questioned Will.

"The—lady is grateful now on earth. She will be more grateful soon in—in heaven."

Will began to make some reply, in a puzzled voice; but became confused, and broke off short. I said nothing. I was wondering at the curious pauses, and, apart from my wonder, I was full of a great sympathy.

The voice continued.

"We—she and I, have talked, as we shared the result of God's tenderness and yours—"

Will interposed; but without coherence.

"I beg of you not to—to belittle your deed of Christian charity this night," said the voice. "Be sure that it has not escaped His notice."

It stopped, and there was a full minute's silence. Then it came again.

"We have spoken together upon that which—which has befallen us. We had thought to go out, without telling any, of the terror which has come into our—lives. She is with me in believing that tonight's happenings are under a special ruling, and that it is God's wish that we should tell to you all that we have suffered since—since—"

"Yes?" said Will softly.

"Since the sinking of the *Albatross.*"

"Ah!" I exclaimed involuntarily. "She left Newcastle for 'Frisco some six months ago, and hasn't been heard of since."

"Yes," answered the voice. "But some few degrees to the north of the line she was caught in a terrible storm, and dismasted. When the day came, it was found that she was leaking badly, and presently, it falling to a calm, the sailors took to the boats, leaving—leaving a young lady—my fiancée—and myself upon the wreck.

"We were below, gathering together a few of our belongings, when they left. They were entirely callous, through fear, and when we came up upon the decks, we saw them only as small shapes afar off upon the horizon. Yet we did not despair, but set to work and constructed a small raft. Upon this we put such few matters as it would hold, including a quantity of water and some ship's biscuit. Then, the vessel being very deep in the water, we got ourselves on to the raft, and pushed off.

"It was later when I observed that we seemed to be in the way of some tide or current, which bore us from the ship at an angle; so that in the course of three hours, by my watch, her hull became invisible to our sight, her broken masts remaining in view for a somewhat longer period. Then, toward evening, it grew misty, and so through the night. The next day we were still encompassed by the mist, the weather remaining quiet.

"For four days we drifted through this strange haze, until, on the evening of the fourth day, there grew upon our ears the murmur of breakers at a distance. Gradually it became plainer, and, somewhat after midnight, it appeared to sound upon either hand at no very great space. The raft was raised upon a swell several times, and then we were in smooth water, and the noise of the breakers was behind.

"When the morning came, we found that we were in a sort of great lagoon; but of this we noticed little at the time; for close before us, through the enshrouding mist, loomed the hull of a large sailing vessel. With one accord, we fell upon our knees and thanked God; for we thought that here was an end to our perils. We had much to learn.

"The raft drew near to the ship, and we shouted on them to take us aboard; but none answered. Presently the raft touched against the side of the vessel, and, seeing a rope hanging downward, I seized it and began to climb. Yet I had much ado to make my way up, because of a kind of gray, lichenous fungus which had seized upon the rope, and which blotched the side of the ship lividly.

"I reached the rail and clambered over it, on to the deck. Here I saw that the decks were covered, in great patches, with the gray masses, some of them rising into nodules several feet in height; but at the time I thought less of this matter than of the possibility of there being people aboard the ship. I shouted; but none answered. Then I went to the door below the poop deck. I opened it, and peered in. There was a great smell of staleness, so that I knew in a moment that nothing living was within, and with the knowledge, I shut the door quickly; for I felt suddenly lonely.

"I went back to the side where I had scrambled up. My—my sweetheart was still sitting quietly upon the raft. Seeing me look down she called up to know whether there were any aboard of the ship. I replied that the vessel had the appearance of having been long deserted; but that if she would wait a little I would see whether there was anything in the shape of a ladder by which she could ascend to the deck. Then we would make a search through the vessel together. A little later, on the opposite side of the decks, I found a rope side ladder. This I carried across, and a minute afterward she was beside me.

"Together we explored the cabins and apartments in the after part of the ship; but nowhere was there any sign of life. Here and there, within the cabins themselves, we came across odd patches of that queer fungus; but this, as my sweetheart said, could be cleansed away.

"In the end, having assured ourselves that the after portion of the vessel was empty, we picked our way to the bows, between the ugly gray nodules of that strange growth; and here we made a further search, which told us that there was indeed none aboard but ourselves.

"This being now beyond any doubt, we returned to the stern of the ship and proceeded to make ourselves as comfortable as possible. Together we cleared out and cleaned two of the cabins; and after that I made examination whether there was anything eatable in the ship. This I soon found was so, and thanked God in my heart for His goodness. In addition to this I discovered the whereabouts of the freshwater pump, and having fixed it I found the water drinkable, though somewhat unpleasant to the taste.

"For several days we stayed aboard the ship, without attempting to get to the shore. We were busily engaged in making the place habitable. Yet even thus early we became aware that our lot was even less to be desired than might have been imagined; for though, as a first step, we scraped away the odd patches of growth that studded the floors and walls of the cabins and saloon, yet they returned almost to their original size within the space of twenty-four hours, which not only discouraged us, but gave us a feeling of vague unease.

"Still we would not admit ourselves beaten, so set to work afresh, and not only scraped away the fungus, but soaked the places where it had been, with carbolic, a canful of which I had found in the pantry. Yet, by the end of the week the growth had returned in full strength, and, in addition it had spread to other places, as though our touching it had allowed germs from it to travel elsewhere.

"On the seventh morning, my sweetheart woke to find a small patch of it growing on her pillow, close to her face. At that, she came to me, so soon as she could get her garments upon her. I was in the galley at the time lighting the fire for breakfast.

" 'Come here, John,' she said, and led me aft. When I saw the thing upon her pillow I shuddered, and then and there we agreed to go right out of the ship and see whether we could not fare to make ourselves more comfortable ashore.

"Hurriedly we gathered together our few belongings, and even among these I found that the fungus had been at work; for one of her shawls had a little lump of it growing near one edge. I threw the whole thing over the side, without saying anything to her.

"The raft was still alongside, but it was too clumsy to guide, and I lowered down a small boat that hung across the stern, and in this we made our way to the shore. Yet, as we drew near to it, I became gradually aware that here the vile fungus, which had driven us from the ship, was growing riot. In places it rose into horrible, fantastic mounds, which seemed almost to quiver, as with a quiet life, when the wind blew across them. Here and there it took on the forms of vast fingers, and in others it just spread out flat and smooth and treacherous. Odd places, it appeared as grotesque stunted trees, seeming extraordinarily kinked and gnarled—the whole quaking vilely at times.

"At first, it seemed to us that there was no single portion of the surrounding shore which was not hidden beneath the masses of the hideous lichen; yet, in this, I found we were mistaken; for somewhat later, coasting along the shore at a little distance, we descried a smooth white patch of what appeared to be fine sand, and there we landed. It was not sand. What it was I do not know. All that I have observed is that upon it the fungus will not grow; while everywhere else, save where the sandlike earth wanders oddly, pathwise, amid the gray desolation of the lichen, there is nothing but that loathsome grayness.

"It is difficult to make you understand how cheered we were to find one place that was absolutely free from the growth, and here we deposited our belongings. Then we went back to the ship for such things as it seemed to us we should need. Among other matters, I managed to bring ashore with me one of the ship's sails, with which I constructed two small tents, which, though exceedingly rough shaped, served the purposes for which they were intended. In these we lived and stored our various necessities, and thus for a matter of some four weeks all went smoothly and without particular unhappiness. Indeed, I may say with much of happiness—for—we were together.

"It was on the thumb of her right hand that the growth first showed. It was only a small circular spot, much like a little gray mole.

My God! how the fear leaped to my heart when she showed me the place. We cleansed it, between us, washing it with carbolic and water. In the morning of the following day she showed her hand to me again. The gray warty thing had returned. For a little while, we looked at one another in silence. Then, still wordless, we started again to remove it. In the midst of the operation she spoke suddenly.

" 'What's that on the side of your face, dear?' Her voice was sharp with anxiety. I put my hand up to feel.

" 'There! Under the hair by your ear. A little to the front a bit.' My finger rested upon the place, and then I knew.

" 'Let us get your thumb done first,' I said. And she submitted, only because she was afraid to touch me until it was cleansed. I finished washing and disinfecting her thumb, and then she turned to my face. After it was finished we sat together and talked awhile of many things; for there had come into our lives sudden, very terrible thoughts. We were, all at once, afraid of something worse than death. We spoke of loading the boat with provisions and water and making our way out onto the sea; yet we were helpless, for many causes, and—and the growth had attacked us already. We decided to stay. God would do with us what was His will. We would wait.

"A month, two months, three months passed and the places grew somewhat, and there had come others. Yet we fought so strenuously with the fear that its headway was but slow, comparatively speaking.

"Occasionally we ventured off to the ship for such stores as we needed. There we found that the fungus grew persistently. One of the nodules on the main deck became soon as high as my head.

"We had now given up all thought or hope of leaving the island. We had realized that it would be unallowable to go among healthy humans, with the thing from which we were suffering.

"With this determination and knowledge in our minds we knew that we should have to husband our food and water; for we did not know, at that time, but that we should possibly live for many years.

"This reminds me that I have told you that I am an old man. Judged by years this is not so. But—but—"

He broke off; then continued somewhat abruptly.

"As I was saying, we knew that we should have to use care in the matter of food. But we had no idea then how little food there was left, of which to take care. It was a week later that I made the discovery that all the other bread tanks—which I had supposed full—were empty, and that (beyond odd tins of vegetables and meat, and some other matters) we had nothing on which to depend, but the bread in the tank which I had already opened.

"After learning this I bestirred myself to do what I could, and set to work at fishing in the lagoon; but with no success. At this I was somewhat inclined to feel desperate until the thought came to me to try outside the lagoon, in the open sea.

"Here, at times, I caught odd fish; but so infrequently that they proved of but little help in keeping us from the hunger which threatened. It seemed to me that our deaths were likely to come by hunger, and not by the growth of the thing which had seized upon our bodies.

"We were in this state of mind when the fourth month wore out. Then I made a very horrible discovery. One morning, a little before midday, I came off from the ship with a portion of the biscuits which were left. In the mouth of her tent I saw my sweetheart sitting, eating something.

" 'What is it, my dear?' I called out as I leaped shore. Yet, on hearing my voice, she seemed confused, and, turning, slyly threw something toward the edge of the little clearing. It fell short, and a vague suspicion having arisen within me, I walked across and picked it up. It was a piece of the gray fungus.

"As I went to her with it in my hand, she turned deadly pale; then a rose red.

"I felt strangely dazed and frightened.

" 'My dear! My dear!' I said, and could say no more. Yet at my words she broke down and cried bitterly. Gradually, as she calmed, I got from her the news that she had tried it the preceding day, and— and liked it. I got her to promise on her knees not to touch it again, however great our hunger. After she had promised she told me that the desire for it had come suddenly, and that, until the moment of desire, she had experienced nothing toward it but the most extreme repulsion.

"Later in the day, feeling strangely restless, and much shaken with the thing which I had discovered, I made my way along one of the twisted paths—formed by the white, sandlike substance—which led among the fungoid growth. I had, once before, ventured along there; but not to any great distance. This time, being involved in perplexing thought, I went much further than hitherto.

"Suddenly I was called to myself by a queer hoarse sound on my left. Turning quickly I saw there was movement among an extraordinarily shaped mass of fungus, close to my elbow. It was swaying uneasily, as though it possessed life of its own. Abruptly, as I stared, the thought came to me that the thing had a grotesque resemblance to the figure of a distorted human creature. Even as the fancy flashed into my brain, there was a slight, sickening noise of tearing, and I saw that one of the branchlike arms was detaching itself from the surrounding gray masses, and coming toward me. The head of the thing —a shapeless gray ball, inclined in my direction. I stood stupidly, and the vile arm brushed across my face. I gave out a frightened cry, and ran back a few paces. There was a sweetish taste upon my lips where the thing had touched me. I licked them, and was immediately filled with an inhuman desire. I turned and seized a mass of the fungus. Then more, and—more. I was insatiable. In the midst of devouring, the remembrance of the morning's discovery swept into my amazed brain. It was sent by God. I dashed the fragment I held to the ground. Then, utterly wretched and feeling a dreadful guiltiness, I made my way back to the little encampment.

"I think she knew, by some marvelous intuition which love must have given, so soon as she set eyes on me. Her quiet sympathy made it easier for me, and I told her of my sudden weakness; yet omitted to mention the extraordinary thing which had gone before. I desired to spare her all unnecessary terror.

"But, for myself, I had added an intolerable knowledge, to breed an incessant terror in my brain; for I doubted not but that I had seen the end of one of these men who had come to the island in the ship in the lagoon; and in that monstrous ending I had seen our own.

"Thereafter we kept from the abominable food, though the desire for it had entered into our blood. Yet our drear punishment was upon us; for, day by day, with monstrous rapidity, the fungoid growth took hold of our poor bodies. Nothing we could do would check

it materially, and so—and so—we who had been human, became—
Well, it matters less each day. Only—only we had been man and
maid!

"And day by day the fight is more dreadful, to withstand the
hunger-lust for the terrible lichen.

"A week ago we ate the last of the biscuit, and since that time I
have caught three fish. I was out here fishing tonight when your
schooner drifted upon me out of the mist. I hailed you. You know the
rest, and may God, out of His great heart, bless you for your goodness to a—a couple of poor outcast souls."

There was the dip of an oar—another. Then the voice came again,
and for the last time, sounding through the slight surrounding mist,
ghostly and mournful.

"God bless you! Good-by!"

"Good-by," we shouted together, hoarsely, our hearts full of
many emotions.

I glanced about me. I became aware that the dawn was upon us.

The sun flung a stray beam across the hidden sea; pierced the
mist dully, and lit up the receding boat with a gloomy fire. Indis-
tinctly I saw something nodding between the oars. I thought of a
sponge—a great, gray nodding sponge— The oars continued to ply.
They were gray—as was the boat—and my eyes searched a moment
vainly for the conjunction of hand and oar. My gaze flashed back
to the—head. It nodded forward as the oars went backward for the
stroke. Then the oars were dipped, the boat shot out of the patch of
light, and the—the thing went nodding into the mist.

HOW LOVE CAME TO PROFESSOR GUILDEA

BY ROBERT S. HICHENS

I

❡ DULL PEOPLE often wondered how it came about that Father Murchison and Professor Frederic Guildea were intimate friends. The one was all faith, the other all skepticism. The nature of the Father was based on love. He viewed the world with an almost child-like tenderness above his long, black cassock; and his mild, yet perfectly fearless, blue eyes seemed always to be watching the goodness that exists in humanity, and rejoicing at what they saw. The Professor, on the other hand, had a hard face like a hatchet, tipped with an aggressive black goatee beard. His eyes were quick, piercing and irreverent. The lines about his small, thin-lipped mouth were almost cruel. His voice was harsh and dry, sometimes, when he grew energetic, almost soprano. It fired off words with a sharp and clipping utterance. His habitual manner was one of distrust and investigation. It was impossible to suppose that, in his busy life, he found any time for love, either of humanity in general or of an individual.

Yet his days were spent in scientific investigations which conferred immense benefits upon the world.

Both men were celibates. Father Murchison was a member of an Anglican order which forbade him to marry. Professor Guildea had a poor opinion of most things, but especially of women. He had formerly held a post as lecturer at Birmingham. But when his fame as a discoverer grew, he removed to London. There, at a lecture he gave in the East End, he first met Father Murchison. They spoke a few words. Perhaps the bright intelligence of the priest appealed to

From *Tongues of Conscience* by Robert S. Hichens. Reprinted by permission of the author's executors and Methuen & Co., Ltd., London.

143

the man of science, who was inclined, as a rule, to regard the clergy with some contempt. Perhaps the transparent sincerity of this devotee, full of common sense, attracted him. As he was leaving the hall he abruptly asked the Father to call on him at his house in Hyde Park Place. And the Father, who seldom went into the West End, except to preach, accepted the invitation.

"When will you come?" said Guildea.

He was folding up the blue paper on which his notes were written in a tiny, clear hand. The leaves rustled dryly in accompaniment to his sharp, dry voice.

"On Sunday week I am preaching in the evening at St. Saviour's, not far off," said the Father.

"I don't go to church."

"No," said the Father, without any accent of surprise or condemnation.

"Come to supper afterward?"

"Thank you, I will."

"What time will you come?"

The Father smiled.

"As soon as I have finished my sermon. The service is at six-thirty."

"About eight then, I suppose. Don't make the sermon too long. My number in Hyde Park Place is 100. Good night to you."

He snapped an elastic band round his papers and strode off without shaking hands.

On the appointed Sunday, Father Murchison preached to a densely crowded congregation at St. Saviour's. The subject of his sermon was sympathy, and the comparative uselessness of man in the world unless he can learn to love his neighbor as himself. The sermon was rather long, and when the preacher, in his flowing, black cloak, and his hard, round hat, with a straight brim over which hung the ends of a black cord, made his way toward the Professor's house, the hands of the illuminated clock disc at the Marble Arch pointed to twenty minutes past eight.

The Father hurried on, pushing his way through the crowd of standing soldiers, chattering women and giggling street boys in their

Sunday best. It was a warm April night, and when he reached number 100 Hyde Park Place, he found the Professor bareheaded on his doorstep, gazing out toward the Park railings, and enjoying the soft, moist air, in front of his lighted passage.

"Ha, a long sermon!" he exclaimed. "Come in."

"I fear it was," said the Father, obeying the invitation. "I am that dangerous thing—an extempore preacher."

"More attractive to speak without notes, if you can do it. Hang your hat and coat—oh, cloak—here. We'll have supper at once. This is the dining room."

He opened a door on the right and they entered a long, narrow room, with gold paper and a black ceiling, from which hung an electric lamp with a gold-colored shade. In the room stood a small oval table with covers laid for two. The Professor rang the bell. Then he said, "People seem to talk better at an oval table than at a square one."

"Really. Is that so?"

"Well, I've had precisely the same party twice, once at a square table, once at an oval table. The first dinner was a dull failure, the second a brilliant success. Sit down, won't you?"

"How d'you account for the difference?" said the Father, sitting down, and pulling the tail of his cassock well under him.

"H'm. I know how you'd account for it."

"Indeed. How then?"

"At an oval table, since there are no corners, the chain of human sympathy—the electric current, is much more complete. Eh! Let me give you some soup."

"Thank you."

The Father took it, and, as he did so, turned his beaming blue eyes on his host. Then he smiled.

"What!" he said, in his pleasant, light tenor voice. "You do go to church sometimes, then?"

"Tonight is the first time for ages. And, mind you, I was tremendously bored."

The Father still smiled, and his blue eyes gently twinkled.

"Dear, dear!" he said, "what a pity!"

"But not by the sermon," Guildea added. "I don't pay a compliment. I state a fact. The sermon didn't bore me. If it had, I should have said so, or said nothing."

"And which would you have done?"

The Professor smiled almost genially.

"Don't know," he said. "What wine d'you drink?"

"None, thank you. I'm a teetotaler. In my profession and *milieu* it is necessary to be one. Yes, I will have some soda water. I think you would have done the first."

"Very likely, and very wrongly. You wouldn't have minded much."

"I don't think I should."

They were intimate already. The Father felt most pleasantly at home under the black ceiling. He drank some soda water and seemed to enjoy it more than the Professor enjoyed his claret.

"You smile at the theory of the chain of human sympathy, I see," said the Father. "Then what is your explanation of the failure of your square party with corners, the success of your oval party without them?"

"Probably on the first occasion the wit of the assembly had a chill on his liver, while on the second he was in perfect health. Yet, you see, I stick to the oval table."

"And that means—"

"Very little. By the way, your omission of any allusion to the notorious part liver plays in love was a serious one tonight."

"Your omission of any desire for close human sympathy in your life is a more serious one."

"How can you be sure I have no such desire?"

"I divine it. Your look, your manner, tell me it is so. You were disagreeing with my sermon all the time I was preaching. Weren't you?"

"Part of the time."

The servant changed the plates. He was a middle-aged, blond, thin man, with a stony white face, pale, prominent eyes, and an accomplished manner of service. When he had left the room the Professor continued.

"Your remarks interested me, but I thought them exaggerated."

"For instance?"

"Let me play the egoist for a moment. I spend most of my time in hard work, very hard work. The results of this work, you will allow, benefit humanity."

"Enormously," assented the Father, thinking of more than one of Guildea's discoveries.

"And the benefit conferred by this work, undertaken merely for its own sake, is just as great as if it were undertaken because I loved my fellow man, and sentimentally desired to see him more comfortable than he is at present. I'm as useful precisely in my present condition of—in my present nonaffectional condition—as I should be if I were as full of gush as the sentimentalists who want to get murderers out of prison, or to put a premium on tyranny—like Tolstoi—by preventing the punishment of tyrants."

"One may do great harm with affection; great good without it. Yes, that is true. Even *le bon motif* is not everything, I know. Still I contend that, given your powers, you would be far more useful in the world with sympathy, affection for your kind, added to them than as you are. I believe even that you would do still more splendid work."

The Professor poured himself out another glass of claret.

"You noticed my butler?" he said.

"I did."

"He's a perfect servant. He makes me perfectly comfortable. Yet he has no feeling of liking for me. I treat him civilly. I pay him well. But I never think about him, or concern myself with him as a human being. I know nothing of his character except what I read of it in his last master's letter. There are, you may say, no truly human relations between us. You would affirm that his work would be better done if I had made him personally like me as man—of any class—can like man—of any other class?"

"I should, decidedly."

"I contend that he couldn't do his work better than he does it at present."

"But if any crisis occurred?"

"What?"

"Any crisis, change in your condition. If you needed his help, not only as a man and a butler, but as a man and a brother? He'd fail you then, probably. You would never get from your servant that finest service which can only be prompted by an honest affection."

"You have finished?"

"Quite."

"Let us go upstairs then. Yes, those are good prints. I picked them up in Birmingham when I was living there. This is my work-room."

They came to a double room lined entirely with books, and brilliantly, rather hardly, lit by electricity. The windows at one end looked onto the Park, at the other onto the garden of a neighboring house. The door by which they entered was concealed from the inner and smaller room by the jutting wall of the outer room, in which stood a huge writing table loaded with letters, pamphlets and manuscripts. Between the two windows of the inner room was a cage in which a large, gray parrot was clambering, using both beak and claws to assist him in his slow and meditative peregrinations.

"You have a pet," said the Father, surprised.

"I possess a parrot," the Professor answered dryly, "I got him for a purpose when I was making a study of the imitative powers of birds, and I have never got rid of him. A cigar?"

"Thank you."

They sat down. Father Murchison glanced at the parrot. It had paused in its journey, and, clinging to the bars of its cage, was regarding them with attentive round eyes that looked deliberately intelligent, but by no means sympathetic. He looked away from it to Guildea, who was smoking, with his head thrown back, his sharp, pointed chin, on which the small black beard bristled, upturned. He was moving his under lip up and down rapidly. This action caused the beard to stir and look peculiarly aggressive. The Father suddenly chuckled softly.

"Why's that?" cried Guildea, letting his chin drop down on his breast and looking at his guest sharply.

"I was thinking it would have to be a crisis indeed that could make you cling to your butler's affection for assistance."

Guildea smiled too.

"You're right. It would. Here he comes."

The man entered with coffee. He offered it gently, and retired like a shadow retreating on a wall.

"Splendid, inhuman fellow," remarked Guildea.

"I prefer the East End lad who does my errands in Bird Street," said the Father. "I know all his worries. He knows some of mine. We are friends. He's more noisy than your man. He even breathes hard when he is especially solicitous, but he would do more for me than put the coals on my fire, or black my square-toed boots."

"Men are differently made. To me the watchful eye of affection would be abominable."

"What about that bird?"

The Father pointed to the parrot. It had got up on its perch and, with one foot uplifted in an impressive, almost benedictory, manner, was gazing steadily at the Professor.

"That's the watchful eye of imitation, with a mind at the back of it, desirous of reproducing the peculiarities of others. No, I thought your sermon tonight very fresh, very clever. But I have no wish for affection. Reasonable liking, of course, one desires—" he tugged sharply at his beard, as if to warn himself against sentimentality—"but anything more would be most irksome, and would push me, I feel sure, toward cruelty. It would also hamper one's work."

"I don't think so."

"The sort of work I do. I shall continue to benefit the world without loving it, and it will continue to accept the benefits without loving me. That's all as it should be."

He drank his coffee. Then he added rather aggressively, "I have neither time nor inclination for sentimentality."

When Guildea let Father Murchison out, he followed the Father onto the doorstep and stood there for a moment. The Father glanced across the damp road into the Park.

"I see you've got a gate just opposite you," he said idly.

"Yes. I often slip across for a stroll to clear my brain. Good night to you. Come again some day."

"With pleasure. Good night."

The priest strode away, leaving Guildea standing on the step.

Father Murchison came many times again to number 100 Hyde

Park Place. He had a feeling of liking for most men and women whom he knew, and of tenderness for all, whether he knew them or not, but he grew to have a special sentiment toward Guildea. Strangely enough, it was a sentiment of pity. He pitied this hard-working, eminently successful man of big brain and bold heart, who never seemed depressed, who never wanted assistance, who never complained of the twisted skein of life or faltered in his progress along its way. The Father pitied Guildea, in fact, because Guildea wanted so little. He had told him so, for the intercourse of the two men, from the beginning, had been singularly frank.

One evening, when they were talking together, the Father happened to speak of one of the oddities of life, the fact that those who do not want things often get them, while those who seek them vehemently are disappointed in their search.

"Then I ought to have affection poured upon me," said Guildea smiling rather grimly. "For I hate it."

"Perhaps some day you will."

"I hope not, most sincerely."

Father Murchison said nothing for a moment. He was drawing together the ends of the broad band round his cassock. When he spoke he seemed to be answering someone.

"Yes," he said slowly, "yes, that *is* my feeling—pity."

"For whom?" said the Professor.

Then, suddenly, he understood. He did not say that he understood, but Father Murchison felt, and saw, that it was quite unnecessary to answer his friend's question. So Guildea, strangely enough, found himself closely acquainted with a man—his opposite in all ways—who pitied him.

The fact that he did not mind this, and scarcely ever thought about it, shows perhaps as clearly as anything could, the peculiar indifference of his nature.

II

One autumn evening, a year and a half after Father Murchison and the Professor had first met, the Father called in Hyde Park

Place and inquired of the blond and stony butler—his name was Pitting—whether his master was at home.

"Yes, sir," replied Pitting. "Will you please come this way?"

He moved noiselessly up the rather narrow stairs, followed by the Father, tenderly opened the library door, and in his soft, cold voice, announced, "Father Murchison."

Guildea was sitting in an armchair, before a small fire. His thin, long-fingered hands lay outstretched upon his knees, his head was sunk down on his chest. He appeared to be pondering deeply. Pitting very slightly raised his voice.

"Father Murchison to see you, sir," he repeated.

The Professor jumped up rather suddenly and turned sharply round as the Father came in.

"Oh," he said. "It's you, is it? Glad to see you. Come to the fire."

The Father glanced at him and thought him looking unusually fatigued.

"You don't look well tonight," the Father said.

"No?"

"You must be working too hard. That lecture you are going to give in Paris is bothering you?"

"Not a bit. It's all arranged. I could deliver it to you at this moment verbatim. Well, sit down."

The Father did so, and Guildea sank once more into his chair and stared hard into the fire without another word. He seemed to be thinking profoundly. His friend did not interrupt him, but quietly lit a pipe and began to smoke reflectively. The eyes of Guildea were fixed upon the fire. The Father glanced about the room, at the walls of soberly bound books, at the crowded writing table, at the windows, before which hung heavy, dark blue curtains of old brocade, at the cage, which stood between them. A green baize covering was thrown over it. The Father wondered why. He had never seen Napoleon—so the parrot was named—covered up at night before. While he was looking at the baize Guildea suddenly jerked up his head and, taking his hands from his knees and clasping them, said abruptly, "D'you think I'm an attractive man?"

Father Murchison jumped. Such a question coming from such a man astounded him.

"Bless me!" he ejaculated. "What makes you ask? Do you mean attractive to the opposite sex?"

"That's what I don't know," said the Professor gloomily, and staring again into the fire. "That's what I don't know."

The Father grew more astonished.

"Don't know!" he exclaimed.

And he laid down his pipe.

"Let's say—d'you think I'm attractive, that there's anything about me which might draw a—a human being, or an animal irresistibly to me?"

"Whether you desired it or not?"

"Exactly—or—no, let us say definitely—if I did not desire it."

Father Murchison pursed up his rather full, cherubic lips, and little wrinkles appeared about the corners of his blue eyes.

"There might be, of course," he said, after a pause. "Human nature is weak, engagingly weak, Guildea. And you're inclined to flout it. I could understand a certain class of lady—the lion-hunting, the intellectual lady, seeking you. Your reputation, your great name—"

"Yes, yes," Guildea interrupted, rather irritably, "I know all that, I know."

He twisted his long hands together, bending the palms outward till his thin, pointed fingers cracked. His forehead was wrinkled in a frown.

"I imagine," he said—he stopped and coughed dryly, almost shrilly—"I imagine it would be very disagreeable to be liked, to be run after—that is the usual expression, isn't it—by anything one objected to."

And now he half turned in his chair, crossed his legs one over the other, and looked at his guest with an unusual, almost piercing interrogation.

"Anything?" said the Father.

"Well—well, anyone. I imagine nothing could be more unpleasant."

"To you—no," answered the Father. "But—forgive me, Guildea,

I cannot conceive your permitting such intrusion. You don't encourage adoration."

Guildea nodded his head gloomily.

"I don't," he said, "I don't. That's just it. That's the curious part of it, that I—"

He broke off deliberately, got up and stretched.

"I'll have a pipe, too," he said.

He went over to the mantelpiece, got his pipe, filled it and lighted it. As he held the match to the tobacco, bending forward with an inquiring expression, his eyes fell upon the green baize that covered Napoleon's cage. He threw the match into the grate, and puffed at the pipe as he walked forward to the cage. When he reached it he put out his hand, took hold of the baize and began to pull it away. Then suddenly he pushed it back over the cage.

"No," he said, as if to himself, "no."

He returned rather hastily to the fire and threw himself once more into his armchair.

"You're wondering," he said to Father Murchison. "So am I. I don't know at all what to make of it. I'll just tell you the facts and you must tell me what you think of them. The night before last, after a day of hard work—but no harder than usual—I went to the front door to get a breath of air. You know I often do that."

"Yes, I found you on the doorstep when I first came here."

"Just so. I didn't put on hat or coat. I just stood on the step as I was. My mind, I remember, was still full of my work. It was rather a dark night, not very dark. The hour was about eleven, or a quarter past. I was staring at the Park, and presently I found that my eyes were directed toward somebody who was sitting, back to me, on one of the benches. I saw the person—if it was a person—through the railings."

"If it was a person!" said the Father. "What do you mean by that?"

"Wait a minute. I say that because it was too dark for me to know. I merely saw some blackish object on the bench, rising into view above the level of the back of the seat. I couldn't say it was man, woman or child. But something there was, and I found that I was looking at it."

"I understand."

"Gradually, I also found that my thoughts were becoming fixed upon this thing or person. I began to wonder, first, what it was doing there; next, what it was thinking; lastly, what it was like."

"Some poor creature without a home, I suppose," said the Father.

"I said that to myself. Still, I was taken with an extraordinary interest about this object, so great an interest that I got my hat and crossed the road to go into the Park. As you know, there's an entrance almost opposite to my house. Well, Murchison, I crossed the road, passed through the gate in the railings, went up to the seat, and found that there was—nothing on it."

"Were you looking at it as you walked?"

"Part of the time. But I removed my eyes from it just as I passed through the gate, because there was a row going on a little way off, and I turned for an instant in that direction. When I saw that the seat was vacant I was seized by a most absurd sensation of disappointment, almost of anger. I stopped and looked about me to see if anything was moving away, but I could see nothing. It was a cold night and misty, and there were few people about. Feeling, as I say, foolishly and unnaturally disappointed, I retraced my steps to this house. When I got here I discovered that during my short absence I had left the hall door open—half open."

"Rather imprudent in London."

"Yes. I had no idea, of course, that I had done so, till I got back. However, I was only away three minutes or so."

"Yes."

"It was not likely that anybody had gone in."

"I suppose not."

"Was it?"

"Why do you ask me that, Guildea?"

"Well, well!"

"Besides, if anybody had gone in, on your return you'd have caught him, surely."

Guildea coughed again. The Father, surprised, could not fail to recognize that he was nervous and that his nervousness was affecting him physically.

"I must have caught cold that night," he said, as if he had read his friend's thought and hastened to contradict it. Then he went on, "I entered the hall, or passage, rather."

He paused again. His uneasiness was becoming very apparent.

"And you did catch somebody?" said the Father.

Guildea cleared his throat.

"That's just it," he said, "now we come to it. I'm not imaginative, as you know."

"You certainly are not."

"No, but hardly had I stepped into the passage before I felt certain that somebody had got into the house during my absence. I felt convinced of it, and not only that, I also felt convinced that the intruder was the very person I had dimly seen sitting upon the seat in the Park. What d'you say to that?"

"I begin to think you are imaginative."

"H'm! It seemed to me that the person—the occupant of the seat—and I, had simultaneously formed the project of interviewing each other, had simultaneously set out to put that project into execution. I became so certain of this that I walked hastily upstairs into this room, expecting to find the visitor awaiting me. But there was no one. I then came down again and went into the dining room. No one. I was actually astonished. Isn't that odd?"

"Very," said the Father, quite gravely.

The Professor's chill and gloomy manner, and uncomfortable, constrained appearance kept away the humor that might well have lurked round the steps of such a discourse.

"I went upstairs again," he continued, "sat down and thought the matter over. I resolved to forget it, and took up a book. I might perhaps have been able to read, but suddenly I thought I noticed—"

He stopped abruptly. Father Murchison observed that he was staring toward the green baize that covered the parrot's cage.

"But that's nothing," he said. "Enough that I couldn't read. I resolved to explore the house. You know how small it is, how easily one can go all over it. I went all over it. I went into every room without exception. To the servants, who were having supper, I made some excuse. They were surprised at my advent, no doubt."

"And Pitting?"

"Oh, he got up politely when I came in, stood while I was there, but never said a word. I muttered 'don't disturb yourselves,' or something of the sort, and came out. Murchison, I found nobody new in the house—yet I returned to this room entirely convinced that somebody had entered while I was in the Park."

"And gone out again before you came back?"

"No, had stayed, and was still in the house."

"But, my dear Guildea," began the Father, now in great astonishment. "Surely—"

"I know what you want to say—what I should want to say in your place. Now, do wait. I am also convinced that this visitor has not left the house and is at this moment in it."

He spoke with evident sincerity, with extreme gravity. Father Murchison looked him full in the face, and met his quick, keen eyes.

"No," he said, as if in reply to an uttered question, "I'm perfectly sane, I assure you. The whole matter seems almost as incredible to me as it must to you. But, as you know, I never quarrel with facts, however strange. I merely try to examine into them thoroughly. I have already consulted a doctor and been pronounced in perfect bodily health."

He paused, as if expecting the Father to say something.

"Go on, Guildea," he said, "you haven't finished."

"No. I felt that night positive that somebody had entered the house, and remained in it, and my conviction grew. I went to bed as usual, and, contrary to my expectation, slept as well as I generally do. Yet directly I woke up yesterday morning I knew that my household had been increased by one."

"May I interrupt you for one moment? How did you know it?"

"By my mental sensation. I can only say that I was perfectly conscious of a new presence within my house, close to me."

"How very strange," said the Father. "And you feel absolutely certain that you are not overworked? Your brain does not feel tired? Your head is quite clear?"

"Quite. I was never better. When I came down to breakfast that morning I looked sharply into Pitting's face. He was as coldly placid and inexpressive as usual. It was evident to me that his mind was in no way distressed. After breakfast I sat down to work, all the time ceaselessly conscious of the fact of this intruder upon my privacy.

Nevertheless, I labored for several hours, waiting for any development that might occur to clear away the mysterious obscurity of this event. I lunched. About half-past two I was obliged to go out to attend a lecture. I therefore took my coat and hat, opened my door, and stepped onto the pavement. I was instantly aware that I was no longer intruded upon, and this although I was now in the street, surrounded by people. Consequently, I felt certain that the thing in my house must be thinking of me, perhaps even spying upon me."

"Wait a moment," interrupted the Father. "What was your sensation? Was it one of fear?"

"Oh, dear no. I was entirely puzzled—as I am now—and keenly interested, but not in any way alarmed. I delivered my lecture with my usual ease and returned home in the evening. On entering the house again I was perfectly conscious that the intruder was still there. Last night I dined alone and spent the hours after dinner in reading a scientific work in which I was deeply interested. While I read, however, I never for one moment lost the knowledge that some mind— very attentive to me—was within hail of mine. I will say more than this—the sensation constantly increased, and, by the time I got up to go to bed, I had come to a very strange conclusion."

"What? What was it?"

"That whoever—or whatever—had entered my house during my short absence in the Park was more than interested in me."

"More than interested in you?"

"Was fond, or was becoming fond, of me."

"Oh!" exclaimed the Father. "Now I understand why you asked me just now whether I thought there was anything about you that might draw a human being or an animal irresistibly to you."

"Precisely. Since I came to this conclusion, Murchison, I will confess that my feeling of strong curiosity has become tinged with another feeling."

"Of fear?"

"No, of dislike, or irritation. No—not fear, not fear."

As Guildea repeated unnecessarily this asseveration he looked again toward the parrot's cage.

"What is there to be afraid of in such a matter?" he added. "I am not a child to tremble before bogies."

In saying the last words he raised his voice sharply; then he walked quickly to the cage, and, with an abrupt movement, pulled the baize covering from it. Napoleon was disclosed, apparently dozing upon his perch with his head held slightly on one side. As the light reached him, he moved, ruffled the feathers about his neck, blinked his eyes, and began slowly to sidle to and fro, thrusting his head forward and drawing it back with an air of complacent, though rather unmeaning, energy. Guildea stood by the cage, looking at him closely, and indeed with an attention that was so intense as to be remarkable, almost unnatural.

"How absurd these birds are!" he said at length, coming back to the fire.

"You have no more to tell me?" asked the Father.

"No. I am still aware of the presence of something in my house. I am still conscious of its close attention to me. I am still irritated, seriously annoyed—I confess it—by that attention."

"You say you are aware of the presence of something at this moment?"

"At this moment—yes."

"Do you mean in this room, with us, now?"

"I should say so—at any rate, quite near us."

Again he glanced quickly, almost suspiciously, toward the cage of the parrot. The bird was sitting still on its perch now. Its head was bent down and cocked sideways, and it appeared to be listening attentively to something.

"That bird will have the intonations of my voice more correctly than ever by tomorrow morning," said the Father, watching Guildea closely with his mild blue eyes. "And it has always imitated me very cleverly."

The Professor started slightly.

"Yes," he said. "Yes, no doubt. Well, what do you make of this affair?"

"Nothing at all. It is absolutely inexplicable. I can speak quite frankly to you, I feel sure."

"Of course. That's why I have told you the whole thing."

"I think you must be overworked, overstrained, without knowing it."

"And that the doctor was mistaken when he said I was all right?"

"Yes."

Guildea knocked his pipe out against the chimney piece.

"It may be so," he said, "I will not be so unreasonable as to deny the possibility, although I feel as well as I ever did in my life. What do you advise then?"

"A week of complete rest away from London, in good air."

"The usual prescription. I'll take it. I'll go tomorrow to Westgate and leave Napoleon to keep house in my absence."

For some reason, which he could not explain to himself, the pleasure which Father Murchison felt in hearing the first part of his friend's final remark was lessened, was almost destroyed, by the last sentence.

He walked toward the City that night, deep in thought, remembering and carefully considering the first interview he had with Guildea in the latter's house a year and a half before.

On the following morning Guildea left London.

III

Father Murchison was so busy a man that he had little time for brooding over the affairs of others. During Guildea's week at the sea, however, the Father thought about him a great deal, with much wonder and some dismay. The dismay was soon banished, for the mild-eyed priest was quick to discern weakness in himself, quicker still to drive it forth as a most undesirable inmate of the soul. But the wonder remained. It was destined to a crescendo. Guildea had left London on a Thursday. On a Thursday he returned, having previously sent a note to Father Murchison to mention that he was leaving Westgate at a certain time. When his train ran into Victoria Station, at five o'clock in the evening, he was surprised to see the cloaked figure of his friend standing upon the gray platform behind a line of porters.

"What, Murchison!" he said. "You here! Have you seceded from your order that you are taking this holiday?"

They shook hands.

"No," said the Father. "It happened that I had to be in this neighborhood today, visiting a sick person. So I thought I would meet you."

"And see if I were still a sick person, eh?"

The Professor glanced at him kindly, but with a dry little laugh.

"Are you?" replied the Father gently, looking at him with interest. "No, I think not. You appear very well."

The sea air had, in fact, put some brownish red into Guildea's always thin cheeks. His keen eyes were shining with life and energy, and he walked forward in his loose gray suit and fluttering overcoat with a vigor that was noticeable, carrying easily in his left hand his well-filled Gladstone bag.

The Father felt completely reassured.

"I never saw you look better," he said.

"I never was better. Have you an hour to spare?"

"Two."

"Good. I'll send my bag up by cab, and we'll walk across the Park to my house and have a cup of tea there. What d'you say?"

"I shall enjoy it."

They walked out of the station yard, past the flower girls and newspaper sellers toward Grosvenor Place.

"And you have had a pleasant time?" the Father said.

"Pleasant enough, and lonely. I left my companion behind me in the passage at number 100, you know."

"And you'll not find him there now, I feel sure."

"H'm!" ejaculated Guildea. "What a precious weakling you think me, Murchison."

As he spoke he strode forward more quickly, as if moved to emphasize his sensation of bodily vigor.

"A weakling—no. But anyone who uses his brain as persistently as you do yours must require an occasional holiday."

"And I required one very badly, eh?"

"You required one, I believe."

"Well, I've had it. And now we'll see."

The evening was closing in rapidly. They crossed the road at Hyde Park Corner, and entered the Park, in which were a number of people going home from work; men in corduroy trousers, caked with dried mud, and carrying tin cans slung over their shoulders, and flat panniers, in which lay their tools. Some of the younger ones talked loudly or whistled shrilly as they walked.

"Until the evening," murmured Father Murchison to himself.

"What?" asked Guildea.

"I was only quoting the last words of the text, which seems written upon life, especially upon the life of pleasure: 'Man goeth forth to his work, and to his labor.' "

"Ah, those fellows are not half bad fellows to have in an audience. There were a lot of them at the lecture I gave when I first met you, I remember. One of them tried to heckle me. He had a red beard. Chaps with red beards are always hecklers. I laid him low on that occasion. Well, Murchison, and now we're going to see."

"What?"

"Whether my companion has departed."

"Tell me—do you feel any expectation of—well—of again thinking something is there?"

"How carefully you choose language. No, I merely wonder."

"You have no apprehension?"

"Not a scrap. But I confess to feeling curious."

"Then the sea air hasn't taught you to recognize that the whole thing came from overstrain."

"No," said Guildea, very dryly.

He walked on in silence for a minute. Then he added, "You thought it would?"

"I certainly thought it might."

"Make me realize that I had a sickly, morbid, rotten imagination—eh? Come now, Murchison, why not say frankly that you packed me off to Westgate to get rid of what you considered an acute form of hysteria?"

The Father was quite unmoved by this attack.

"Come now, Guildea," he retorted, "what did you expect me to think? I saw no indication of hysteria in you. I never have. One would suppose you the last man likely to have such a malady. But which is more natural—for me to believe in your hysteria or in the truth of such a story as you told me?"

"You have me there. No, I mustn't complain. Well, there's no hysteria about me now, at any rate."

"And no stranger in your house, I hope."

Father Murchison spoke the last words with earnest gravity, dropping the half-bantering tone—which they had both assumed.

"You take the matter very seriously, I believe," said Guildea, also speaking more gravely.

"How else can I take it? You wouldn't have me laugh at it when you tell it me seriously?"

"No. If we find my visitor still in the house, I may even call upon you to exorcise it. But first I must do one thing."

"And that is?"

"Prove to you, as well as to myself, that it is still there."

"That might be difficult," said the Father, considerably surprised by Guildea's matter-of-fact tone.

"I don't know. If it has remained in my house I think I can find a means. And I shall not be at all surprised if it is still there—despite the Westgate air."

In saying the last words the Professor relapsed into his former tone of dry chaff. The Father could not quite make up his mind whether Guildea was feeling unusually grave or unusually gay. As the two men drew near to Hyde Park Place their conversation died away and they walked forward silently in the gathering darkness.

"Here we are!" said Guildea at last.

He thrust his key into the door, opened it and let Father Murchison into the passage, following him closely, and banging the door.

"Here we are!" he repeated in a louder voice.

The electric light was turned on in anticipation of his arrival. He stood still and looked round.

"We'll have some tea at once," he said. "Ah, Pitting!"

The pale butler, who had heard the door bang, moved gently forward from the top of the stairs that led to the kitchen, greeted his master respectfully, took his coat and Father Murchison's cloak, and hung them on two pegs against the wall.

"All's right, Pitting? All's as usual?" said Guildea.

"Quite so, sir."

"Bring us up some tea to the library."

"Yes, sir."

Pitting retreated. Guildea waited till he had disappeared, then opened the dining-room door, put his head into the room and kept it there for a moment, standing perfectly still. Presently he drew back into the passage, shut the door, and said, "Let's go upstairs."

Father Murchison looked at him inquiringly, but made no remark. They ascended the stairs and came into the library. Guildea glanced rather sharply round. A fire was burning on the hearth. The blue curtains were drawn. The bright gleam of the strong electric light fell on the long rows of books, on the writing table—very orderly in consequence of Guildea's holiday—and on the uncovered cage of the parrot. Guildea went up to the cage. Napoleon was sitting humped up on his perch with his feathers ruffled. His long toes, which looked as if they were covered with crocodile skin, clung to the bar. His round and blinking eyes were filmy, like old eyes. Guildea stared at the bird very hard, and then clucked with his tongue against his teeth. Napoleon shook himself, lifted one foot, extended his toes, sidled along the perch to the bars nearest to the Professor and thrust his head against them. Guildea scratched it with his forefinger two or three times, still gazing attentively at the parrot; then he returned to the fire just as Pitting entered with the tea tray.

Father Murchison was already sitting in an armchair on one side of the fire. Guildea took another chair and began to pour out tea, as Pitting left the room, closing the door gently behind him. The Father sipped his tea, found it hot and set the cup down on a little table at his side.

"You're fond of that parrot, aren't you?" he asked his friend.

"Not particularly. It's interesting to study sometimes. The parrot mind and nature are peculiar."

"How long have you had him?"

"About four years. I nearly got rid of him just before I made your acquaintance. I'm very glad now I kept him."

"Are you? Why is that?"

"I shall probably tell you in a day or two."

The Father took his cup again. He did not press Guildea for an immediate explanation, but when they had both finished their tea he said, "Well, has the sea air had the desired effect?"

"No," said Guildea.

The Father brushed some crumbs from the front of his cassock and sat up higher in his chair.

"Your visitor is still here?" he asked, and his blue eyes became almost ungentle and piercing as he gazed at his friend.

"Yes," answered Guildea calmly.

"How do you know it, when did you know it—when you looked into the dining room just now?"

"No. Not until I came into this room. It welcomed me here."

"Welcomed you! In what way?"

"Simply by being here, by making me feel that it is here, as I might feel that a man was if I came into the room when it was dark."

He spoke quietly, with perfect composure in his usual dry manner.

"Very well," the Father said, "I shall not try to contend against your sensation, or to explain it away. Naturally, I am in amazement."

"So am I. Never has anything in my life surprised me so much. Murchison, of course I cannot expect you to believe more than that I honestly suppose—imagine, if you like—that there is some intruder here, of what kind I am totally unaware. I cannot expect you to believe that there really is anything. If you were in my place, I in yours, I should certainly consider you the victim of some nervous delusion. I could not do otherwise. But—wait. Don't condemn me as a hysteria patient, or as a madman, for two or three days. I feel convinced that —unless I am indeed unwell, a mental invalid, which I don't think is possible—I shall be able very shortly to give you some proof that there is a newcomer in my house."

"You don't tell me what kind of proof?"

"Not yet. Things must go a little farther first. But, perhaps even tomorrow I may be able to explain myself more fully. In the meanwhile, I'll say this, that if, eventually, I can't bring any kind of proof that I'm not dreaming, I'll let you take me to any doctor you like, and I'll resolutely try to adopt your present view—that I'm suffering from an absurd delusion. That is your view, of course?"

Father Murchison was silent for a moment. Then he said, rather doubtfully, "It ought to be."

"But isn't it?" asked Guildea, surprised.

"Well, you know, your manner is enormously convincing. Still, of course, I doubt. How can I do otherwise? The whole thing must be fancy."

The Father spoke as if he were trying to recoil from a mental position he was being forced to take up.

"It must be fancy," he repeated.

"I'll convince you by more than my manner, or I'll not try to convince you at all," said Guildea.

When they parted that evening, he said, "I'll write to you in a day or two probably. I think the proof I am going to give you has been accumulating during my absence. But I shall soon know."

Father Murchison was extremely puzzled as he sat on the top of the omnibus going homeward.

IV

In two days' time he received a note from Guildea asking him to call, if possible, the same evening. This he was unable to do as he had an engagement to fulfill at some East End gathering. The following day was Sunday. He wrote saying he would come on the Monday, and got a wire shortly afterward: "YES, MONDAY COME TO DINNER SEVEN-THIRTY GUILDEA." At half-past seven he stood on the doorstep of number 100.

Pitting let him in.

"Is the Professor quite well, Pitting?" the Father inquired as he took off his cloak.

"I believe so, sir. He has not made any complaint," the butler formally replied. "Will you come upstairs, sir?"

Guildea met them at the door of the library. He was very pale and somber, and shook hands carelessly with his friend.

"Give us dinner," he said to Pitting.

As the butler retired, Guildea shut the door rather cautiously. Father Murchison had never before seen him look so disturbed.

"You're worried, Guildea," the Father said. "Seriously worried."

"Yes, I am. This business is beginning to tell on me a good deal."

"Your belief in the presence of something here continues then?"

"Oh, dear, yes. There's no sort of doubt about the matter. The night I went across the road into the Park something got into the house, though what the devil it is I can't yet find out. But now, before we go down to dinner, I'll just tell you something about that proof I promised you. You remember?"

"Naturally."

"Can't you imagine what it might be?"

Father Murchison moved his head to express a negative reply.

"Look about the room," said Guildea. "What do you see?"

The Father glanced round the room, slowly and carefully.

"Nothing unusual. You do not mean to tell me there is any appearance of—"

"Oh, no, no, there's no conventional, white-robed, cloudlike figure. Bless my soul, no! I haven't fallen so low as that."

He spoke with considerable irritation.

"Look again."

Father Murchison looked at him, turned in the direction of his fixed eyes and saw the gray parrot clambering in its cage, slowly and persistently.

"What?" he said, quickly. "Will the proof come from there?"

The Professor nodded.

"I believe so," he said. "Now let's go down to dinner. I want some food badly."

They descended to the dining room. While they ate and Pitting waited upon them, the Professor talked about birds, their habits, their curiosities, their fears and their powers of imitation. He had evidently studied this subject with the thoroughness that was characteristic of him in all that he did.

"Parrots," he said presently, "are extraordinarily observant. It is a pity that their means of reproducing what they see are so limited. If it were not so, I have little doubt that their echo of gesture would be as remarkable as their echo of voice often is."

"But hands are missing."

"Yes. They do many things with their heads, however. I once knew an old woman near Goring on the Thames. She was afflicted with the palsy. She held her head perpetually sideways and it trembled, moving from right to left. Her sailor son brought her home a parrot from one of his voyages. It used to reproduce the old woman's palsied movement of the head exactly. Those gray parrots are always on the watch."

Guildea said the last sentence slowly and deliberately, glancing sharply over his wine at Father Murchison, and, when he had spoken it, a sudden light of comprehension dawned in the priest's mind. He opened his lips to make a swift remark. Guildea turned his bright eyes toward Pitting, who at the moment was tenderly bearing a cheese meringue from the lift that connected the dining room with the lower regions. The Father closed his lips again. But presently, when the butler had placed some apples on the table, had meticulously arranged the decanters, brushed away the crumbs and evaporated, he said, quickly, "I begin to understand. You think Napoleon is aware of the intruder?"

"I know it. He has been watching my visitant ever since the night of that visitant's arrival."

Another flash of light came to the priest.

"That was why you covered him with green baize one evening?"

"Exactly. An act of cowardice. His behavior was beginning to grate upon my nerves."

Guildea pursed up his thin lips and drew his brows down, giving to his face a look of sudden pain.

"But now I intend to follow his investigations," he added, straightening his features. "The week I wasted at Westgate was not wasted by him in London, I can assure you. Have an apple."

"No, thank you; no, thank you."

The Father repeated the words without knowing that he did so. Guildea pushed away his glass.

"Let us come upstairs, then."

"No, thank you," reiterated the Father.

"Eh?"

"What am I saying?" exclaimed the Father, getting up. "I was thinking over this extraordinary affair."

"Ah, you're beginning to forget the hysteria theory?"

They walked out into the passage.

"Well, you are so very practical about the whole matter."

"Why not? Here's something very strange and abnormal come into my life. What should I do but investigate it closely and calmly?"

"What, indeed?"

The Father began to feel rather bewildered, under a sort of compulsion which seemed laid upon him to give earnest attention to a matter that ought to strike him—so he felt—as entirely absurd. When they came into the library his eyes immediately turned, with profound curiosity, toward the parrot's cage. A slight smile curled the Professor's lips. He recognized the effect he was producing upon his friend. The Father saw the smile.

"Oh, I'm not won over yet," he said in answer to it.

"I know. Perhaps you may be before the evening is over. Here comes the coffee. After we have drunk it we'll proceed to our experiment. Leave the coffee, Pitting, and don't disturb us again."

"No, sir."

"I won't have it black tonight," said the Father, "plenty of milk, please. I don't want my nerves played upon."

"Suppose we don't take coffee at all?" said Guildea. "If we do, you may trot out the theory that we are not in a perfectly normal condition. I know you, Murchison, devout priest and devout skeptic."

The Father laughed and pushed away his cup.

"Very well, then. No coffee."

"One cigarette, and then to business."

The gray-blue smoke curled up.

"What are we going to do?" said the Father.

He was sitting bolt upright as if ready for action. Indeed there was no suggestion of repose in the attitudes of either of the men.

"Hide ourselves, and watch Napoleon. By the way—that reminds me."

He got up, went to a corner of the room, picked up a piece of green baize and threw it over the cage.

"I'll pull that off when we are hidden."

"And tell me first if you have had any manifestation of this supposed presence during the last few days?"

"Merely an increasingly intense sensation of something here, perpetually watching me, perpetually attending to all my doings."

"Do you feel that it follows you about?"

"Not always. It was in this room when you arrived. It is here now—I feel. But, in going down to dinner, we seemed to get away from it. The conclusion is that it remained here. Don't let us talk about it just now."

They spoke of other things till their cigarettes were finished. Then, as they threw away the smoldering ends, Guildea said, "Now, Murchison, for the sake of this experiment, I suggest that we should conceal ourselves behind the curtains on either side of the cage, so that the bird's attention may not be drawn toward us and so distracted from that which we want to know more about. I will pull away the green baize when we are hidden. Keep perfectly still, watch the bird's proceedings, and tell me afterward how you feel about them, how you explain them. Tread softly."

The Father obeyed, and they stole toward the curtains that fell before the two windows. The Father concealed himself behind those on the left of the cage, the Professor behind those on the right. The latter, as soon as they were hidden, stretched out his arm, drew the baize down from the cage, and let it fall on the floor.

The parrot, which had evidently fallen asleep in the warm darkness, moved on its perch as the light shone upon it, ruffled the feathers round its throat, and lifted first one foot and then the other. It turned its head round on its supple, and apparently elastic, neck, and, diving its beak into the down upon its back, made some searching investigations with, as it seemed, a satisfactory result, for it soon lifted its head again, glanced around its cage, and began to address itself to a nut which had been fixed between the bars for its refreshment. With its curved beak it felt and tapped the nut, at first gently, then with severity. Finally it plucked the nut from the bars, seized it with its rough, gray toes, and, holding it down firmly on the perch, cracked it and pecked out its contents, scattering some on the floor of the cage and letting the fractured shell fall into the china bath that was fixed against the bars. This accomplished, the bird paused meditatively, extended one leg backward, and went through an elaborate process of wing-stretching that made it look as if it were lopsided and deformed. With its head reversed, it again applied itself to a subtle and exhaustive search among the feathers of its wing. This time its investigation seemed interminable, and Father Murchison had time to realize the absurdity of the whole position, and to wonder why he had lent himself to it. Yet he did not find his sense of humor laughing at it. On the contrary, he was smitten by a sudden gust of horror. When he was talking to his friend and watching him, the Professor's manner, generally so calm, even so prosaic, vouched for the truth of his story and the well-adjusted balance of his mind. But when he was hidden this was not so. And Father Murchison, standing behind his curtain, with his eyes upon the unconcerned Napoleon, began to whisper to himself the word—madness, with a quickening sensation of pity and of dread.

The parrot sharply contracted one wing, ruffled the feathers around its throat again, then extended its other leg backward, and proceeded to the cleaning of its other wing. In the still room the dry sound of the feathers being spread was distinctly audible. Father Murchison saw the blue curtains behind which Guildea stood tremble slightly, as if a breath of wind had come through the window they shrouded. The clock in the far room chimed, and a coal dropped into the grate, making a noise like dead leaves stirring abruptly on hard ground. And again a gust of pity and of dread swept over the Father. It seemed to him that he had behaved very foolishly, if not wrongly, in encouraging what must surely be the strange dementia of his friend. He ought to have declined to lend himself to a proceeding that, ludicrous, even childish in itself, might well be dangerous in the encouragement it gave to a diseased expectation. Napoleon's protruding leg, extended wing and twisted neck, his busy and unconscious devotion to the arrangement of his person, his evident sensation of complete loneliness, most comfortable solitude, brought home with vehemence to the Father the undignified buffoonery of his conduct; the more piteous buffoonery of his friend. He seized the curtains with his hand and was about to thrust them aside and issue forth, when an abrupt movement of the parrot stopped him. The bird, as if sharply attracted by something, paused in its pecking, and, with its head still bent backward and twisted sideways on its neck, seemed to listen intently. Its round eye looked glistening and strained, like the eye of a disturbed pigeon. Contracting its wing, it lifted its head and sat for a moment erect on its perch, shifting its feet mechanically up and down, as if a dawning excitement produced in it an uncontrollable desire of movement. Then it thrust its head forward in the direction of the further room and remained perfectly still. Its attitude so strongly suggested the concentration of its attention on something immediately before it, that Father Murchison instinctively stared about the room, half expecting to see Pitting advance softly, having entered through the hidden door. He did not come, and there was no sound in the chamber. Nevertheless, the parrot was obviously getting excited and increasingly attentive. It bent its head lower and lower, stretching out its neck until, almost falling from the perch, it half extended its wings, raising them slightly from its back, as if about to take flight, and fluttering them rapidly up and down. It continued this fluttering movement for what seemed to the Father an immense time. At length, raising its wings as far as possible, it dropped them slowly and deliberately down to its back, caught hold of the edge of its bath with its beak, hoisted itself onto the floor of the cage, waddled to the bars, thrust its head against them, and stood quite still in the exact attitude it always assumed when its head was being scratched by the Professor. So complete was the suggestion of this delight conveyed by the bird, that Father Murchison felt as if he saw a white finger gently pushed among the soft feathers of its head, and he was seized by a most strong conviction that something, unseen by him but seen and welcomed by Napoleon, stood immediately before the cage.

The parrot presently withdrew its head, as if the coaxing finger had been lifted from it, and its pronounced air of acute physical enjoyment faded into one of marked attention and alert curiosity. Pulling itself up by the bars it climbed again upon its perch, sidled to the left side of the cage, and began apparently to watch something with profound interest. It bowed its head oddly, paused for a moment, then bowed its head again. Father Murchison found himself conceiving—from this elaborate movement of the head—a distinct idea of a personality. The bird's proceedings suggested extreme sentimentality combined with that sort of weak determination which is often the most persistent. Such weak determination is a very common attribute of persons who are partially idiotic. Father Murchison was moved to think of these poor creatures who will often, so strangely and un reasonably, attach themselves with persistence to those who love them least. Like many priests, he had had some experience of them, for the amorous idiot is peculiarly sensitive to the attraction of preachers. This bowing movement of the parrot recalled to his memory a terrible, pale woman who for a time haunted all churches in which he ministered, who was perpetually endeavoring to catch his eye, and who always bent her head with an obsequious and cunningly conscious smile when she did so. The parrot went on bowing, making a short pause between each genuflection, as if it waited for a signal to be given that called into play its imitative faculty.

"Yes, yes, it's imitating an idiot," Father Murchison caught himself saying as he watched.

And he looked again about the room, but saw nothing; except the furniture, the dancing fire, and the serried ranks of the books. Presently the parrot ceased from bowing, and assumed the concentrated and stretched attitude of one listening very keenly. He opened his beak, showing his black tongue, shut it, then opened it again. The Father thought he was going to speak, but he remained silent, although it was obvious that he was trying to bring out something. He bowed again two or three times, paused, and then, again opening his beak, made some remark. The Father could not distinguish any words, but the voice was sickly and disagreeable, a cooing and, at the same time, querulous voice, like a woman's, he thought. And he put his ear nearer to the curtain, listening with almost feverish attention. The bowing was resumed, but this time Napoleon added to it a sidling movement, affectionate and affected, like the movement of a silly and eager thing, nestling up to someone, or giving someone a gentle and furtive nudge. Again the Father thought of that terrible, pale woman who had haunted churches. Several times he had come upon her waiting for him after evening services. Once she had hung her head smiling, and lolled out her tongue and pushed against him sideways in the dark. He remembered how his flesh had shrunk from the poor thing, the sick loathing of her that he could not banish by remembering that her mind was all astray. The parrot paused, listened, opened his beak, and again said something in the same dovelike, amorous voice, full of sickly suggestion and yet hard, even dangerous, in its intonation. A loathsome voice, the Father thought it. But this time, although he heard the voice more distinctly than before, he could not make up his mind whether it was like a woman's voice or a man's—or perhaps a child's. It seemed to be a human voice, and yet oddly sexless. In order to resolve his doubt he withdrew into the darkness of the curtains, ceased to watch Napoleon and simply listened with keen attention, striving to forget that he was listening to a bird, and to imagine that he was overhearing a human being in conversation. After two or three minutes' silence the voice spoke again, and at some length, apparently repeating several times an affectionate series of ejaculations with a cooing emphasis that was unutterably mawkish and offensive. The sickliness of the voice, its falling intonations and its strange indelicacy, combined with a die-away softness and meretricious refinement, made the Father's flesh creep. Yet he could not distinguish any words, nor could he decide on the voice's sex or age. One thing alone he was certain of as he stood still in the darkness— that such a sound could only proceed from something peculiarly loathsome, could only express a personality unendurably abominable to him, if not to everybody. The voice presently failed, in a sort of husky gasp, and there was a prolonged silence. It was broken by the Professor, who suddenly pulled away the curtains that hid the Father and said to him, "Come out now, and look."

The Father came into the light, blinking, glanced toward the cage, and saw Napoleon poised motionless on one foot with his head under his wing. He appeared to be asleep. The Professor was pale, and his mobile lips were drawn into an expression of supreme disgust.

"Faugh!" he said.

He walked to the windows of the further room, pulled aside the curtains and pushed the glass up, letting in the air. The bare trees were visible in the gray gloom outside. Guildea leaned out for a minute drawing the night air into his lungs. Presently he turned round to the Father, and exclaimed abruptly, "Pestilent! Isn't it?"

"Yes—most pestilent."

"Ever hear anything like it?"

"Not exactly."

"Nor I. It gives me nausea, Murchison, absolute physical nausea."

He closed the window and walked uneasily about the room.

"What d'you make of it?" he asked, over his shoulder.

"How d'you mean exactly?"

"Is it man's, woman's, or child's voice?"

"I can't tell, I can't make up my mind."

"Nor I."

"Have you heard it often?"

"Yes, since I returned from Westgate. There are never any words that I can distinguish. What a voice!"

He spat into the fire.

"Forgive me," he said, throwing himself down in a chair. "It turns my stomach—literally."

"And mine," said the Father truly.

"The worst of it is," continued Guildea, with a high, nervous accent, "that there's no brain with it, none at all—only the cunning of idiocy."

The Father started at this exact expression of his own conviction by another.

"Why d'you start like that?" said Guildea, with a quick suspicion which showed the unnatural condition of his nerves.

"Well, the very same idea had occurred to me."

"What?"

"That I was listening to the voice of something idiotic."

"Ah! That's the devil of it, you know, to a man like me. I could fight against brain—but this!"

He sprang up again, poked the fire violently, then stood on the hearth rug with his back to it, and his hands thrust into the high pockets of his trousers.

"That's the voice of the thing that's got into my house," he said. "Pleasant, isn't it?"

And now there was really horror in his eyes, and his voice.

"I must get it out," he exclaimed. "I must get it out. But how?"

He tugged at his short black beard with a quivering hand.

"How?" he continued. "For what is it? Where is it?"

"You feel it's here—now?"

"Undoubtedly. But I couldn't tell you in what part of the room."

He stared about, glancing rapidly at everything.

"Then you consider yourself haunted?" said Father Murchison.

He, too, was much moved and disturbed, although he was not conscious of the presence of anything near them in the room.

"I have never believed in any nonsense of that kind, as you know," Guildea answered. "I simply state a fact, which I cannot understand, and which is beginning to be very painful to me. There is something here. But whereas most so-called hauntings have been described to me as inimical, what I am conscious of is that I am admired, loved, desired. This is distinctly horrible to me, Murchison, distinctly horrible."

Father Murchison suddenly remembered the first evening he had spent with Guildea, and the latter's expression almost of disgust, at the idea of receiving warm affection from anyone. In the light of that long-ago conversation, the present event seemed supremely strange, and almost like a punishment for an offense committed by the Professor against humanity. But, looking up at his friend's twitching face, the Father resolved not to be caught in the net of his hideous belief.

"There can be nothing here," he said. "It's impossible."

"What does that bird imitate, then?"

"The voice of someone who has been here."

"Within the last week then. For it never spoke like that before, and mind, I noticed that it was watching and striving to imitate something before I went away, since the night that I went into the Park, only since then."

"Somebody with a voice like that must have been here while you were away," Father Murchison repeated, with a gentle obstinacy.

"I'll soon find out."

Guildea pressed the bell. Pitting stole in almost immediately.

"Pitting," said the Professor, speaking in a high, sharp voice, "did anyone come into this room during my absence at the sea?"

"Certainly not, sir, except the maids—and me, sir."

"Not a soul? You are certain?"

"Perfectly certain, sir."

The cold voice of the butler sounded surprised, almost resentful. The Professor flung out his hand toward the cage.

"Has the bird been here the whole time?"

"Yes, sir."

"He was not moved, taken elsewhere, even for a moment?"

Pitting's pale face began to look almost expressive, and his lips were pursed.

"Certainly not, sir."

"Thank you. That will do."

The butler retired, moving with a sort of ostentatious rectitude. When he had reached the door, and was just going out, his master called, "Wait a minute, Pitting."

The butler paused. Guildea bit his lips, tugged at his beard uneasily two or three times, and then said, "Have you noticed—er—the parrot talking lately in a—a very peculiar, very disagreeable voice?"

"Yes, sir—a soft voice like, sir."

"Ha! Since when?"

"Since you went away, sir. He's always at it."

"Exactly. Well, and what did you think of it?"

"Beg pardon, sir?"

"What do you think about his talking in this voice?"

"Oh, that it's only his play, sir."

"I see. That's all, Pitting."

The butler disappeared and closed the door noiselessly behind him.

Guildea turned his eyes on his friend.

"There, you see!" he ejaculated.

"It's certainly very odd," said the Father. "Very odd indeed. You are certain you have no maid who talks at all like that?"

"My dear Murchison! Would you keep a servant with such a voice about you for two days?"

"No."

"My housemaid has been with me for five years, my cook for seven. You've heard Pitting speak. The three of them make up my entire household. A parrot never speaks in a voice it has not heard. Where has it heard that voice?"

"But we hear nothing?"

"No. Nor do we see anything. But it does. It feels something too. Didn't you observe it presenting its head to be scratched?"

"Certainly it seemed to be doing so."

"It was doing so."

Father Murchison said nothing. He was full of increasing discomfort that almost amounted to apprehension.

"Are you convinced?" said Guildea, rather irritably.

"No. The whole matter is very strange. But till I hear, see or feel
—as you do—the presence of something, I cannot believe."

"You mean that you will not?"

"Perhaps. Well, it is time I went."

Guildea did not try to detain him, but said, as he let him out,
"Do me a favor, come again tomorrow night."

The Father had an engagement. He hesitated, looked into the
Professor's face and said, "I will. At nine I'll be with you. Good night."

When he was on the pavement he felt relieved. He turned round,
saw Guildea stepping into his passage, and shivered.

v

Father Murchison walked all the way home to Bird Street that
night. He required exercise after the strange and disagreeable evening
he had spent, an evening upon which he looked back already as a man
looks back upon a nightmare. In his ears, as he walked, sounded the
gentle and intolerable voice. Even the memory of it caused him physical discomfort. He tried to put it from him, and to consider the whole
matter calmly. The Professor had offered his proof that there was
some strange presence in his house. Could any reasonable man accept
such proof? Father Murchison told himself that no reasonable man
could accept it. The parrot's proceedings were, no doubt, extraordinary. The bird had succeeded in producing an extraordinary illusion
of an invisible presence in the room. But that there really was such a
presence the Father insisted on denying to himself. The devoutly
religious, those who believe implicitly in the miracles recorded in the
Bible, and who regulate their lives by the messages they suppose themselves to receive directly from the Great Ruler of a hidden World, are
seldom inclined to accept any notion of supernatural intrusion into
the affairs of daily life. They put it from them with anxious determination. They regard it fixedly as hocus-pocus, childish if not wicked.

Father Murchison inclined to the normal view of the devoted
churchman. He was determined to incline to it. He could not—so he
now told himself—accept the idea that his friend was being super-
naturally punished for his lack of humanity, his deficiency in affec-

tion, by being obliged to endure the love of some horrible thing, which could not be seen, heard, or handled. Nevertheless, retribution did certainly seem to wait upon Guildea's condition. That which he had unnaturally dreaded and shrunk from in his thought he seemed to be now forced unnaturally to suffer. The Father prayed for his friend that night before the little, humble altar in the barely furnished, cell-like chamber where he slept.

On the following evening, when he called in Hyde Park Place, the door was opened by the housemaid, and Father Murchison mounted the stairs, wondering what had become of Pitting. He was met at the library door by Guildea and was painfully struck by the alteration in his appearance. His face was ashen in hue, and there were lines beneath his eyes. The eyes themselves looked excited and horribly forlorn. His hair and dress were disordered and his lips twitched continually, as if he were shaken by some acute nervous apprehension.

"What has become of Pitting?" asked the Father, grasping Gildea's hot and feverish hand.

"He has left my service."

"Left your service!" exclaimed the Father in utter amazement.

"Yes, this afternoon."

"May one ask why?"

"I'm going to tell you. It's all part and parcel of this—this most odious business. You remember once discussing the relations men ought to have with their servants?"

"Ah!" cried the Father, with a flash of inspiration. "The crisis has occurred?"

"Exactly," said the Professor, with a bitter smile. "The crisis has occurred. I called upon Pitting to be a man and a brother. He responded by declining the invitation. I upbraided him. He gave me warning. I paid him his wages and told him he could go at once. And he has gone. What are you looking at me like that for?"

"I didn't know," said Father Murchison, hastily dropping his eyes, and looking away. "Why," he added. "Napoleon is gone too."

"I sold him today to one of those shops in Shaftesbury Avenue."

"Why?"

"He sickened me with his abominable imitation of—his intercourse with—well, you know what he was at last night. Besides, I have no further need of his proof to tell me I am not dreaming. And, being convinced as I now am, that all I have thought to have happened has actually happened, I care very little about convincing others. Forgive me for saying so, Murchison, but I am now certain that my anxiety to make you believe in the presence of something here really arose from some faint doubt on that subject—within myself. All doubt has now vanished."

"Tell me why."

"I will."

Both men were standing by the fire. They continued to stand while Guildea went on.

"Last night I felt it."

"What?" cried the Father.

"I say that last night, as I was going upstairs to bed, I felt something accompanying me and nestling up against me."

"How horrible!" exclaimed the Father, involuntarily.

Guildea smiled drearily.

"I will not deny the horror of it. I cannot, since I was compelled to call on Pitting for assistance."

"But—tell me—what was it, at least what did it seem to be?"

"It seemed to be a human being. It seemed, I say; and what I mean exactly is that the effect upon me was rather that of human contact than of anything else. But I could see nothing, hear nothing. Only, three times, I felt this gentle, but determined, push against me, as if to coax me and to attract my attention. The first time it happened I was on the landing outside this room, with my foot on the first stair. I will confess to you, Murchison, that I bounded upstairs like one pursued. That is the shameful truth. Just as I was about to enter my bedroom, however, I felt the thing entering with me, and, as I have said, squeezing, with loathsome, sickening tenderness, against my side. Then—"

He paused, turned toward the fire and leaned his head on his arm. The Father was greatly moved by the strange helplessness and despair of the attitude. He laid his hand affectionately on Guildea's shoulder.

"Then?"

Guildea lifted his head. He looked painfully abashed.

"Then, Murchison, I am ashamed to say, I broke down, suddenly, unaccountably, in a way I should have thought wholly impossible to me. I struck out with my hands to thrust the thing away. It pressed more closely to me. The pressure, the contact became unbearable to me. I shouted out for Pitting. I—I believe I must have cried —'Help.' "

"He came, of course?"

"Yes, with his usual soft, unemotional quiet. His calm—its opposition to my excitement of disgust and horror—must, I suppose, have irritated me. I was not myself, no, no!"

He stopped abruptly. Then—

"But I need hardly tell you that," he added, with most piteous irony.

"And what did you say to Pitting?"

"I said that he should have been quicker. He begged my pardon. His cold voice really maddened me, and I burst out into some foolish, contemptible diatribe, called him a machine, taunted him, then— as I felt that loathsome thing nestling once more to me—begged him to assist me, to stay with me, not to leave me alone—I meant in the company of my tormentor. Whether he was frightened, or whether he was angry at my unjust and violent manner and speech a moment before, I don't know. In any case he answered that he was engaged as a butler, and not to sit up all night with people. I suspect he thought I had taken too much to drink. No doubt that was it. I believe I swore at him as a coward—I! This morning he said he wished to leave my service. I gave him a month's wages, a good character as a butler, and sent him off at once."

"But the night? How did you pass it?"

"I sat up all night."

"Where? In your bedroom?"

"Yes—with the door open—to let it go."

"You felt that it stayed?"

"It never left me for a moment, but it did not touch me again. When it was light I took a bath, lay down for a little while, but did not close my eyes. After breakfast I had the explanation with Pitting and paid him. Then I came up here. My nerves were in a very shattered condition. Well, I sat down, tried to write, to think. But the silence was broken in the most abominable manner."

"How?"

"By the murmur of that appalling voice, that voice of a lovesick idiot, sickly but determined. Ugh!"

He shuddered in every limb. Then he pulled himself together, assumed, with a self-conscious effort, his most determined, most aggressive, manner, and added, "I couldn't stand that. I had come to the end of my tether; so I sprang up, ordered a cab to be called, seized the cage and drove with it to a bird shop in Shaftesbury Avenue. There I sold the parrot for a trifle. I think, Murchison, that I must have been nearly mad then, for, as I came out of the wretched shop, and stood for an instant on the pavement among the cages of rabbits, guinea pigs, and puppy dogs, I laughed aloud. I felt as if a load was lifted from my shoulders, as if in selling that voice I had sold the cursed thing that torments me. But when I got back to the house it was here. It's here now. I suppose it will always be here."

He shuffled his feet on the rug in front of the fire.

"What on earth am I to do?" he said. "I'm ashamed of myself, Murchison, but—but I suppose there are things in the world that certain men simply can't endure. Well, I can't endure this, and there's an end of the matter."

He ceased. The Father was silent. In the presence of this extraordinary distress he did not know what to say. He recognized the uselessness of attempting to comfort Guildea, and he sat with his eyes turned, almost moodily, to the ground. And while he sat there he tried to give himself to the influences within the room, to feel all that was within it. He even, half unconsciously, tried to force his imagination to play tricks with him. But he remained totally unaware of any third person with them. At length he said, "Guildea, I cannot pretend to doubt the reality of your misery here. You must go away, and at once. When is your Paris lecture?"

"Next week. In nine days from now."

"Go to Paris tomorrow then; you say you have never had any consciousness that this—this thing pursued you beyond your own front door?"

"Never—hitherto."

"Go tomorrow morning. Stay away till after your lecture. And then let us see if the affair is at an end. Hope, my dear friend, hope."

He had stood up. Now he clasped the Professor's hand.

"See all your friends in Paris. Seek distractions. I would ask you also to seek—other help."

He said the last words with a gentle, earnest gravity and simplicity that touched Guildea, who returned his handclasp almost warmly.

"I'll go," he said. "I'll catch the ten o'clock train, and tonight I'll sleep at a hotel, at the Grosvenor—that's close to the station. It will be more convenient for the train."

As Father Murchison went home that night he kept thinking of that sentence: "It will be more convenient for the train." The weakness in Guildea that had prompted its utterance appalled him.

VI

No letter came to Father Murchison from the Professor during the next few days, and this silence reassured him, for it seemed to betoken that all was well. The day of the lecture dawned, and passed. On the following morning, the Father eagerly opened the *Times*, and scanned its pages to see if there were any report of the great meeting of scientific men which Guildea had addressed. He glanced up and down the columns with anxious eyes, then suddenly his hands stiffened as they held the sheets. He had come upon the following paragraph:

We regret to announce that Professor Frederic Guildea was suddenly seized with severe illness yesterday evening while addressing a scientific meeting in Paris. It was observed that he looked very pale and nervous when he rose to his feet. Nevertheless, he spoke in French fluently for about a quarter of an hour. Then he appeared to become uneasy. He faltered and glanced about like a man apprehensive, or in severe distress. He even stopped once or twice, and seemed unable to go on, to remember what he wished to say. But, pulling himself together with an obvious effort, he continued to address the audience. Suddenly, however, he paused again, edged furtively along the platform, as if pursued by something which he feared, struck out with his hands, uttered a loud, harsh cry and fainted. The sensation in the hall was indescribable. People rose from their seats. Women screamed, and, for a moment, there was a veritable panic. It is feared that the Professor's mind must have temporarily given way owing to overwork. We understand that he will return to England as soon as possible, and we sincerely hope that necessary rest and quiet will soon have the desired effect, and that he will be completely restored to health and enabled to prosecute further the investigations which have already so benefited the world.

The Father dropped the paper, hurried out into Bird Street, sent a wire of inquiry to Paris, and received the same day the following reply: "RETURNING TOMORROW. PLEASE CALL EVENING. GUILDEA." On that evening the Father called in Hyde Park Place, was at once admitted, and found Guildea sitting by the fire in the library, ghastly pale, with a heavy rug over his knees. He looked like a man emaciated by a long and severe illness, and in his wide-open eyes there was an expression of fixed horror. The Father started at the sight of him, and could scarcely refrain from crying out. He was beginning to express his sympathy when Guildea stopped him with a trembling gesture.

"I know all that," Guildea said, "I know. This Paris affair—" He faltered and stopped.

"You ought never to have gone," said the Father. "I was wrong. I ought not to have advised your going. You were not fit."

"I was perfectly fit," he answered, with the irritability of sickness. "But I was—I was accompanied by that abominable thing."

He glanced hastily round him, shifted his chair and pulled the rug higher over his knees. The Father wondered why he was thus wrapped up. For the fire was bright and red and the night was not very cold.

"I was accompanied to Paris," he continued, pressing his upper teeth upon his lower lip.

He paused again, obviously striving to control himself. But the effort was vain. There was no resistance in the man. He writhed in his chair and suddenly burst forth in a tone of hopeless lamentation.

"Murchison, this being, thing—whatever it is—no longer leaves me even for a moment. It will not stay here unless I am here, for it loves me, persistently, idiotically. It accompanied me to Paris, stayed with me there, pursued me to the lecture hall, pressed against me, caressed me while I was speaking. It has returned with me here. It is here now—" he uttered a sharp cry—"now, as I sit here with you. It is nestling up to me, fawning upon me, touching my hands. Man, man, can't you feel that it is here?"

"No," the Father answered truly.

"I try to protect myself from its loathsome contact," Guildea continued, with fierce excitement, clutching the thick rug with both hands. "But nothing is of any avail against it. Nothing. What is it? What can it be? Why should it have come to me that night?"

"Perhaps as a punishment," said the Father, with a quick softness.

"For what?"

"You hated affection. You put human feeling aside with contempt. You had, you desired to have, no love for anyone. Nor did you desire to receive any love from anything. Perhaps this is a punishment."

Guildea stared into his face.

"D'you believe that?" he cried.

"I don't know," said the Father. "But it may be so. Try to endure it, even to welcome it. Possibly then the persecution will cease."

"I know it means me no harm," Guildea exclaimed, "it seeks me out of affection. It was led to me by some amazing attraction which I exercise over it ignorantly. I know that. But to a man of my nature that is the ghastly part of the matter. If it would hate me, I could bear it. If it would attack me, if it would try to do me some dreadful harm, I should become a man again. I should be braced to fight against it. But this gentleness, this abominable solicitude, this brainless worship of an idiot, persistent, sickly, horribly physical, I cannot endure. What does it want of me? What would it demand of me? It nestles to me. It leans against me. I feel its touch, like the touch of a feather, trembling about my heart, as if it sought to number my pulsations, to find out the inmost secrets of my impulses and desires. No privacy is left to me." He sprang up excitedly. "I cannot withdraw," he cried, "I cannot be alone, untouched, unworshiped, unwatched for even one-half second. Murchison, I am dying of this, I am dying."

He sank down again in his chair, staring apprehensively on all sides, with the passion of some blind man, deluded in the belief that by his furious and continued effort he will attain sight. The Father knew well that he sought to pierce the veil of the invisible, and have knowledge of the thing that loved him.

"Guildea," the Father said, with insistent earnestness, "try to endure this—do more—try to give this thing what it seeks."

"But it seeks my love."

"Learn to give it your love and it may go, having received what it came for."

"T'sh! You talk like a priest. Suffer your persecutors. Do good to them that despitefully use you. You talk as a priest."

"As a friend I spoke naturally, indeed, right out of my heart. The idea suddenly came to me that all this—truth or seeming, it doesn't matter which—may be some strange form of lesson. I have had lessons—painful ones. I shall have many more. If you could welcome—"

"I can't! I can't!" Guildea cried fiercely. "Hatred! I can give it that—always that, nothing but that—hatred, hatred."

He raised his voice, glared into the emptiness of the room, and repeated, "Hatred!"

As he spoke the waxen pallor of his cheeks increased, until he looked like a corpse with living eyes. The Father feared that he was going to collapse and faint, but suddenly he raised himself upon his chair and said, in a high and keen voice, full of suppressed excitement, "Murchison, Murchison!"

"Yes. What is it?"

An amazing ecstasy shone in Guildea's eyes.

"It wants to leave me," he cried. "It wants to go! Don't lose a moment! Let it out! The window—the window!"

The Father, wondering, went to the near window, drew aside the curtains and pushed it open. The branches of the trees in the garden creaked dryly in the light wind. Guildea leaned forward on the arms of his chair. There was silence for a moment. Then Guildea, speaking in a rapid whisper, said, "No, no. Open this door—open the hall door. I feel—I feel that it will return the way it came. Make haste —ah, go!"

The Father obeyed—to soothe him, hurried to the door and opened it wide. Then he glanced back to Guildea. He was standing up, bent forward. His eyes were glaring with eager expectation, and, as the Father turned, he made a furious gesture toward the passage with his thin hands.

The Father hastened out and down the stairs. As he descended in the twilight he fancied he heard a slight cry from the room behind him, but he did not pause. He flung the hall door open, standing back against the wall. After waiting a moment—to satisfy Guildea, he was about to close the door again, and had his hand on it, when he was attracted irresistibly to look forth toward the park. The night was lit by a young moon, and, gazing through the railings, his eyes fell upon a bench beyond them.

Upon the bench something was sitting, huddled together very strangely.

The Father remembered instantly Guildea's description of that former night, that night of Advent, and a sensation of horror-stricken curiosity stole through him.

Was there then really something that had indeed come to the Professor? And had it finished its work, fulfilled its desire and gone back to its former existence?

The Father hesitated a moment in the doorway. Then he stepped out resolutely and crossed the road, keeping his eyes fixed upon this black or dark object that leaned so strangely upon the bench. He could not tell yet what it was like, but he fancied it was unlike anything with which his eyes were acquainted. He reached the opposite path, and was about to pass through the gate in the railings, when his arm was brusquely grasped. He started, turned round, and saw a policeman eyeing him suspiciously.

"What are you up to?" said the policeman.

The Father was suddenly aware that he had no hat upon his head, and that his appearance, as he stole forward in his cassock, with his eyes intently fixed upon the bench in the Park, was probably unusual enough to excite suspicion.

"It's all right, policeman," he answered quickly, thrusting some money into the constable's hand.

Then, breaking from him, the Father hurried toward the bench, bitterly vexed at the interruption. When he reached it, nothing was there. Guildea's experience had been almost exactly repeated and, filled with unreasonable disappointment, the Father returned to the house, entered it, shut the door and hastened up the narrow stairway into the library.

On the hearth rug, close to the fire, he found Guildea lying with his head lolled against the armchair from which he had recently risen. There was a shocking expression of terror on his convulsed face. On examining him the Father found that he was dead.

The doctor, who was called in, said that the cause of death was failure of the heart.

When Father Murchison was told this, he murmured, "Failure of the heart! It was that then!"

He turned to the doctor and said, "Could it have been prevented?"

The doctor drew on his gloves and answered, "Possibly, if it had been taken in time. Weakness of the heart requires a great deal of care. The Professor was too much absorbed in his work. He should have lived very differently."

The Father nodded.

"Yes, yes," he said, sadly.

THE MOMENT OF DECISION

BY STANLEY ELLIN

❧ HUGH LOZIER was the exception to the rule that people who are completely sure of themselves cannot be likable. We have all met the sure ones, of course—those controlled but penetrating voices which cut through all others in a discussion, those hard forefingers jabbing home opinions on your chest, those living Final Words on all issues— and I imagine we all share the same amalgam of dislike and envy for them. Dislike, because no one likes to be shouted down or prodded in the chest, and envy, because everyone wishes he himself were so rich in self-assurance that he could do the shouting down and the prodding.

For myself, since my work took me regularly to certain places in this atomic world where the only state was confusion and the only steady employment that of splitting political hairs, I found absolute judgments harder and harder to come by. Hugh once observed of this that it was a good thing my superiors in the Department were not cut of the same cloth, because God knows what would happen to the country then. I didn't relish that, but—and there was my curse again—I had to grant him his right to say it.

Despite this, and despite the fact that Hugh was my brother-in-law—a curious relationship when you come to think of it—I liked him immensely, just as everyone else did who knew him. He was a big, good-looking man, with clear blue eyes in a ruddy face, and with a quick, outgoing nature eager to appreciate whatever you had to offer. He was overwhelmingly generous, and his generosity was ɔf that rare and excellent kind which makes you feel as if you are doing the donor a favor by accepting it.

I wouldn't say he had any great sense of humor, but plain good humor can sometimes be an adequate substitute for that, and in Hugh's case it was. His stormy side was largely reserved for those times when he thought you might have needed his help in something and failed to call on him for it. Which meant that ten minutes after Hugh had met you and liked you, you were expected to ask him for anything he might be able to offer. A month or so after he married my sister Elizabeth she mentioned to him my avid interest in a fine Copley he had hanging in his gallery at Hilltop, and I can still vividly recall my horror when it suddenly arrived, heavily crated and with his gift card attached, at my barren room-and-a-half. It took considerable effort, but I finally managed to return it to him by foregoing the argument that the picture was undoubtedly worth more than the entire building in which I lived and by complaining that it simply didn't show to advantage on my wall. I think he suspected I was lying, but being Hugh he would never dream of charging me with that in so many words.

Of course, Hilltop and the two hundred years of Lozier tradition that went into it did much to shape Hugh this way. The first Loziers had carved the estate from the heights overlooking the river, had worked hard and flourished exceedingly; its successive generations had invested their income so wisely that money and position eventually erected a towering wall between Hilltop and the world outside. Truth to tell, Hugh was very much a man of the eighteenth century who somehow found himself in the twentieth, and simply made the best of it.

Hilltop itself was almost a replica of the celebrated, but long untenanted, Dane house nearby, and was striking enough to open anybody's eyes at a glance. The house was weathered stone, graceful despite its bulk, and the vast lawns reaching to the river's edge were tended with such fanatic devotion over the years that they had become carpets of purest green which magically changed luster under any breeze. Gardens ranged from the other side of the house down to the groves which half hid the stables and outbuildings, and past the far side of the groves ran the narrow road which led to town. The road was a courtesy road, each estate holder along it maintaining his share, and I think it safe to say that for all the crushed rock he laid in it Hugh made less use of it by far than any of his neighbors.

Hugh's life was bound up in Hilltop; he could be made to leave it only by dire necessity; and if you did meet him away from it you were made acutely aware that he was counting off the minutes until he could return. And if you weren't wary you would more than likely find yourself going along with him when he did return, and totally unable to tear yourself away from the place while the precious weeks rolled by. I know. I believe I spent more time at Hilltop than at my own apartment after my sister brought Hugh into the family.

At one time I wondered how Elizabeth took to this marriage, considering that before she met Hugh she had been as restless and flighty as she was pretty. When I put the question to her directly, she said, "It's wonderful, darling. Just as wonderful as I knew it would be when I first met him."

It turned out that their first meeting had taken place at an art exhibition, a showing of some ultramodern stuff, and she had been intently studying one of the more bewildering concoctions on display when she became aware of this tall, good-looking man staring at her. And, as she put it, she had been about to set him properly in his place when he said abruptly, "Are you admiring that?"

This was so unlike what she had expected that she was taken completely aback. "I don't know," she said weakly. "Am I supposed to?"

"No," said the stranger, "it's damned nonsense. Come along now, and I'll show you something which isn't a waste of time."

"And," Elizabeth said to me, "I came along like a pup at his heels, while he marched up and down and told me what was good and what was bad, and in a good loud voice, too, so that we collected quite a crowd along the way. Can you picture it, darling?"

"Yes," I said, "I can." By now I had shared similar occasions with Hugh, and learned at firsthand that nothing could dent his cast-iron assurance.

"Well," Elizabeth went on, "I must admit that at first I was a little put off, but then I began to see that he knew exactly what he was talking about, and that he was terribly sincere. Not a bit self-conscious about anything, but just eager for me to understand things the way he did. It's the same way with everything. Everybody else in the world is always fumbling and bumbling over deciding anything—what to order for dinner, or how to manage his job, or whom to vote for—but Hugh always *knows*. It's *not* knowing that makes for all those nerves and complexes and things you hear about, isn't that so? Well, Ill take Hugh, thank you, and leave everyone else to the psychiatrists."

So there it was. An Eden with flawless lawns and no awful nerves and complexes, and not even the glimmer of a serpent in the offing. That is, not a glimmer until the day Raymond made his entrance on the scene.

We were out on the terrace that day, Hugh and Elizabeth and I, slowly being melted into a sort of liquid torpor by the August sunshine, and all of us too far gone to make even a pretense at talk. I lay there with a linen cap over my face, listening to the summer noises around me and being perfectly happy.

There was the low, steady hiss of the breeze through the aspens nearby, the plash and drip of oars on the river below, and now and then the melancholy *tink-tunk* of a sheep bell from one of the flock on the lawn. The flock was a fancy of Hugh's. He swore that nothing was better for a lawn than a few sheep grazing on it, and every summer five or six fat sleepy ewes were turned out on the grass to serve this purpose and to add a pleasantly pastoral note to the view.

My first warning of something amiss came from the sheep—from the sudden sound of their bells clanging wildly and then a baa-ing which suggested an assault by a whole pack of wolves. I heard Hugh say, "Damn!" loudly and angrily, and I opened my eyes to see something more incongruous than wolves. It was a large black poodle in the full glory of a clownish haircut, a bright red collar, and an ecstasy of high spirits as he chased the frightened sheep around the lawn. It was clear the poodle had no intention of hurting them—he probably found them the most wonderful playmates imaginable—but it was just as clear that the panicky ewes didn't understand this, and would very likely end up in the river before the fun was over.

In the bare second it took me to see all this, Hugh had already leaped the low terrace wall and was among the sheep, herding them away from the water's edge, and shouting commands at the dog who had different ideas.

"Down, boy!" he yelled. "Down!" And then as he would to one of his own hounds, he sternly commanded, "Heel!"

He would have done better, I thought, to have picked up a stick or stone and made a threatening gesture, since the poodle paid no attention whatever to Hugh's words. Instead, continuing to bark happily, the poodle made for the sheep again, this time with Hugh in futile pursuit. An instant later the dog was frozen into immobility by a voice from among the aspens near the edge of the lawn.

"*Assieds!*" the voice called breathlessly. "*Assieds-toi!*"

Then the man appeared, a small, dapper figure trotting across the grass. Hugh stood waiting, his face darkening as we watched.

Elizabeth squeezed my arm. "Let's get down there," she whispered. "Hugh doesn't like being made a fool of."

We got there in time to hear Hugh open his big guns. "Any man," he was saying, "who doesn't know how to train an animal to its place shouldn't own one."

The man's face was all polite attention. It was a good face, thin and intelligent, and webbed with tiny lines at the corners of the eyes. There was also something behind those eyes that couldn't quite be masked. A gentle mockery. A glint of wry perception turned on the world like a camera lens. It was nothing anyone like Hugh would have noticed, but it was there all the same, and I found myself warming to it on the spot. There was also something tantalizingly familiar about the newcomer's face, his high forehead, and his thinning gray hair, but much as I dug into my memory during Hugh's long and solemn lecture I couldn't come up with an answer. The lecture ended with a few remarks on the best methods of dog training, and by then it was clear that Hugh was working himself into a mood of forgiveness.

"As long as there's no harm done—" he said.

The man nodded soberly. "Still, to get off on the wrong foot with one's new neighbors—"

Hugh looked startled. "Neighbors?" he said almost rudely. "You mean that you live around here?"

The man waved toward the aspens. "On the other side of those woods."

"The *Dane* house?" The Dane house was almost as sacred to Hugh as Hilltop, and he had once explained to me that if he were ever offered a chance to buy the place he would snap it up. His tone now was not so much wounded as incredulous. "I don't believe it!" he exclaimed.

"Oh, yes," the man assured him, "the Dane house. I performed there at a party many years ago, and always hoped that some day I might own it."

It was the word *performed* which gave me my clue—that and the accent barely perceptible under the precise English. He had been born and raised in Marseilles—that would explain the accent—and long before my time he had already become a legend.

"You're Raymond, aren't you?" I said. "Charles Raymond."

"I prefer Raymond alone." He smiled in deprecation of his own small vanity. "And I am flattered that you recognize me."

I don't believe he really was. Raymond the Magician, Raymond the Great, would, if anything, expect to be recognized wherever he went. As the master of sleight of hand who had paled Thurston's star, as the escape artist who had almost outshone Houdini, Raymond would not be inclined to underestimate himself.

He had started with the standard box of tricks which makes up the repertoire of most professional magacians; he had gone far beyond that to those feats of escape which, I suppose, are known to us all by now. The lead casket sealed under a foot of lake ice, the welded-steel strait jackets, the vaults of the Bank of England, the exquisite suicide knot which nooses throat and doubles legs together so that the motion of a leg draws the noose tighter around the throat—all these Raymond had known and escaped from. And then at the pinnacle of fame he had dropped from sight and his name had become relegated to the past.

When I asked him why, he shrugged.

"A man works for money or for the love of his work. If he has all the wealth he needs and has no more love for his work, why go on?"

"But to give up a great career—" I protested.

"It was enough to know that the house was waiting here."

"You mean," Elizabeth said, "that you never intended to live any place but here?"

"Never—not once in all these years." He laid a finger along his nose and winked broadly at us. "Of course, I made no secret of this to the Dane estate, and when the time came to sell I was the first and only one approached."

"You don't give up an idea easily," Hugh said in an edged voice.

Raymond laughed. "Idea? It became an obsession really. Over the years I traveled to many parts of the world, but no matter how fine the place, I knew it could not be as fine as that house on the edge of the woods there, with the river at its feet and the hills beyond. Some day, I would tell myself, when my travels are done I will come here, and, like Candide, cultivate my garden."

He ran his hand abstractedly over the poodle's head and looked around with an air of great satisfaction. "And now," he said, "here I am."

Here he was, indeed, and it quickly became clear that his arrival was working a change on Hilltop. Or, since Hilltop was so completely a reflection of Hugh, it was clear that a change was being worked on Hugh. He became irritable and restless, and more aggressively sure of himself than ever. The warmth and good nature were still there —they were as much part of him as his arrogance—but he now had to work a little harder at them. He reminded me of a man who is bothered by a speck in the eye, but can't find it, and must get along with it as best he can.

Raymond, of course, was the speck, and I got the impression at times that he rather enjoyed the role. It would have been easy enough for him to stay close to his own house and cultivate his garden, or paste up his album, or whatever retired performers do, but he evidently found that impossible. He had a way of drifting over to Hilltop at odd times, just as Hugh was led to find his way to the Dane house and spend long and troublesome sessions there.

Both of them must have known that they were so badly suited to each other that the easy and logical solution would have been to stay apart. But they had the affinity of negative and positive forces, and when they were in a room together the crackling of the antagonistic current between them was so strong you could almost see it in the air.

Any subject became a point of contention for them, and they would duel over it bitterly: Hugh armored and weaponed with his massive assurance, Raymond flicking away with a rapier, trying to find a chink in the armor. I think that what annoyed Raymond most was the discovery that there was no chink in the armor. As someone with an obvious passion for searching out all sides to all questions and for going deep into motives and causes, he was continually being outraged by Hugh's single-minded way of laying down the law.

He didn't hesitate to let Hugh know that. "You are positively medieval," he said. "And of all things men should have learned since that time, the biggest is that there are no easy answers, no solutions one can give with a snap of the fingers. I can only hope for you that some day you may be faced with the perfect dilemma, the unanswerable question. You would find that a revelation. You would learn more in that minute than you dreamed possible."

And Hugh did not make matters any better when he coldly answered: "And *I* say, that for any man with a brain and the courage to use it there is no such thing as a perfect dilemma."

It may be that this was the sort of episode that led to the trouble that followed, or it may be that Raymond acted out of the most innocent and aesthetic motives possible. But, whatever the motives, the results were inevitable and dangerous.

They grew from the project Raymond outlined for us in great detail one afternoon. Now that he was living in the Dane house he had discovered that it was too big, too overwhelming. "Like a museum," he explained. "I find myself wandering through it like a lost soul through endless galleries."

The grounds also needed landscaping. The ancient trees were handsome, but, as Raymond put it, there were just too many of them. "Literally," he said, "I cannot see the river for the trees, and I am one devoted to the sight of running water."

Altogether there would be drastic changes. Two wings of the house would come down, the trees would be cleared away to make a broad aisle to the water, the whole place would be enlivened. It would no longer be a museum, but the perfect home he had envisioned over the years.

At the start of this recitative Hugh was slouched comfortably in his chair. Then as Raymond drew the vivid picture of what was to be, Hugh sat up straighter and straighter until he was as rigid as a trooper in the saddle. His lips compressed. His face became blood-red. His hands clenched and unclenched in a slow, deadly rhythm. Only a miracle was restraining him from an open outburst, but it was not the kind of miracle to last. I saw from Elizabeth's expression that she understood this, too, but was as helpless as I to do anything about it. And when Raymond, after painting the last glowing strokes of his description, said complacently, "Well, now, what do you think?" there was no holding Hugh.

He leaned forward with deliberation and said, "Do you really want to know what I think?"

"Now, Hugh," Elizabeth said in alarm. "Please, Hugh—"

He brushed that aside.

"Do you really want to know?" he demanded of Raymond.

Raymond frowned. "Of course."

"Then I'll tell you," Hugh said. He took a deep breath. "I think that nobody but a damned iconoclast could even conceive the atrocity you're proposing. I think you're one of those people who take pleasure in smashing apart anything that's stamped with tradition or stability. You'd kick the props from under the whole world if you could!"

"I beg your pardon," Raymond said. He was very pale and angry. "But I think you are confusing change with destruction. Surely, you must comprehend that I do not intend to destroy anything, but only wish to make some necessary changes."

"Necessary?" Hugh gibed. "Rooting up a fine stand of trees that's been there for centuries? Ripping apart a house that's as solid as a rock? *I* call it wanton destruction."

"I'm afraid I do not understand. To refresh a scene, to reshape it—"

"I have no intention of arguing," Hugh cut in. "I'm telling you straight out that you don't have the right to tamper with that property!"

They were on their feet now, facing each other truculently, and the only thing that kept me from being really frightened was the conviction that Hugh would not become violent, and that Raymond was far too level-headed to lose his temper. Then the threatening moment was magically past. Raymond's lips suddenly quirked in amusement, and he studied Hugh with courteous interest.

"I see," he said. "I was quite stupid not to have understood at once. This property, which, I remarked, was a little too much like a museum, is to remain that way, and I am to be its custodian. A caretaker of the past, one might say, a curator of its relics."

He shook his head smilingly. "But I am afraid I am not quite suited to that role. I lift my hat to the past, it is true, but I prefer to court the present. For that reason I will go ahead with my plans, and hope they do not make an obstacle to our friendship."

I remember thinking, when I left next day for the city and a long hot week at my desk, that Raymond had carried off the affair very nicely, and that, thank God, it had gone no further than it did. So I was completely unprepared for Elizabeth's call at the end of the week.

It was awful, she said. It was the business of Hugh and Raymond and the Dane house, but worse than ever. She was counting on my coming down to Hilltop the next day; there couldn't be any question about that. She had planned a way of clearing up the whole thing, but I simply had to be there to back her up. After all, I was one of the few people Hugh would listen to, and she was depending on me.

"Depending on me for what?" I said. I didn't like the sound of it. "And as for Hugh's listening to me, Elizabeth, isn't that stretching it a good deal? I can't see him wanting my advice on his personal affairs."

"If you're going to be touchy about it—"

"I'm *not* touchy about it," I retorted. "I just don't like getting mixed up in this thing. Hugh's quite capable of taking care of himself."

"Maybe too capable."

"And what does that mean?"

"Oh, I can't explain now," she wailed. "I'll tell you everything tomorrow. And, darling, if you have any brotherly feelings you'll be here on the morning train. Believe me, it's serious."

I arrived on the morning train in a bad state. My imagination is one of the overactive kind that can build a cosmic disaster out of very little material, and by the time I arrived at the house I was prepared for almost anything.

But, on the surface, at least, all was serene. Hugh greeted me warmly, Elizabeth was her cheerful self, and we had an amiable lunch and a long talk which never came near the subject of Raymond or the Dane house. I said nothing about Elizabeth's phone call, but thought of it with a steadily growing sense of outrage until I was alone with her.

"Now," I said, "I'd like an explanation of all this mystery. The Lord knows what I expected to find out here, but it certainly wasn't anything I've seen so far. And I'd like some accounting for the bad time you've given me since that call."

"All right," she said grimly, "and that's what you'll get. Come along."

She led the way on a long walk through the gardens and past the stables and outbuildings. Near the private road which lay beyond the last grove of trees she suddenly said, "When the car drove you up to the house didn't you notice anything strange about this road?"

"No, I didn't."

"I suppose not. The driveway to the house turns off too far away from here. But now you'll have a chance to see for yourself."

I did see for myself. A chair was set squarely in the middle of the road and on the chair sat a stout man placidly reading a magazine. I recognized the man at once: he was one of Hugh's stable hands, and he had the patient look of someone who has been sitting for a long time and expects to sit a good deal longer. It took me only a second to realize what he was there for, but Elizabeth wasn't leaving anything to my deductive powers. When we walked over to him, the man stood up and grinned at us.

"William," Elizabeth said, "would you mind telling my brother what instructions Mr. Lozier gave you?"

"Sure," the man said cheerfully. "Mr. Lozier told us there was always supposed to be one of us sitting right here, and any truck we saw that might be carrying construction stuff or suchlike for the Dane house was to be stopped and turned back. All we had to do is tell them it's private property and they were trespassing. If they laid a finger on us we just call in the police. That's the whole thing."

"Have you turned back any trucks?" Elizabeth asked for my benefit.

The man looked surprised. "Why, you know that, Mrs. Lozier," he said. "There was a couple of them the first day we were out here, and that was all. There wasn't any fuss either," he explained to me. "None of those drivers wants to monkey with trespass."

When we were away from the road again I clapped my hand to my forehead. "It's incredible!" I said. "Hugh must know he can't get away with this. That road is the only one to the Dane place, and it's been in public use so long that it isn't even a private thoroughfare any more!"

Elizabeth nodded. "And that's exactly what Raymond told Hugh a few days back. He came over here in a fury, and they had quite an argument about it. And when Raymond said something about hauling Hugh off to court, Hugh answered that he'd be glad to spend the rest of his life in litigation over this business. But that wasn't the worst of it. The last thing Raymond said was that Hugh ought to know that force only invites force, and ever since then I've been expecting a war to break out here any minute. Don't you see? That man blocking the road is a constant provocation, and it scares me."

I could understand that. And the more I considered the matter, the more dangerous it looked.

"But I have a plan," Elizabeth said eagerly, "and that's why I wanted you here. I'm having a dinner party tonight, a very small, informal dinner party. It's to be a sort of peace conference. You'll be there, and Dr. Wynant—Hugh likes you both a great deal—and," she hesitated, "Raymond."

"No!" I said. "You mean he's actually coming?"

"I went over to see him yesterday and we had a long talk. I explained everything to him—about neighbors being able to sit down and come to an understanding, and about brotherly love and—oh, it must have sounded dreadfully inspirational and sticky, but it worked. He said he would be there."

I had a foreboding. "Does Hugh know about this?"

"About the dinner? Yes."

"I mean, about Raymond's being there."

"No, he doesn't." And then when she saw me looking hard at her, she burst out defiantly with, "Well, *something* had to be done, and I did it, that's all! Isn't it better than just sitting and waiting for God knows what?"

Until we were all seated around the dining-room table that evening I might have conceded the point. Hugh had been visibly shocked by Raymond's arrival, but then, apart from a sidelong glance at Elizabeth which had volumes written in it, he managed to conceal his feelings well enough. He had made the introductions gracefully, kept up his end of the conversation, and, all in all, did a creditable job of playing host.

Ironically, it was the presence of Dr. Wynant which made even this much of a triumph possible for Elizabeth, and which then turned it into disaster. The doctor was an eminent surgeon, stocky and gray-haired, with an abrupt, positive way about him. Despite his own position in the world he seemed pleased as a schoolboy to meet Raymond, and in no time at all they were as thick as thieves.

It was when Hugh discovered during dinner that nearly all attention was fixed on Raymond and very little on himself that the mantle of good host started to slip, and the fatal flaws in Elizabeth's plan showed through. There are people who enjoy entertaining lions and who take pleasure in reflected glory, but Hugh was not one of them. Besides, he regarded the doctor as one of his closest friends, and I have noticed that it is the most assured of men who can be the most jealous of their friendships. And when a prized friendship is being impinged on by the man one loathes more than anything else in the world—! All in all, by simply imagining myself in Hugh's place and looking across the table at Raymond who was gaily and unconcernedly holding forth, I was prepared for the worst.

The opportunity for it came to Hugh when Raymond was deep in a discussion of the devices used in effecting escapes. They were innumerable, he said. Almost anything one could seize on would serve as such a device. A wire, a scrap of metal, even a bit of paper—at one time or another he had used them all.

"But of them all," he said with a sudden solemnity, "there is only one I would stake my life on. Strange, it is one you cannot see, cannot hold in your hand—in fact, for many people it does not even exist. Yet, it is the one I have used most often and which has never failed me."

The doctor leaned forward, his eyes bright with interest. "And it is—?"

"It is a knowledge of people, my friend. Or, as it may be put, a knowledge of human nature. To me it is as vital an instrument as the scalpel is to you."

"Oh?" said Hugh, and his voice was so sharp that all eyes were instantly turned on him. "You make sleight of hand sound like a department of psychology."

"Perhaps," Raymond said, and I saw he was watching Hugh now, gauging him. "You see there is no great mystery in the matter. My profession—my art, as I like to think of it—is no more than the art of misdirection, and I am but one of its many practitioners."

"I wouldn't say there were many escape artists around nowadays," the doctor remarked.

"True," Raymond said, "but you will observe I referred to the art of misdirection. The escape artist, the master of legerdemain, these are a handful who practice the most exotic form of that art. But what of those who engage in the work of politics, of advertising, of salesmanship?" He laid his finger along his nose in the familiar gesture, and winked. "I am afraid they have all made my art their business."

The doctor smiled. "Since you haven't dragged medicine into it I'm willing to go along with you," he said. "But what I want to know is, exactly how does this knowledge of human nature work in your profession?"

"In this way," Raymond said. "One must judge a person carefully. Then, if he finds in that person certain weaknesses, he can state a false premise and it will be accepted without question. Once the false premise is swallowed, the rest is easy. The victim will then see only what the magician wants him to see, or will give his vote to that politician, or will buy merchandise because of that advertising." He shrugged. "And that is all there is to it."

"Is it?" Hugh said. "But what happens when you're with people who have some intelligence and won't swallow your false premise? How do you do your tricks then? Or do you keep them on the same level as selling beads to the savages?"

"Now that's uncalled for, Hugh," the doctor said. "The man's expressing his ideas. No reason to make an issue of them."

"Maybe there is," Hugh said, his eyes fixed on Raymond. "I have found he's full of interesting ideas. I was wondering how far he'd want to go in backing them up."

Raymond touched the napkin to his lips with a precise little flick, and then laid it carefully on the table before him. "In short," he said, addressing himself to Hugh, "you want a small demonstration of my art."

"It depends," Hugh said. "I don't want any trick cigarette cases or rabbits out of hats or any damn nonsense like that. I'd like to see something good."

"Something good," echoed Raymond reflectively. He looked around the room, studied it, and then turned to Hugh, pointing toward the huge oak door which was closed between the dining room and the living room, where we had gathered before dinner.

"That door is not locked, is it?"

"No," Hugh said, "it isn't. It hasn't been locked for years."

"But there is a key to it?"

Hugh pulled out his key chain, and with an effort detached a heavy, old-fashioned key. "Yes, it's the same one we use for the butler's pantry." He was becoming interested despite himself.

"Good. No, do not give it to me. Give it to the doctor. You have faith in the doctor's honor, I am sure?"

"Yes," said Hugh dryly, "I have."

"Very well. Now, Doctor, will you please go to that door and lock it."

The doctor marched to the door, with his firm, decisive tread, thrust the key into the lock, and turned it. The click of the bolt snapping into place was loud in the silence of the room. The doctor returned to the table holding the key, but Raymond motioned it away. "It must not leave your hand or everything is lost," he warned.

"Now," Raymond said, "for the finale I approach the door, I flick my handkerchief at it—" the handkerchief barely brushed the keyhole— "and presto, the door is unlocked!"

The doctor went to it. He seized the doorknob, twisted it dubiously, and then watched with genuine astonishment as the door swung silently open.

"Well, I'll be damned," he said.

"Somehow," Elizabeth laughed, "a false premise went down easy as an oyster."

Only Hugh reflected a sense of personal outrage. "All right," he demanded, "how was it done? How did you work it?"

"I?" Raymond said reproachfully, and smiled at all of us with obvious enjoyment. "It was you who did it all. I used only my little knowledge of human nature to help you along the way."

I said, "I can guess part of it. That door was set in advance, and when the doctor thought he was locking it, he wasn't. He was really unlocking it. Isn't that the answer?"

Raymond nodded. "Very much the answer. The door *was* locked in advance. I made sure of that, because with a little forethought I suspected there would be such a challenge during the evening, and this was the simplest way of preparing for it. I merely made certain that I was the last one to enter this room, and when I did I used this." He held up his hand so that we could see the sliver of metal in it. "An ordinary skeleton key, of course, but sufficient for an old and primitive lock."

For a moment Raymond looked grave, then he continued brightly, "It was our host himself who stated the false premise when he said the door was unlocked. He was a man so sure of himself that he would not think to test anything so obvious. The doctor is also a man who is sure, and he fell into the same trap. It is, as you now see, a little dangerous always to be so sure."

"I'll go along with that," the doctor said ruefully, "even though it's heresy to admit it in my line of work." He playfully tossed the key he had been holding across the table to Hugh who let it fall in front of him and made no gesture toward it. "Well, Hugh, like it or not, you must admit the man has proved his point."

"Do I?" said Hugh softly. He sat there smiling a little now, and it was easy to see he was turning some thought over and over in his head.

"Oh, come on, man," the doctor said with some impatience. "You were taken in as much as we were. You know that."

"Of course you were, darling," Elizabeth agreed.

I think that she suddenly saw her opportunity to turn the proceedings into the peace conference she had aimed at, but I could have told her she was choosing her time badly. There was a look in Hugh's eye I didn't like—a veiled look which wasn't natural to him. Ordinarily, when he was really angered, he would blow up a violent storm, and once the thunder and lightning had passed he would be honestly apologetic. But this present mood of his was different. There was a slumbrous quality in it which alarmed me.

He hooked one arm over the back of his chair and rested the other on the table, sitting halfway around to fix his eyes on Raymond. "I seem to be a minority of one," he remarked, "but I'm sorry to say I found your little trick disappointing. Not that it wasn't cleverly done—I'll grant that, all right—but because it wasn't any more than you'd expect from a competent locksmith."

"Now there's a large helping of sour grapes," the doctor jeered.

Hugh shook his head. "No, I'm simply saying that where there's a lock on a door and the key to it in your hand, it's no great trick to open it. Considering our friend's reputation, I thought we'd see more from him than that."

Raymond grimaced. "Since I had hoped to entertain," he said, "I must apologize for disappointing."

"Oh, as far as entertaining goes I have no complaints. But for a real test—"

"A real test?"

"Yes, something a little different. Let's say, a door without any locks or keys to tamper with. A closed door which can be opened with a fingertip, but which is nevertheless impossible to open. How does that sound to you?"

Raymond narrowed his eyes thoughtfully, as if he were considering the picture being presented to him. "It sounds most interesting," he said at last. "Tell me more about it."

"No," Hugh said, and from the sudden eagerness in his voice I felt that this was the exact moment he had been looking for. "I'll do better than that. I'll *show* it to you."

He stood up brusquely and the rest of us followed suit—except Elizabeth, who remained in her seat. When I asked her if she wanted to come along, she only shook her head and sat there watching us hopelessly as we left the room.

We were bound for the cellars, I realized when Hugh picked up a flashlight along the way, but for a part of the cellars I had never seen before. On a few occasions I had gone downstairs to help select a bottle of wine from the racks there, but now we walked past the wine vault and into a long, dimly lit chamber behind it. Our feet scraped loudly on the rough stone, the walls around us showed the stains of seepage, and warm as the night was outside, I could feel the chill of dampness turning my chest to gooseflesh. When the doctor shuddered and said hollowly, "These are the very tombs of Atlantis," I knew I wasn't alone in my feeling, and felt some relief at that.

We stopped at the very end of the chamber, before what I can best describe as a stone closet built from floor to ceiling in the farthest angle of the walls. It was about four feet wide and not quite twice that in length, and its open doorway showed impenetrable blackness inside. Hugh reached into the blackness and pulled a heavy door into place.

"That's it," he said abruptly. "Plain solid wood, four inches thick, fitted flush into the frame so that it's almost airtight. It's a beautiful piece of carpentry, too, the kind they practiced two hundred years ago. And no locks or bolts. Just a ring set into each side to use as a handle." He pushed the door gently and it swung open noiselessly at his touch. "See that? The whole thing is balanced so perfectly on the hinges that it moves like a feather."

"But what's it for?" I asked. "It must have been made for a reason."

Hugh laughed shortly. "It was. Back in the bad old days, when a servant committed a crime—and I don't suppose it had to be more of a crime than talking back to one of the ancient Loziers—he was put in here to repent. And since the air inside was good for only a few hours at the most, he either repented damn soon or not at all."

"And that door?" the doctor said cautiously. "That impressive door of yours which opens at a touch to provide all the air needed— what prevented the servant from opening it?"

"Look," Hugh said. He flashed his light inside the cell and we crowded behind him to peer in. The circle of light reached across the cell to its far wall and picked out a short, heavy chain hanging a little above head level with a U-shaped collar dangling from its bottom link.

"I see," Raymond said, and they were the first words I had heard him speak since we had left the dining room. "It is truly ingenious. The man stands with his back against the wall, facing the door. The collar is placed around his neck, and then—since it is clearly not made for a lock—it is clamped there, hammered around his neck. The door is closed, and the man spends the next few hours like someone on an invisible rack, reaching out with his feet to catch the ring on the door which is just out of reach. If he is lucky he may not strangle himself in his iron collar, but may live until someone chooses to open the door for him."

"My God," the doctor said. "You make me feel as if I were living through it."

Raymond smiled faintly. "I have lived through many such experiences, and, believe me, the reality is always a little worse than the worst imaginings. There is always the ultimate moment of terror, of panic, when the heart pounds so madly you think it will burst through your ribs, and the cold sweat soaks clear through you in the space of one breath. That is when you must take yourself in hand, must dispel all weakness, and remember all the lessons you have ever learned. If not—!" He whisked the edge of his hand across his lean throat. "Unfortunately for the usual victim of such a device," he concluded sadly, "since he lacks the essential courage and knowledge to help himself, he succumbs."

"But you wouldn't," Hugh said.

"I have no reason to think so."

"You mean," and the eagerness was creeping back into Hugh's voice, stronger than ever, "that under the very same conditions as someone chained in there two hundred years ago you could get this door open?"

The challenging note was too strong to be brushed aside lightly. Raymond stood silent for a long minute, face strained with concentration, before he answered.

"Yes," he said. "It would not be easy—the problem is made formidable by its very simplicity—but it could be solved."

"How long do you think it would take you?"

"An hour at the most."

Hugh had come a long way around to get to this point. He asked the question slowly, savoring it. "Would you want to bet on that?"

"Now, wait a minute," the doctor said. "I don't like any part of this."

"And I vote we adjourn for a drink," I put in. "Fun's fun, but we'll all wind up with pneumonia, playing games down here."

Neither Hugh nor Raymond appeared to hear a word of this. They stood staring at each other—Hugh waiting on pins and needles, Raymond deliberating—until Raymond said, "What is this bet you offer?"

"This. If you lose, you get out of the Dane house inside of a month, and sell it to me."

"And if I win?"

It was not easy for Hugh to say it, but he finally got it out. "Then I'll be the one to get out. And if you don't want to buy Hilltop I'll arrange to sell it to the first comer."

For anyone who knew Hugh it was so fantastic, so staggering a statement to hear from him, that none of us could find words at first. It was the doctor who recovered most quickly.

"You're not speaking for yourself, Hugh," he warned. "You're a married man. Elizabeth's feelings have to be considered."

"Is it a bet?" Hugh demanded of Raymond. "Do you want to go through with it?"

"I think before I answer that, there is something to be explained." Raymond paused, then went on slowly, "I'm afraid I gave the impression—out of false pride, perhaps—that when I retired from my work it was because of a boredom, a lack of interest in it. That was not altogether the truth. In reality, I was required to go to a doctor some years ago, the doctor listened to the heart, and suddenly my heart became the most important thing in the world. I tell you this because, while your challenge strikes me as being a most unusual and interesting way of settling differences between neighbors, I must reject it for reasons of health."

"You were healthy enough a minute ago," Hugh said in a hard voice.

"Perhaps not as much as you would want to think, my friend."

"In other words," Hugh said bitterly, "there's no accomplice handy, no keys in your pocket to help out, and no way of tricking anyone into seeing what isn't there! So you have to admit you're beaten."

Raymond stiffened. "I admit no such thing. All the tools I would need even for such a test as this I have with me. Believe me, they would be enough."

Hugh laughed aloud, and the sound of it broke into small echoes all down the corridors behind us. It was that sound, I am sure—the living contempt in it rebounding from wall to wall around us—which sent Raymond into the cell.

Hugh wielded the hammer, a short-handled but heavy sledge, which tightened the collar into a circlet around Raymond's neck, hitting with hard even strokes at the iron which was braced against the wall. When he was finished I saw the pale glow of the radium-painted numbers on a watch as Raymond studied it in his pitch darkness.

"It is now eleven," he said calmly. "The wager is that by midnight this door must be opened, and it does not matter what means are used. Those are the conditions, and you gentlemen are the witnesses to them."

Then the door was closed, and the walking began.

Back and forth we walked—the three of us—as if we were being compelled to trace every possible geometric figure on that stony floor, the doctor with his quick, impatient step, and I matching Hugh's long, nervous strides. A foolish, meaningless march, back and forth across our own shadows, each of us marking the time by counting off the passing seconds, and each ashamed to be the first to look at his watch.

For a while there was a counterpoint to this scraping of feet from inside the cell. It was a barely perceptible clinking of chain coming at brief, regular intervals. Then there would be a long silence, followed by a renewal of the sound. When it stopped again I could not restrain myself any longer. I held up my watch toward the dim yellowish light of the bulb overhead and saw with dismay that barely twenty minutes had passed.

After that there was no hesitancy in the others about looking at the time, and, if anything, this made it harder to bear than just wondering. I caught the doctor winding his watch with small, brisk turns, and then a few minutes later he would try to wind it again, and suddenly drop his hand with disgust as he realized he had already done it. Hugh walked with his watch held up near his eyes, as if by concentration on it he could drag that crawling minute hand faster around the dial.

Thirty minutes had passed.

Forty.

Forty-five.

I remember that when I looked at my watch and saw there were less than fifteen minutes to go I wondered if I could last out even that short time. The chill had sunk so deep into me that I ached with it. I was shocked when I saw that Hugh's face was dripping with sweat, and that beads of it gathered and ran off while I watched.

It was while I was looking at him in fascination that it happened. The sound broke through the walls of the cell like a wail of agony heard from far away, and shivered over us as if it were spelling out the words.

"*Doctor!*" it cried. "*The air!*"

It was Raymond's voice, but the thickness of the wall blocking it off turned it into a high, thin sound. What was clearest in it was the note of pure terror, the plea growing out of that terror.

"*Air!*" it screamed, the word bubbling and dissolving into a long-drawn sound which made no sense at all.

And then it was silent.

We leaped for the door together, but Hugh was there first, his back against it, barring the way. In his upraised hand was the hammer which had clinched Raymond's collar.

"Keep back!" he cried. "Don't come any nearer, I warn you!"

The fury in him, brought home by the menace of the weapon, stopped us in our tracks.

"Hugh," the doctor pleaded, "I know what you're thinking, but you can forget that now. The bet's off, and I'm opening the door on my own responsibility. You have my word for that."

"Do I? But do you remember the terms of the bet, Doctor? This door must be opened within an hour—*and it doesn't matter what means are used*! Do you understand now? He's fooling both of you. He's faking a death scene, so that you'll push open the door and win his bet for him. But it's my bet, not yours, and I have the last word on it!"

I saw from the way he talked, despite the shaking tension in his voice, that he was in perfect command of himself, and it made everything seem that much worse.

"How do you know he's faking?" I demanded. "The man said he had a heart condition. He said there was always a time in a spot like this when he had to fight panic and could feel the strain of it. What right do you have to gamble with his life?"

"Damn it, don't you see he never mentioned any heart condition until he smelled a bet in the wind? Don't you see he set his trap that way, just as he locked the door behind him when he came into dinner! But this time nobody will spring it for him—nobody!"

"Listen to me," the doctor said, and his voice cracked like a whip. "Do you concede that there's one slim possibility of that man being dead in there, or dying?"

"Yes, it is possible—anything is possible."

"I'm not trying to split hairs with you! I'm telling you that if that man is in trouble every second counts, and you're stealing that time from him. And if that's the case, by God, I'll sit in the witness chair at your trial and swear you murdered him! Is that what you want?"

Hugh's head sank forward on his chest, but his hand still tightly gripped the hammer. I could hear the breath drawing heavily in his throat, and when he raised his head, his face was gray and haggard. The torment of indecision was written in every pale sweating line of it.

And then I suddenly understood what Raymond had meant that day when he told Hugh about the revelation he might find in the face of a perfect dilemma. It was the revelation of what a man may learn about himself when he is forced to look into his own depths, and Hugh had found it at last.

In that shadowy cellar, while the relentless seconds thundered louder and louder in our ears, we waited to see what he would do.

A JUNGLE GRADUATE

BY JAMES FRANCIS DWYER

❡ THE MOONLIGHT fell upon Schreiber's bald head as he jerked his body out of the depths of the roughhewn lounge chair. His eyes were turned to the blue-black smear of jungle, but his ears were absorbing the faint sounds that came from the interior of the bungalow. The path, like a whitewashed strip, reached toward the weird tree masses, and alongside it the coarse rirro grass stood up haughtily, as if protesting against the man-made barrenness. The jungle resents a cleared space; it speaks of the presence of human beings.

"What is it?" I asked softly.

"Nothing," murmured the naturalist, but his grip on the unplaned pine limbs, which formed the frame upon which the Dyak mat was stretched, did not relax. He gave one the impression of a man sifting the noises of the night with his whole body.

Suddenly his head came sharply down between his shoulders, and the chair seemed to groan protestingly as he left it with a spring. A black line appeared upon the moon-whitened path, and the heavy German pounced upon it with the agility of a cat.

"It is that damn vermilion snake," he grunted, holding the wriggling thing up by the tail as he shuffled toward the door. "This is the second time he has escaped."

When the chair had again received him with a long-drawn creaking sound, I put a question.

"Did you see him before he started across the path?" I asked.

"No!" snapped Schreiber. "I just felt that things are not right. That is easy. When he escaped, it caused a little silence and just a

From *The Story-Teller*, 1932.

212

little change in the note of those that didn't keep altogether quiet. Listen, please, now."

From inside the darkened bungalow came a peculiar wasplike buzzing that filtered unceasingly into the mysterious night. The surrounding jungle appeared to be listening to it. At first it defied the attempts of the ear when it sought to analyze the medley, then the different noises asserted themselves slowly. It was the inarticulate cry of the German's prisoners. There was the soft moaning of the wakeful gibbon, the *pat-pat* of the civet, the whimper of the black monkey, the snuffling of caged small things, and the rustle of snakes that crawled wearily around their boxes. The sounds seemed to bring to the place a peculiar aura that put the bungalow apart from the untrammeled jungle that surrounded it on all sides.

"They are all right now," murmured the German contentedly. "They are quiet, so."

"But how did they know that the vermilion snake had escaped?" I asked. "They're in the dark, and the snake made no noise."

The naturalist laughed, the pleasant laugh of the man to whom a question like mine brings the thrill of subtle flattery.

"How?" he repeated. "My friend, the gibbon in there felt it in his blood, *ja*. He whimper softly, oh, so softly, and the news ran along the cages. The dark makes no difference to the wild people. Every little bit of their bodies is an eye. Every little hair listens and tells them something. That is as it should be. I felt the change in their notes. I was dreaming of Jan Wyck's place in Amsterdam just then, and I wake up mighty quick. The black monkey is wise, but the tune of the others changed to pianissimo very, very sudden. A snake is a fellow that can get in anywhere. Listen to them now. I did not tell them that he was back, but they know."

A feeling of nausea crept over me as the German spoke haltingly, groping for the words to express himself. To me the bungalow appeared as a leprous spot in the jungle of wild, waving tapang, pandanus, and sandalwood, laced together with riotous creepers. The whimpering, snuffling, and protesting rustling made me shiver, and I surprised myself by voicing my thoughts.

"It seems so infernally cruel," I stammered. "If you look at—"

The naturalist interrupted me with a quiet laugh, and I remained silent. The big meerschaum was being puffed vigorously.

"It is not cruel," he said slowly. "Out there—" he waved a hand at the blue-black smear of jungle that looked like a foundation upon which the pearly sky reared itself—"they are dining on each other. My prisoners are safe and have plenty. Did you not hear just now how it troubled them when the snake escaped? So! The black monkey has a little one, and she was afraid. The jungle life is not a lengthy one for the weak. I was at Amsterdam five years ago—*ach Gott!* it seems fifty years ago—and at Hagenbeck's I see a one-eared *mias* that I trapped years ago. She looked well. Would she be alive here? I do not know."

The irritating droning noise continued to pour out of the bungalow. It floated out into the night that appeared to be all ears, in an effort to absorb it.

"No, captivity is not bad if they are treated right," continued the naturalist, "and can you tell me where they are not treated well?"

I did not answer. Confronted with a request for reasons to back up my stammered protest, I found myself without any. Schreiber's captives were well fed. The baby monkey was guarded from the snake.

The big German smoked silently for several minutes, his eyes fixed on the jungle belt in front.

"The zoological people treat their animals better than society treats human beings," he said gently. "And the naturalists? Well, they treat them well. I never knew one who did not."

He stopped for a moment, and then gave a little throaty gurgle. Memory had pushed forward something that displeased him.

"I made a mistake," he remarked harshly. "I did know of one. The night is young; I will tell you of him. It happened a long while ago, when I first came to the Samarahan River—Fogelberg and I came together. This man's name was Lesohn—Pierre Lesohn—and he was a naturalist of a kind. That is, his heart was not in his work. *Nein!* He was always thinking of other ways of making money, and no man who calls himself a naturalist can do that. This business calls for everything—heart, soul, brains, all. That is why I said Lesohn was not a naturalist. The devil of discontent was gnawing at him, and in this work there should be no discontent. No, my friend.

"One day I pulled down the river to Lesohn's place, and he pushed at me an illustrated paper from Paris. He laughed, too, very excitedly. He was nearly always excited; the discontented people always are.

" 'What do you think of that?' he said.

"I read the piece in the paper, and I looked at the picture that went with it. It was the picture of an orangoutang, and it had under it the brute's name. He had two names, just like you and me. There he was, sitting at a desk, smoking a cigar and making a bluff that he was writing a letter. It turned me sick. It was not good to me. I handed the paper back to Lesohn and I said nothing.

" 'Well?' he snapped. 'I asked you what you thought of it.'

" 'Not much,' I said. 'It interests me not.'

" 'You old fool!' he cried out. 'That monkey is earning two hundred pounds a week at the Royal Music Hall, in Piccadilly. He is making a fortune for his trainer.'

" 'I do not care,' I said; 'I am not concerned one little bit.'

" 'Ho, ho!' he sneered. 'You want to work in this foul jungle till you die, eh? I have other things in my mind, Schreiber.' I knew he had, but I didn't interrupt him just then. 'Yes,' he cried out, 'I do not want to be buried out here with the wahwahs singing the "Dead March" over my grave. I want to die in Paris. And I want to have some fun before I die, Schreiber. There is a little girl whose father keeps the Café des Primroses—*Mon Dieu*! Why did I come to this wilderness?'

" 'And how will that help you?' I asked, pointing to the paper that had the picture of the smart monkey in it.

" 'How?' he screamed. 'How? Why, you old stupid, I, Pierre Lesohn, will train an orangoutang, too.'

" 'It is not good to make a brute into a human,' I said. 'I would not try if I were you.'

"Lesohn laughed himself nearly into convulsions when I said that. It was a great joke to him. He fell on the bed and laughed for ten minutes. He was a smart man, was Pierre Lesohn—too smart to come out of Paris. The smart men should always stay in the cities.

The jungle is not for them. It agrees only with men who have made a proper assay of their faculties. Lesohn never had time to make an assay. He was too busy scheming."

Schreiber stopped and again leaned forward in the big chair. Something had gone astray in the buzzing noise from the prison house, and like a maestro he listened for the jarring note. Softly he rose from his seat and disappeared into the interior darkness.

When he returned he relit his pipe slowly—the jungle life makes a man's movements composed and deliberate—then he settled himself back in the seat of his own manufacture.

"The little one of the black monkey is ill," he explained. "If it was in the jungle it would die. Here it will live, I think. But we will get back to Lesohn, the smart Frenchman, who should have stayed in Paris. He pasted that picture of the man-ape over his cot, and he looked at it every day. It got between him and his sleep.

" 'Two hundred pounds a week,' he would cry out. 'Think of that, you old, squareheaded German. That is nearly five thousand francs! That is four thousand marks! Could we not train one, too?'

" 'Not me,' I said. 'I like the orangoutang just as he is. He suits me like that. If he got so clever that he could smoke my cigars and read my letters. I would not like him one bit. He would be out of the place that God gave him in the animal kingdom.'

"I annoyed Lesohn by telling him that. I annoyed him very much. Three days afterward a Dyak trapped an orangoutang that was just getting out of its babyhood, and the Frenchman bought it quick.

" 'It is just the size I want,' he said to Fogelberg and me. I want to train it as quick as I can. Ho, ho, you two fools, just wait! There is a little girl whose father keeps the Café des Primroses—wait, German, and see things. Professor Pierre Lesohn and his wonderful trained orangoutang! Five thousand francs a week! Is it not good?'

"But Fogelberg and I said nothing. We knew the status of the orangoutang in the animal kingdom, and we were content to leave him on his proper plane. Mother Nature fixes the grades, and she knows that the orang is not the fellow that shall send notes to his sweetheart or puff cigars when he is sitting in tight boots that squeeze his toes that have been made for swinging him through the palm trees. From the ant-eating manis, with his horn armor, right up to Pierre

Lesohn, Mother Nature has settled things very properly and very quietly.

"Lesohn was not the man for the wilderness. No, my friend. He was all bubble, all nerves, and he wanted to feed on excitement ten times a day. And there is no excitement here. Not a bit. People in the cities think that there is, but they are mistaken. This is a cradle where you get a rest if you sit quiet. Do you understand? The Frenchman could not sit quiet. His imagination made him a millionaire after he had that orangoutang two days. It did so. It bought him a house at Passy, and a carriage and pair, and the smiles of the ballet girls at the Grand Casino. Some men are like that. They make their imaginations into gas-wagons, and ride to the devil. And Lesohn was taking something that didn't improve things. He kept a square bottle under his cot, and he toasted the monkey and the good times that he was going to have in Paris—toasted them much too often for my liking.

"That monkey learned things mighty fast. He was a great mimic. Every time Fogelberg and I pulled down to Lesohn's place, the Frenchman trotted the damn hairy brute out to do things for our approval. Fogelberg didn't like it. I didn't like it. *Nein!* We told Lesohn, and he laughed and made fun of us.

" 'Oh, you two old fools!' he cried out. 'Oh, you two old monkey-snarers! You wait! Professor Pierre Lesohn and his trained orangoutang at five thousand francs a week! Five thousand francs! Think of it! In the Café des Primroses I will think sometimes of you two fools on the stinking mudbanks of the Samarahan.'

"He was going mad thinking of the good times he would have on the boulevards. He drank—*Gott im Himmel,* how he drank! He saw himself strutting in Europe with the monkey bringing in the money. He was mad, all right. And I think that orangoutang began to think that he was mad. He would sit alongside Lesohn and puzzle his old head to know what the Frenchman was so excited about. The brute didn't know of the dreams of Monsieur Pierre Lesohn. No, my friend. He didn't know that the Frenchman was going to make a pedestal of his wisdom, upon which he could climb and kiss his fingers to the Milky Way. Oh, no! He was only an orangoutang, and he didn't know that people would pay four thousand marks a week to see him stick his blue nose into a stein and puff at a cigarette. *Ach!* it sickens me.

"Then one day the monkey got sulky, and would not do a single thing. I think Lesohn was drunk that day. He must have been. The brute was sulky and the Frenchman was drunk. Pierre told me of it afterward. The *mias* knocked over the specimen cases, and went cranky. Lesohn went cranky, too. He saw the boulevards and house at Passy and the ballet girls and the Café des Primroses floating away on the monkey's tantrums, and he got sick. He got very sick. He swigged away at the flat bottle till he went nearly mad, and then he done something."

The blue depths of the jungle appeared to pulsate as Schreiber halted in his story to listen again to the sounds that came from within. There was witchery in the soft night. It touched one with mysterious fingers. It watched outside the lonely bungalow, wondering, inquisitive, wide-eyed.

"He must have been mad," continued the German, "mad or drunk. The Samarahan flowed right by Lesohn's bungalow, and the Samarahan was alive at that place. Dirty, ugly, scaly-backed crocodiles slept in the mud there all day long. Ugh! I hate crocodiles. They turn me sick. The Frenchman, he was mad, though—mad with drink and mad because he thought the orangoutang was turning stupid."

"Well," I asked, "what happened?" The night was listening to the story. The buzzing noise from the prisoners died down to the faintest murmur.

"Well," repeated the naturalist, "Pierre Lesohn taught that orangoutang a lesson in obedience. He tied the animal to the trunk of a tree near the mudbanks—yes, near the stinking, slimy mudbanks that smell like asafetida, and then he, Pierre, laid himself down on the veranda of his bungalow with his Winchester rifle in his lap.

"The orangoutang whimpered, and Lesohn laughed. He told me of this afterward. The orang whimpered again and again. Then he cried out with fear. A bit of the mud started to move, and the big *mias* was afraid, very much afraid. You know the cold eye of the crocodile? It is the icicle eye. It is the eye of the monte shark. No animal has such a cold eye. The shark? *Nein!* The shark has a fighting eye. The crocodile doesn't fight. He waits till all the cards are his way. He is a devil. That tied-up pet of Lesohn's attracted the dirty brute in the mud, and the orangoutang had been fool enough to tell him by that whimper that he was helpless. See?

"The crocodile watched him for one hour—for two hours—for three hours. He thought it might be a trap. Lesohn watched, too. He was teaching the monkey what mighty smart fellows come out of Paris.

"The crocodile knocked the mud off his back to get a better view, and the orang screamed out to Pierre to save him. He screamed mighty hard. He chattered of the things he would learn if Lesohn came to his aid quick, but Lesohn smiled to himself and sat quiet.

"The crocodile dug himself out of the mud and looked at the *mias* and the *mias* shivered in every bit of his body. Lesohn told me all about it afterward. He said the monkey cursed him when the crocodile flicked the water out of his eye and moved a little farther up the bank. That icicle eye had the orangoutang fascinated. He lost his nerve. He shrieked and he prayed in monkey gibberish, and that gave the crocodile plenty heart. *Ach, yes!* He thought that he held four aces in the little game with the orang, and he thinks it good to take a chance. He made a big rush at the tree, but Pierre was waiting for that rush. He threw the rifle forward quick, the bullet took the brute in the eye, and he flopped back into the stinking mud with a grunt.

"You see what Lesohn was? He was a madman. Next day, when Fogelberg and I went down there, he told us all about it, and laughed a lot. The orangoutang was so mighty afraid that Lesohn would repeat the stunt that he was hopping round doing everything that he could. *Gott!* He was much afraid was that monkey. I bet he dreamed of nights of the icicle eye of that crocodile. Every time Lesohn looked at him he shivered as if he was going to take a fit, and he whimpered like a baby. That crocodile had watched him for three hours. See?

" 'Look at him!' screamed the Frenchman. 'No more sulks from him! I tamed him! Here!' he yelled to the orang. 'Bring me my bottle!'

"Didn't that monkey rush to get it? You bet he did. He went as if it was a matter of life and death to him, and I suppose it was, to his thinking. And Lesohn shrieked with laughter till you could hear him at Brunei. He reckoned that the cold eye of a crocodile was the very best thing in the world to bring a monkey to his senses.

" 'I will take him over to Singapore next week,' said Lesohn, 'and from there I will get a boat to Colombo, and then ship by the Messageries Maritimes to Paris. Five thousand francs a week! You will read to me. *Mon Dieu!* Yes! You will read of Pierre Lesohn—Professor Pierre Lesohn and his trained orangoutang!' "

Schreiber halted in his recital. A wind came out of the China Sea, charged down upon the jungle and slashed the fronds of the big palms like a regiment of cuirassiers thundering through space. It died away suddenly, leaving an atmosphere of weird expectancy that put one's nerves on a tension. The night seemed to listen for something that it knew was coming.

"Go on!" I cried excitedly. "Tell me! Tell me what happened!"

"Four days after that night," said Schreiber quietly, "I pulled down the Samarahan. When I came in front of Lesohn's bungalow I called out to him, but I got no answer. 'He is in the forest,' I said to myself; 'I will go up to the hut and get a drink.' It was a mighty hot day, and the Samarahan is not a summer resort. *Nein!* It is not.

"Did you ever feel that a silence can be too much a silence? Sometimes in the jungle I feel a hush that is not nice. It was here tonight when the vermilion snake escaped. Often in the forest it chokes the whistle of the cicada and it seems to stop the little blades of grass from waving. *Ja!* It is strange. Whenever I feel that silence I am careful. I am not afraid, but I know that other things that can feel in a way that I cannot feel are much afraid.

"It was that kind of a silence that I feel when I was going up the path to Lesohn's bungalow. It touched me like ten thousand cold hands. I am not imaginative, no, but in the jungle one gets a skin that feels and sees and hears. And my skin was working overtime just then. . . . It was telling my brain something that my brain could not understand.

"I walked on my toes through the mangrove bushes at the top of that path. I know not why, but I did. I was near to making a discovery. I knew that. I stopped and peeped through the branches and I saw something. *Gott!* Yes! I saw something that made me reach out for the news that my skin was trying to tell me. I knew, and I did not know. Do you understand? I chased that thing all around in my brain, and I was getting closer to it each minute. The things I thought of made it come closer, and my lips got dry. I thought of what Lesohn had done to that orang, how he had tied him to the tree and frightened him into a fit with the cold stare of that scaly-backed crocodile, and while I thought of that I watched the veranda of the bungalow. I seemed to see that monkey tied to the tree and that icicle eye looking at him from the mud, and then—why, I knew! It came on me like a flash. I felt as if I was hit with a sandbag.

"For three minutes I could not move, then I staggered toward the veranda. Do you know what was there? *That big ugly mias was fumbling with the Frenchman's rifle, and he was crying like a human.* " 'Where is Lesohn?' I cried out. 'Where is he?' And then I laughed like a madman at my own question. My skin, that was all eyes and ears, had told me where Lesohn was. *Ja!* It was so.

"The big *mias* sprang up on his feet and he looked at me just as if he understood every word I said. My legs were as weak as two blades of grass. I had not seen the thing done. *Ach!* It was strange. I thought I had dreamed about it, but then I knew I hadn't. It was the silence, and the crying *mias*, and something inside me which told me it is not good to teach a brute too much. 'Where is he?' I cried out again. 'Show me where is he.'

"The orang wiped the tears from his ugly blue nose and touched me with his big, hairy arm, and then he started to shamble toward the mudbanks where the Frenchman had tied him to give him that little lesson in obedience.

"I was sick, then. That atmosphere turned me all upside down. I knew what had happened. Yes, I knew. My mind had pieced things together like the pieces of a picture puzzle. I knew what Lesohn had done to the brute. I knew the imitative ways of the *mias*, and I knew that Pierre was often drunk—very often drunk. And then there was the knowledge which my skin had strained out of the silence. A cold sweat ran from me as I followed the orang, and I clutched the rifle tight as I got near the mudbank and looked around for something to confirm the horror my soul had sensed. And the proof was there. It was a coat sleeve tied to the tree where the Frenchman had tied the *mias* a week before, and the sleeve wasn't empty. *Nein!* The cords had been tied around the wrist of Pierre Lesohn, and the cords were very strong. They had stood the strain of the pull, and—and it was there as a proof of what had happened.

"It was all so plain to me. Lesohn must have been drunk, see? Well, while he was drunk it had come into the ugly head of that brute to let Pierre get a thrill from the icicle eyes of the scaly-backed devils in the mud. He had tied Lesohn to the tree, and then he got the rifle and copied the Frenchman by sitting on the veranda to watch for the first one of those things that would find out that Pierre was helpless. It was plain—oh, so plain to me. But the Frenchman, in educating that orang, had forgotten to teach him how to load a rifle. It was unfortunate, was it not? The rifle was empty, and when the dirty brutes came out of the mud, the *mias* could do nothing. *Gott*, no! He just fumbled with the breech and cried like a human being till I came along, and then it was too late."

"What did you do then?" I cried, as the German's heavy bass tones were pursued and throttled by the palpitating silence.

"I did nothing," said Schreiber quietly. "Lesohn had told me what he had done to that brute. Fate—Nemesis—call it what you will—has funny ways. I looked at the orangoutang, and he backed away from me crying. And he looked back a dozen times, still crying, till the jungle swallowed him up. Somewhere out there—" the German waved a hand at the dark forest that was watching and listening —"there is an orangoutang with a tragedy on his mind."

RECIPE FOR MURDER

BY C. P. DONNEL, JR.

❡ JUST AS THE VILLA, clamorous with flowers, was not what he had expected, so was its owner a new quantity in his calculations. Madame Chalon, at forty, fitted no category of murderess; she was neither Cleopatra nor beldame. A Minerva of a woman, he told himself instantly, whose large, liquid eyes were but a shade lighter than the cobalt blue of the Mediterranean twinkling outside the tall windows of the salon where they sat.

Not quite a Minerva, he decided upon closer inspection. Her cheeks had the peach bloom of eighteen, and she was of a roundness, a smoothness, a desirability that rendered her, if less regal, infinitely more interesting. An ungraceful woman of her weight might be considered as journeying toward stoutness, but with Madame Chalon, he knew by instinct, the body was static with regard to weight and outline, and she would be at sixty what she was this day, neither more nor less.

"Dubonnet, Inspector Miron?" As he spoke, she prepared to pour. His reflex of hesitation lit a dim glow of amusement in her eyes, which her manners prevented from straying to her lips.

"Thank you." Annoyed with himself, he spoke forcefully.

Madame Chalon made a small, barely perceptible point of drinking first, as though to say, "See, M. Miron, you are quite safe." It was neat. Too neat?

With a tiny smile now: "You have called about my poisoning of my husbands," she stated flatly.

"Madame!" Again he hesitated, nonplused. "Madame, I . . ."

"You must already have visited the Prefecture. All Villefranche believes it," she said placidly.

He adjusted his composure to an official calm. "Madame, I come to ask your permission to disinter the body of M. Charles Wesser, deceased January 1939, and M. Etienne Chalon, deceased May 1946, for official analysis of certain organs. You have already refused Sergeant Luchaire of the local station this permission. Why?"

"Luchaire is a type without politeness. I found him repulsive. He is, unlike you, without finesse. I refuse the attitude of the man, not the law." She raised the small glass to her full lips. "I shall not refuse you, Inspector Miron." Her eyes were almost admiring.

"You are most flattering."

"Because," she continued gently, "I am quite sure, knowing the methods of you Paris police, that the disinterment has already been conducted secretly." She waited for his color to deepen, affecting not to notice the change. "And the analyses," she went on, as though there had been no break, "completed. You are puzzled. You found nothing. So now you, new to the case, wish to estimate me, my character, my capacity for self-control—and incidentally your own chances of maneuvering me into talk that will guide you in the direction of my guilt."

So accurately did these darts strike home that it would be the ultimate stupidity to deny the wounds. Better a disarming frankness, Miron decided quickly. "Quite true, Madame Chalon. True to the letter. But—" he regarded her closely—"when one loses two husbands of some age—but not old—to a fairly violent gastric disturbance, each within two years of marriage, each of a substantial fortune and leaving all to the widow . . . you see . . . ?"

"Of course." Madame Chalon went to the window, let her soft profile, the grand line of her bosom be silhouetted against the blue water. "Would you care for a full confession, Inspector Miron?" She was very much woman, provocative woman, and her tone, just short of caressing, warned Miron to keep a grip on himself.

"If you would care to make one, Madame Chalon," he said, as casually as he could. A dangerous woman. A consumedly dangerous woman.

"Then I shall oblige." Madame Chalon was not smiling. Through the open window a vagrant whiff of air brought him the scent of her. Or was it the scent of the garden? Caution kept his hand from his notebook. Impossible that she would really talk so easily. And yet . . .

"You know something of the art of food, M. Miron?"

"I am from Paris, you remember?"

"And love, too?"

"As I said, I am from Paris."

"Then—" the bosom swelled with her long breath—"I can tell you that I, Hortense Eugenie Villerois Wesser Chalon, did slowly and deliberately, with full purpose, kill and murder my first husband, M. Wesser, aged 57, and likewise my second, M. Chalon, aged 65."

"For some reason, no doubt." Was this a dream? Or insanity?

"M. Wesser I married through persuasion of family. I was no longer a girl. M. Wesser, I learned within a fortnight, was a pig—a pig of insatiable appetites. A crude man, Inspector; a belcher, a braggart, cheater of the poor, deceiver of the innocent. A gobbler of food, an untidy man of unappetizing habits—in short, with all the revolting faults of advancing age and none of its tenderness or dignity. Also, because of these things, his stomach was no longer strong."

Having gone thoroughly into the matter of M. Wesser in Paris and obtained much the same picture, he nodded. "And M. Chalon?"

"Older—as I was older when I wed him."

With mild irony. "And also with a weak stomach?"

"No doubt. Say, rather a weak will. Perhaps less brutish than Wesser. Perhaps, *au fond*, worse, for he knew too many among the Germans here. Why did they take plains to see that we had the very best, the most unobtainable of foods and wines, when, daily, children fainted in the street? Murderess I may be, Inspector, but also a Frenchwoman. So I decided without remorse that Chalon should die, as Wesser died."

Very quietly, not to disturb the thread. "How, Madame Chalon?"

She turned, her face illumined by a smile. "You are familiar, perhaps with such dishes as *'Dindonneau Forci aux Marrons'*? Or *'Supremes de Volaille à l'Indienne'*? Or *'Tournedos Mascotte'*? Or *'Omelette en Surprise à la Napolitaine'*? Or *'Potage Bagration Gras,'* *'Aubergines à la Turcque,' 'Chaud-Froid de Cailles en Belle Vue,'* or . . . ?"

"Stop, Madame Chalon! I am simultaneously ravenous and smothering in food. Such richness of food! Such . . ."

"You asked my methods, Inspector Miron. I used these dishes and a hundred others. And in each of them, I concealed a bit of . . ." Her voice broke suddenly.

Inspector Miron, by a mighty effort, steadied his hand as he finished his Dubonnet. "You concealed a bit of what, Madame Chalon?"

"You have investigated me. You know who was my father."

"Jean-Marie Villerois, chef superb, matchless disciple of the matchless Escoffier. Once called Escoffier's sole worthy successor."

"Yes. And before I was twenty-two, my father—just before his death—admitted that outside of a certain negligible weakness in the matter of braising, he would not be ashamed to own me as his equal."

"Most interesting. I bow to you." Miron's nerves tightened at this handsome woman's faculty for irrelevancy. "But you said you concealed in each of these incomparable dishes a bit of . . . ?"

Madame Chalon turned her back to him. Fine shoulders, he noted; a waist not to be ignored; hips that delighted. She addressed the sea: "A bit of my art, and no more. That and no more, Inspector. The art of Escoffier, or Villerois. What man like Wesser or Chalon could resist? Three, four times a day I fed them rich food of the richest; varied irresistibly. I forced them to gorge to bursting, sleep, gorge again; and drink too much wine that they might gorge still more. How could they, at their ages, live—even as long as they did?"

A silence like the ticking of a far-off clock. "And love, Madame Chalon? Forgive me, but it was you who mentioned it."

"Rich food breeds love—or the semblance of it. What they called love, Inspector. They had me. Nor did I discourage them having also some little friends. And so they died—M. Wesser, aged 57, M. Chalon, aged 65. That is all."

Another silence, one that hummed. Inspector Miron stood up, so abruptly that she started, whirled. She was paler.

"You will come with me to Nice this evening, Madame Chalon."

"To the police station, Inspector Miron?"

"To the Casino, Madame Chalon. For champagne and music. We shall talk some more."

"But Inspector Miron . . . !"

"Listen to me, Madame. I am a bachelor. Of forty-four. Not too bad to look at, I have been told. I have a sum put away. I am not a great catch, but still, not one to be despised." He looked into her eyes. "I wish to die."

He straightened his shoulders, set his figure at its best as Madame Chalon's eloquent eyes roamed over him in the frankest of frank appraisals.

"The diets," said Madame Chalon finally and thoughtfully, "if used in moderation, are not necessarily fatal. Would you care to kiss my hand, Inspector Miron."

NUNC DIMITTIS

BY ROALD DAHL

❡ IT IS NEARLY MIDNIGHT, and I can see that if I don't make a start with writing this story now, I never shall. All evening I have been sitting here trying to force myself to begin, but the more I have thought about it, the more appalled and ashamed and distressed I have become by the whole thing.

My idea—and I believe it was a good one—was to try, by a process of confession and analysis, to discover a reason or at any rate some justification for my outrageous behavior toward Janet de Pelagia. I wanted, essentially, to address myself to an imaginary and sympathetic listener, a kind of mythical *you*, someone gentle and understanding to whom I might tell unashamedly every detail of this unfortunate episode. I can only hope that I am not too upset to make a go of it.

If I am to be quite honest with myself, I suppose I shall have to admit that what is disturbing me most is not so much the sense of my own shame, or even the hurt that I have inflicted upon poor Janet; it is the knowledge that I have made a monstrous fool of myself and that all my friends—if I can still call them that—all those warm and lovable people who used to come so often to my house, must now be regarding me as nothing but a vicious, vengeful old man. Yes, that surely hurts. When I say to you that my friends were my whole life— everything, absolutely everything in it—then perhaps you will begin to understand.

Originally published under the title of "The Devious Bachelor" in *Collier's*. Reprinted from *Someone Like You* by Roald Dahl, by permission of Alfred A. Knopf, Inc. Copyright 1953 by Roald Dahl.

Will you? I doubt it—unless I digress for a minute to tell you roughly the sort of person I am.

Well—let me see. Now that I come to think of it, I suppose I am, after all, a type; a rare one, mark you, but nevertheless a quite definite type—the wealthy, leisurely, middle-aged man of culture, adored (I choose the word carefully) by his many friends for his charm, his money, his air of scholarship, his generosity and, I sincerely hope, for himself also. You will find him (this type) only in the big capitals, London, Paris, New York; of that I am certain. The money he has was earned by his dead father whose memory he is inclined to despise. This is not his fault, for there is something in his make-up that compels him secretly to look down upon all people who never had the wit to learn the difference between Rockingham and Spode, Waterford and Venetian, Sheraton and Chippendale, Monet and Manet, or even Pommard and Montrachet.

He is, therefore, a connoisseur, possessing above all things an exquisite taste. His Constables, Boningtons, Lautrecs, Redons, Veuillards, Mathew Smiths are as fine as anything in the Tate; and because they are so fabulous and beautiful, they create an atmosphere of suspense around him in the home, something tantalizing, breathtaking, faintly frightening—frightening to think that he has the power and the right, if he feels inclined, to slash, tear, plunge his fist right through a superb Dedham Vale, a Mont Saint-Victoire, an Arles corn field, a Tahiti maiden, a portrait of Madame Cézanne. And from the walls on which these wonders hang there issues a little golden glow of splendor, a subtle emanation of grandeur in which he lives and moves and entertains with a sly nonchalance that is not entirely unpracticed.

He is invariably a bachelor, yet he never appears to get entangled with the women who surround him, who love him so dearly. It it just possible—and this you may or may not have noticed—that there is a frustration, a discontent, a regret somewhere inside him. Even a slight aberration.

I don't think I need say any more. I have been very frank. You should know me well enough by now to judge me fairly—and dare I hope it?—to sympathize with me when you hear my story. You may even decide that much of the blame for what has happened should be placed, not upon me, but upon a lady called Gladys Ponsonby. After all, she was the one who started it. Had I not escorted Gladys Ponsonby back to her house that night nearly six months ago, and had she not spoken so freely to me about certain people, certain things, then this tragic business could never have taken place.

It was last December, if I remember rightly, and I had been dining with the Ashendens in that lovely house of theirs that overlooks the southern fringe of Regents Park. There were a fair number of people there, but Gladys Ponsonby was the only one beside myself who had come alone. So when it was time for us to leave, I naturally offered to see her safely back to her house. She accepted and we left together in my car; but unfortunately, when we arrived at her place she insisted that I come in and have "one for the road," as she put it. I didn't wish to seem stuffy, so I told the chauffeur to wait and followed her in.

Gladys Ponsonby is an unusually short woman, certainly not more than four feet nine or ten, maybe even less than that—one of those tiny persons who gives me, when I am beside her, the comical, rather wobbly feeling that I am standing on a chair. She is a widow, a few years younger than I—maybe fifty-three or four, and it is possible that thirty years ago she was quite a fetching little thing. But now the face is loose and puckered with nothing distinctive about it whatsoever. The individual features, the eyes, the nose, the mouth, the chin, are buried in the folds of fat around the puckered little face and one does not notice them. Except perhaps the mouth, which reminds me—I cannot help it—of a salmon.

In the living room, as she gave me my brandy, I noticed that her hand was a trifle unsteady. The lady is tired, I told myself, so I mustn't stay long. We sat down together on the sofa and for a while discussed the Ashendens' party and the people who were there. Finally I got up to go.

"Sit down, Lionel," she said. "Have another brandy."

"No, really, I must go."

"Sit down and don't be so stuffy. *I'm* having another one, and the least you can do is keep me company while I drink it."

I watched her as she walked over to the sideboard, this tiny woman, faintly swaying, holding her glass out in front of her with both hands as though it were an offering; and the sight of her walking like that, so incredibly short and squat and stiff, suddenly gave me the ludicrous notion that she had no legs at all above the knees.

"Lionel, what are you chuckling about?" She half turned to look at me as she poured the drink, and some of it slopped over the side of the glass.

"Nothing, my dear. Nothing at all."

"Well, stop it, and tell me what you think of my new portrait." She indicated a large canvas hanging over the fireplace that I had been trying to avoid with my eye ever since I entered the room. It was a hideous thing, painted, as I well knew, by a man who was now all the rage in London, a very mediocre painter called John Royden. It was a full length portrait of Gladys Lady Ponsonby, painted with a certain technical cunning that made her out to be a tall and quite alluring creature.

"Charming," I said.

"Isn't it, though! I'm so glad you like it."

"Quite charming."

"I think John Royden is a genius. Don't you think he's a genius, Lionel?"

"Well—that might be going a bit far."

"You mean it's a little early to say for sure?"

"Exactly."

"But listen, Lionel—and I think this will surprise you. John Royden is so sought after now that he won't even *consider* painting anyone for less than a thousand guineas!"

"Really?"

"Oh yes! And everyone's queuing up, simply *queuing up* to get themselves done."

"Most interesting."

"Now take your Mr. Cézanne or whatever his name is. I'll bet *he* never got that sort of money in *his* lifetime."

"Never."

"And you say *he* was a genius?"

"Sort of—yes."

"Then so is Royden," she said, settling herself again on the sofa. "The money proves it."

She sat silent for a while, sipping her brandy, and I couldn't help noticing how the unsteadiness of her hand was causing the rim of the glass to jog against her lower lip. She knew I was watching her, and without turning her head she swiveled her eyes and glanced at me cautiously out of the corners of them. "A penny for your thoughts?"

Now, if there is one phrase in the world I cannot abide, it is this. It gives me an actual physical pain in the chest and I begin to cough.

"Come on, Lionel. A penny for them."

I shook my head, quite unable to answer. She turned away abruptly and placed the brandy glass on a small table to her left; and the manner in which she did this seemed to suggest—I don't know why—that she felt rebuffed and was now clearing the decks for action. I waited, rather uncomfortable in the silence that followed, and because I had no conversation left in me, I made a great play about smoking my cigar, studying the ash intently and blowing the smoke up slowly toward the ceiling. But she made no move. There was beginning to be something about this lady I did not much like, a mischievous, brooding air that made me want to get up quickly and go away. When she looked around again, she was smiling at me slyly with those little buried eyes of hers, but the mouth—oh, just like a salmon's—was absolutely rigid.

"Lionel, I think I'll tell you a secret."

"Really, Gladys, I simply must get home."

"Don't be frightened, Lionel. I won't embarrass you. You look so frightened all of a sudden."

"I'm not very good at secrets."

"I've been thinking," she said, "you're such a great expert on pictures, this ought to interest you." She sat quite still except for her fingers which were moving all the time. She kept them perpetually twisting and twisting around each other, and they were like a bunch of small white snakes wriggling in her lap.

"Don't you want to hear my secret, Lionel?"

"It isn't that, you know. It's just that it's so awfully late . . ."

"This is probably the best kept secret in London. A woman's secret. I suppose it's known to about—let me see—about thirty or forty women altogether. And not a single man. Except him, of course —John Royden."

I didn't wish to encourage her, so I said nothing.

"But first of all, promise—*promise* you won't tell a soul?"

"Dear me!"

"You *promise*, Lionel?"

"Yes, Gladys, all right, I promise."

"Good! Now listen." She reached for the brandy glass and settled back comfortably in the far corner of the sofa. "I suppose you know John Royden paints only women?"

"I didn't."

"And they're always full-length portraits, either standing or sitting—like mine there. Now take a good look at it, Lionel. Do you see how beautifully the dress is painted?"

"Well . . ."

"Go over and look carefully, please."

I got up reluctantly and went over and examined the painting. To my surprise I noticed that the paint of the dress was laid on so heavily it was actually raised out from the rest of the picture. It was a trick, quite effective in its way, but neither difficult to do nor entirely original.

"You see?" she said. "It's thick, isn't it, where the dress is?"

"Yes."

"But there's a bit more to it than that, you know, Lionel. I think the best way is to describe what happened the very first time I went along for a sitting."

Oh, what a bore this woman is, I thought, and how can I get away?

"That was about a year ago, and I remember how excited I was to be going in to the studio of the great painter. I dressed myself up in a wonderful new thing I'd just got from Norman Hartnell, and a special little red hat, and off I went. Mr. Royden met me at the door, and of course I was fascinated by him at once. He had a small pointed beard and thrilling blue eyes, and he wore a black velvet jacket. The studio was huge, with red velvet sofas and velvet chairs—he loves velvet—and velvet curtains and even a velvet carpet on the floor. He sat me down, gave me a drink and came straight to the point. He told me about how he painted quite differently from other artists. In his opinion, he said, there was only one method of attaining perfection when painting a woman's body and I mustn't be shocked when I heard what it was.

" 'I don't think I'll be shocked, Mr. Royden,' I told him.

" 'I'm sure you won't either,' he said. He had the most marvelous white teeth and they sort of shone through his beard when he smiled. 'You see, it's like this,' he went on. 'You examine any painting you like of a woman—I don't care who it's by—and you'll see that although the dress may be well painted, there is an effect of artificiality, of flatness about the whole thing, as though the dress were draped over a log of wood. And you know why?'

" 'No, Mr. Royden, I don't.'

" 'Because the painters themselves didn't really know what was underneath! ' "

Gladys Ponsonby paused to take a few more sips of brandy. "Don't look so startled, Lionel," she said to me. "There's nothing wrong about this. Keep quiet and let me finish. So then Mr. Royden said, 'That's why I insist on painting my subjects first of all in the nude.'

" 'Good Heavens, Mr. Royden!' I exclaimed.

" 'If you object to that, I don't mind making a slight concession, Lady Ponsonby,' he said. 'But I prefer it the other way.'

" 'Really, Mr. Royden, I don't know.'

" 'And when I've done you like that,' he went on, 'we'll have to wait a few weeks for the paint to dry. Then you come back and I paint on your underclothing. And when that's dry, I paint on the dress. You see, it's quite simple.' "

"The man's an absolute bounder!" I cried.

"No, Lionel, no! You're quite wrong. If only you could have heard him, so charming about it all, so genuine and sincere. Anyone could see he really *felt* what he was saying."

"I tell you, Gladys, the man's a bounder!"

"Don't be so silly, Lionel. And anyway, let me finish. The first thing I told him was that my husband (who was alive then) would never agree.

" 'Your husband need never know,' he answered. 'Why trouble him. No one knows my secret except the women I've painted.'

"And when I protested a bit more, I remember he said, 'My dear Lady Ponsonby, there's nothing immoral about this. Art is only immoral when practiced by amateurs. It's the same with medicine. You wouldn't refuse to undress before your doctor, would you?' "I told him I would if I'd gone to him for earache. That made him laugh. But he kept on at me about it and I must say he was very convincing, so after a while I gave in and that was that. So now Lionel, my sweet, you know the secret." She got up and went over to fetch herself some more brandy.

"Gladys, is this really true?"

"Of course it's true."

"You mean to say that's the way he paints all his subjects?"

"Yes. And the joke is the husbands never know anything about it. All they see is a nice fully clothed portrait of their wives. Of course, there's nothing wrong with being painted in the nude; artists do it all the time. But our silly husbands have a way of objecting to that sort of thing."

"By gad, the fellow's got a nerve!"

"I think he's a genius."

"I'll bet he got the idea from Goya."

"Nonsense, Lionel."

"Of course he did. But listen, Gladys. I want you to tell me something. Did you by any chance know about this . . . this peculiar technique of Royden's before you went to him?"

When I asked the question she was in the act of pouring the brandy, and she hesitated and turned her head to look at me, a little silky smile moving the corners of her mouth. "Damn you, Lionel," she said. "You're far too clever. You never let me get away with a single thing."

"So you knew?"

"Of course. Hermione Girdlestone told me."

"Exactly as I thought!"

"There's still nothing wrong."

"Nothing," I said. "Absolutely nothing." I could see it all quite clearly now. This Royden was indeed a bounder, practicing as neat a piece of psychological trickery as ever I'd seen. The man knew only too well that there was a whole set of a wealthy indolent women in the city who got up at noon and spent the rest of the day trying to relieve their boredom with bridge and canasta and shopping until the cocktail hour came along. All they craved was a little excitement, something out of the ordinary, and the more expensive the better. Why—the news of an entertainment like this would spread through their ranks like smallpox. I could just see the great plump Hermione Girdlestone leaning over the canasta table and telling them about it. . . . "But my dear, it's *simp*-ly fascinating . . . I can't *tell* you how intriguing it is . . . *much* more fun than going to your doctor . . ."

"You won't tell anyone, Lionel, will you? You promised."

"No, of course not. But now I must go, Gladys, I really must."

"Don't be so silly. I'm just beginning to enjoy myself. Stay till I've finished this drink anyway."

I sat patiently on the sofa while she went on with her interminable brandy sipping. The little buried eyes still watching me out of their corners in that mischievous, canny way, and I had a strong feeling that the woman was now hatching out some further unpleasantness or scandal. There was the look of serpents in those eyes and a queer curl around the mouth; and in the air—although maybe I only imagined it—the faint smell of danger.

Then suddenly, so suddenly that I jumped, she said, "Lionel, what's this I hear about you and Janet de Pelagia?"

"Now, Gladys, please . . ."

"Lionel, you're blushing!"

"Nonsense."

"Don't tell me the old bachelor has really taken a tumble at last?"

"Gladys, this is too absurd." I began making movements to go, but she put a hand on my knee and stopped me.

"Don't you know by now, Lionel, that there *are* no secrets?"

"Janet is a fine girl."

"You can hardly call her a *girl*." Gladys Ponsonby paused, staring down into the large brandy glass that she held cupped in both hands. "But of course, I agree with you, Lionel, she's a wonderful person in every way. Except," and now she spoke very slowly, "except that she *does* say some rather peculiar things occasionally."

"What sort of things?"

"Just things, you know—things about people. About you."

"What did she say about me?"

"Nothing at all, Lionel. It wouldn't interest you."

"What did she say about me?"

"It's not even worth repeating, honestly it isn't. It's only that it struck me as being rather odd at the time."

"Gladys—what did she say?" While I waited for her to answer, I could feel the sweat breaking out all over my body.

"Well now, let me see. Of course, she was only joking or I couldn't dream of telling you, but I suppose she *did* say how it was all a wee bit of a bore."

"What was?"

"Sort of going out to dinner with you nearly every night—that kind of thing."

"She said it was a bore?"

"Yes." Gladys Ponsonby drained the brandy glass with one last big gulp, and sat up straight. "If you really want to know, she said it was a crashing bore. And then . . ."

"What did she say then?"

"Now look, Lionel—there's no need to get excited. I'm only telling you this for your own good."

"Then please hurry up and tell it."

"It's just that I happened to be playing canasta with Janet this afternoon and I asked her if she was free to dine with me tomorrow. She said no, she wasn't."

"Go on."

"Well—actually what she said was, 'I'm dining with that crashing old bore Lionel Lampson.' "

"Janet said that?"

"Yes, Lionel dear."

"What else?"

"Now, that's enough. I don't think I should tell the rest."

"Finish it, please!"

"Why, Lionel, don't keep shouting at me like that. Of course I'll tell you if you insist. As a matter of fact, I wouldn't consider myself a true friend if I didn't. Don't you think it's the sign of true friendship when two people like us . . ."

"Gladys! *Please* hurry."

"Good Heavens, you must give me time to *think*. Let me see now—so far as I can remember, what she *actually* said was this—" and Gladys Ponsonby, sitting upright on the sofa with her feet not quite touching the floor, her eyes away from me now, looking at the wall, began cleverly to mimic the deep tone of that voice I knew so well—" 'Such a bore, my dear, because with Lionel one can *always* tell exactly what will happen *right* from beginning to end. For dinner we'll go to the Savoy Grill—it's *always* the Savoy Grill—and for two hours I'll have to listen to the pompous old . . . I mean I'll have to listen to him droning away about pictures and porcelain—*always* pictures and porcelain. Then in the taxi going home he'll reach out for my hand, and he'll lean closer, and I'll get a whiff of stale cigar smoke and brandy, and he'll start burbling about how he wished—oh how he wished he was just twenty years younger. And I will say "Could you open a window, do you mind?" And when we arrive at my house I'll tell him to keep the taxi, but he'll pretend he hasn't heard and pay it off quickly. And then at the front door, while I fish for my key, he'll stand beside me with a sort of silly spaniel look in his eyes, and I'll slowly put the key in the lock, and slowly turn it, and then— very quickly, before he has time to move—I'll say good night and skip inside and shut the door behind me . . .' Why Lionel! What's the matter, dear? You look positively ill. . . ."

At that point, mercifully, I must have swooned clear away. I can remember practically nothing of the rest of that terrible night except for a vague and disturbing suspicion that when I regained consciousness I broke down completely and permitted Gladys Ponsonby to comfort me in a variety of different ways. Later, I believe I walked out of the house and was driven home, but I remained more or less unconscious of everything around me until I woke up in my bed the next morning.

I awoke feeling weak and shaken. I lay still with my eyes closed, trying to piece together the events of the night before—Gladys Ponsonby's living room, Gladys on the sofa sipping brandy, the little puckered face, the mouth that was like a salmon's mouth, the things she had said. . . . What was it she had said. Ah yes. About me. My

God, yes! About Janet and me! Those outrageous, unbelievable remarks! Could Janet really have made them? Could she?

I can remember with what terrifying swiftness my hatred of Janet de Pelagia now began to grow. It all happened in a few minutes —a sudden, violent welling up of a hatred that filled me till I thought I was going to burst. I tried to dismiss it but it was on me like a fever, and in no time at all I was hunting around, as would some filthy gangster, for a method of revenge.

A curious way to behave, you may say, for a man such as I; to which I would answer—no, not really, if you consider the circumstances. To my mind, this was the sort of thing that could drive a man to murder. As a matter of fact, had it not been for a small sadistic streak that caused me to seek a more subtle and painful punishment for my victim, I might well have become a murderer myself. But mere killing, I decided, was too good for this woman, and far too crude for my own taste. So I began looking for a superior alternative.

I am not normally a scheming person; I consider it an odious business and have had no practice in it whatsoever. But fury and hate can concentrate a man's mind to an astonishing degree, and in no time at all a plot was forming and unfolding in my head—a plot so superior and exciting that I began to be quite carried away at the idea of it. By the time I had filled in the details and overcome one or two minor objections, my brooding vengeful mood had changed to one of extreme elation, and I remember how I started bouncing up and down absurdly on my bed and clapping my hands. The next thing I knew I had the telephone directory on my lap and was searching eagerly for a name. I found it, picked up the phone, and dialed the number.

"Hello," I said. "Mr. Royden? Mr. John Royden?"

"Speaking."

Well—it wasn't difficult to persuade the man to call around and see me for a moment. I had never met him, but of course he knew my name, both as an important collector of paintings and as a person of some consequence in society. I was a big fish for him to catch.

"Let me see now, Mr. Lampson," he said, "I think I ought to be free in about a couple of hours. Will that be all right?"

I told him it would be fine, gave my address, and rang off.

I jumped out of bed. It was really remarkable how exhilarated I felt all of a sudden. One moment I had been in agony of despair, contemplating murder and suicide and I don't know what; the next, I was whistling an aria from Puccini in my bath. Every now and again I caught myself rubbing my hands together in a devilish fashion, and once, during my exercises, when I overbalanced doing a double-knee-bend, I sat on the floor and giggled like a schoolboy.

At the appointed time Mr. John Royden was shown in to my library and I got up to meet him. He was a small neat man with a slightly ginger goatee beard. He wore a black velvet jacket, a rust-brown tie, a red pullover, and black suède shoes. I shook his small neat hand.

"Good of you to come along so quickly, Mr. Royden."

"Not at all, sir." The man's lips—like the lips of nearly all bearded men—looked wet and naked, a trifle indecent, shining pink in among all that hair. After telling him again how much I admired his work, I got straight down to business.

"Mr. Royden," I said. "I have a rather unusual request to make of you, something quite personal in its way."

"Yes, Mr. Lampson?" He was sitting in the chair opposite me and he cocked his head over to one side, quick and perky like a bird.

"Of course, I know I can trust you to be discreet about anything I say."

"Absolutely, Mr. Lampson."

"All right. Now my proposition is this: there is a certain lady in town here whose portrait I would like you to paint. I very much want to possess a fine painting of her. But there are certain complications. For example, I have my own reasons for not wishing her to know that it is I who am commissioning the portrait."

"You mean . . ."

"Exactly, Mr. Royden. That is exactly what I mean. As a man of the world I'm sure you will understand."

He smiled, a crooked little smile that only just came through his beard, and he nodded his head knowingly up and down.

"Is it not possible," I said, "that a man might be—how shall I put it?—extremely fond of a lady and at the same time have his own good reasons for not wishing her to know about it yet?"

"More than possible, Mr. Lampson."

"Sometimes a man has to stalk his quarry with great caution, waiting patiently for the right moment to reveal himself."

"Precisely, Mr. Lampson."

"There are better ways of catching a bird than by chasing it through the woods."

"Yes indeed, Mr. Lampson."

"Putting salt on its tail, for instance."

"Ha-ha!"

"All right, Mr. Royden. I think you understand. Now—do you happen by any chance to know a lady called Janet de Pelagia?"

"Janet de Pelagia? Let me see now—yes. At least, what I mean is I've heard of her. I couldn't exactly say I know her."

"That's a pity. It makes it a little more difficult. Do you think you could get to meet her—perhaps at a cocktail party or something like that?"

"Shouldn't be too tricky, Mr. Lampson."

"Good, because what I suggest is this: that you go up to her and tell her she's the sort of model you've been searching for for years—just the right face, the right figure, the right colored eyes. You know the sort of thing. Then ask her if she'd mind sitting for you free of charge. Say you'd like to do a picture of her for next year's Academy. I feel sure she'd be delighted to help you, and honored too, if I may say so. Then you will paint her and exhibit the picture and deliver it to me after the show is over. No one but you need know that I have bought it."

The small round eyes of Mr. John Royden were watching me shrewdly, I thought, and the head was again cocked over to one side. He was sitting on the edge of his chair, and in this position, with the pullover making a flash of red down his front, he reminded me of a robin on a twig listening for a suspicious noise.

"There's really nothing wrong about it at all," I said. "Just call it—if you like—a harmless little conspiracy being perpetrated by a . . . well . . . by a rather romantic old man."

"I know, Mr. Lampson, I know . . ." He still seemed to be hesitating, so I said quickly, "I'll be glad to pay you double your usual fee."

That did it. The man actually licked his lips. "Well, Mr. Lampson, I must say this sort of thing's not really in my line, you know. But all the same, it'd be a very heartless man who refused such a—shall I say such a romantic assignment?"

"I should like a full length portrait, Mr. Royden, please. A large canvas—let me see—about twice the size of that Manet on the wall there."

"About sixty by thirty-six?"

"Yes. And I should like her to be standing. That, to my mind, is her most graceful attitude."

"I quite understand, Mr. Lampson. And it'll be a pleasure to paint such a lovely lady."

I expect it will, I told myself. The way you go about it, my boy, I'm quite sure it will. But I said, "All right, Mr. Royden, then I'll leave it all to you. And don't forget, please—this is a little secret between ourselves."

When he had gone I forced myself to sit still and take twenty-five deep breaths. Nothing else would have restrained me from jumping up and shouting for joy like an idiot. I have never in my life felt so exhilarated. My plan was working! The most difficult part was already accomplished. There would be a wait now, a long wait. The way this man painted, it would take him several months to finish the picture. Well, I would just have to be patient, that's all.

I now decided on the spur of the moment that it would be best if I were to go abroad in the interim; and the very next morning, after sending a message to Janet (with whom, you will remember, I was due to dine that night) telling her I had been called away, I left for Italy.

There, as always, I had a delightful time, marred only by a constant nervous excitement caused by the thought of returning to the scene of action.

I eventually arrived back, four months later, in July, on the day after the opening of the Royal Academy, and I found to my relief that everything had gone according to plan during my absence. The picture of Janet de Pelagia had been painted and hung in the Exhibition, and it was already the subject of much favorable comment both by the critics and the public. I myself refrained from going to see it but Royden told me on the telephone that there had been several inquiries by persons who wished to buy it, all of whom had been informed that it was not for sale. When the show was over, Royden delivered the picture to my house and received his money.

I immediately had it carried up to my workroom, and with mounting excitement I began to examine it closely. The man had painted her standing up in a black evening dress and there was a red plush sofa in the background. Her left hand was resting on the back of a heavy chair, also of red plush, and there was a huge crystal chandelier hanging from the ceiling.

My God, I thought, what a hideous thing! The portrait itself wasn't so bad. He had caught the woman's expression—the forward drop of the head, the wide blue eyes, the large, ugly-beautiful mouth with the trace of a smile in one corner. He had flattered her, of course. There wasn't a wrinkle on her face or the slightest suggestion of fat under her chin. I bent forward to examine the painting of the dress. Yes—here the paint was thicker, much thicker. At this point, unable to wait another moment, I threw off my coat and prepared to go to work.

I should mention here that I am myself an expert cleaner and restorer of paintings. The cleaning, particularly, is a comparatively simple process provided one has patience and a gentle touch, and those professionals who make such a secret of their trade and charge such shocking prices get no business from me. Where my own pictures are concerned I always do the job myself.

I poured out the turpentine and added a few drops of alcohol. I dipped a small wad of cotton-wool in the mixture, squeezed it out, and then gently, so very gently, with a circular motion, I began to work upon the black paint of the dress. I could only hope that Royden had allowed each layer to dry thoroughly before applying the next, otherwise the two would merge and the process I had in mind would be impossible. Soon I would know. I was working on one square inch of black dress somewhere around the lady's stomach and I took plenty of time, cautiously testing and teasing the paint, adding a drop or two more of alcohol to my mixture, testing again, adding another drop until finally it was just strong enough to loosen the pigment.

For perhaps a whole hour I worked away on this little square of black, proceeding more and more gently as I came closer to the layer below. Then, a tiny pink spot appeared, and gradually it spread and spread until the whole of my square inch was a clear shining patch of pink. Quickly I neutralized with pure turps.

So far so good. I knew now that the black paint could be removed without disturbing what was underneath. So long as I was patient and industrious I would easily be able to take it all off. Also, I had discovered the right mixture to use and just how hard I could safely rub, so things should go much quicker now.

I must say it was rather an amusing business. I worked first from the middle of her body downward, and as the lower half of her dress came away bit by bit onto my little wads of cotton, a queer pink undergarment began to reveal itself. I didn't for the life of me know what the thing was called, but it was a formidable apparatus constructed of what appeared to be a strong thick elastic material, and its purpose was apparently to contain and to compress the woman's bulging figure into a neat streamlined shape, giving a quite false impression of slimness. As I traveled lower and lower down, I came upon a striking arrangement of suspenders, also pink, which were attached to this elastic armor and hung downward four or five inches to grip the tops of the stockings.

Quite fantastic the whole thing seemed to me as I stepped back a pace to survey it. It gave me a strong sense of having somehow been cheated; for had I not, during all these past months, been admiring the sylphlike figure of this lady? She was a faker. No question about it. But do many other females practice this sort of deception, I wondered. I knew, of course, that in the days of stays and corsets it was usual for ladies to strap themselves up; yet for some reason I was under the impression that nowadays all they had to do was diet.

When the whole of the lower half of the dress had come away, I immediately turned my attention to the upper portion, working my way slowly upward from the lady's middle. Here, around the midriff, there was an area of naked flesh; then higher up upon the bosom itself and actually containing it, I came upon a contrivance made of some heavy black material edged with frilly lace. This, I knew very well, was the brassière—another formidable appliance upheld by an arrangement of black straps as skillfully and scientifically rigged as the supporting cables of a suspension bridge.

Dear me, I thought. One lives and learns.

But now at last the job was finished, and I stepped back again to take a final look at the picture. It was truly an astonishing sight! This woman, Janet de Pelagia, almost life size, standing there in her underwear—in a sort of drawing room, I suppose it was—with a great chandelier above her head and a red plush chair by her side; and she herself—this was the most disturbing part of all—looking so completely unconcerned, with the wide placid blue eyes, the faintly smiling, ugly-beautiful mouth. Also I noticed, with something of a shock, that she was exceedingly bow-legged, like a jockey. I tell you frankly, the whole thing embarrassed me. I felt as though I had no right to be in the room, certainly no right to stare. So after a while I went out and shut the door behind me. It seemed like the only decent thing to do.

Now, for the next and final step! And do not imagine simply because I have not mentioned it lately that my thirst for revenge had in any way diminished during the last few months. On the contrary, it had if anything increased; and with the last act about to be performed, I can tell you I found it hard to contain myself. That night, for example, I didn't even go to bed.

You see, I couldn't wait to get the invitations out. I sat up all night preparing them and addressing the envelopes. There were twenty-two of them in all, and I wanted each to be a personal note. "I'm having a little dinner on Friday night, the twenty-second, at eight. I do hope you can come along . . . I'm so looking forward to seeing you again. . . ."

The first, the most carefully phrased, was to Janet de Pelagia. In it I regretted not having seen her for so long . . . I had been abroad . . . It was time we got together again, etc., etc. The next was to Gladys Ponsonby. Then one to Hermione Lady Girdlestone, another to Princess Bicheno, Mrs. Cudbird, Sir Hubert Kaul, Mrs. Galbally, Peter Euan-Thomas, James Pisker, Sir Eustace Piegrome, Peter van Santen, Elizabeth Moynihan, Lord Mulherrin, Bertram Sturt, Philip Cornelius, Jack Hill, Lady Akeman, Mrs. Icely, Humphrey

King-Howard, Johnny O'Coffey, Mrs. Uvary, and the Dowager Countess of Waxworth.

It was a carefully selected list, containing as it did the most distinguished men, the most brilliant and influential women in the top crust of our society.

I was well aware that a dinner at my house was regarded as quite an occasion; everybody liked to come. And now, as I watched the point of my pen moving swiftly over the paper, I could almost see the ladies in their pleasure picking up their bedside telephones the morning the invitations arrived, shrill voices calling to shriller voices over the wires . . . "Lionel's giving a party . . . he's asked you too? My dear, how nice . . . his food is always *so* good . . . and *such* a lovely man, isn't he though, yes. . . ."

Is that really what they would say? It suddenly occurred to me that it might not be like that at all. More like this perhaps: "I agree, my dear, yes, not a bad old man . . . but a bit of a bore, don't you think? . . . What did you say? . . . dull? But desperately, my dear. You've hit the nail right on the head . . . did you ever hear what Janet de Pelagia once said about him? . . . Ah yes, I thought you'd heard that one . . . screamingly funny, don't you think? . . . poor Janet . . . how she stood it as long as she did I don't know. . . ."

Anyway, I got the invitations off, and within a couple of days everybody with the exception of Mrs. Cudbird and Sir Hubert Kaul, who were away, had accepted with pleasure.

At eight-thirty on the evening of the twenty-second, my large drawing room was filled with people. They stood about the room admiring the pictures, drinking their martinis, talking with loud voices. The women smelled strongly of scent, the men were pink-faced and carefully buttoned up in their dinner jackets. Janet de Pelagia was wearing the same black dress she had used for the portrait, and every time I caught sight of her, a kind of huge bubble-vision—as in those absurd cartoons—would float up above my head, and in it I would see Janet in her underclothes, the black brassière, the pink elastic belt, the suspenders, the jockey's legs.

I moved from group to group, chatting amiably with them all, listening to their talk. Behind me I could hear Mrs. Galbally telling Sir Eustace Piegrome and James Pisker how the man at the next table to hers at Claridges the night before had had red lipstick on his white mustache. "Simply *plastered* with it," she kept saying, "and the old boy was ninety if he was a day. . . ." On the other side, Lady Girdlestone was telling somebody where one could get truffles cooked in brandy, and I could see Mrs. Icely whispering something to Lord Mulherrin while his Lordship kept shaking his head slowly from side to side like an old and dispirited metronome.

Dinner was announced, and we all moved out.

"My goodness!" they cried as they entered the dining room. "How dark and sinister!"

"I can hardly see a thing!"

"What divine little candles!"

"But Lionel, how romantic!"

There were six very thin candles set about two feet apart from each other down the center of the long table. Their small flames made a little glow of light around the table itself, but left the rest of the room in darkness. It was an amusing arrangement and apart from the fact that it suited my purpose well, it made a pleasant change. The guests soon settled themselves in their right places and the meal began.

They all seemed to enjoy the candlelight and things went famously, though for some reason the darkness caused them to speak much louder than usual. Janet de Pelagia's voice struck me as being particularly strident. She was sitting next to Lord Mulherrin, and I could hear her telling him about the boring time she had had at Cap Ferrat the week before. "Nothing but Frenchmen," she kept saying. "Nothing but Frenchmen in the whole place. . . ."

For my part, I was watching the candles. They were so thin that I knew it would not be long before they burned down to their bases. Also I was mighty nervous—I will admit that—but at the same time intensely exhilarated, almost to the point of drunkenness. Every time I heard Janet's voice or caught sight of her face shadowed in the light of the candles, a little ball of excitement exploded inside me and I felt the fire of it running under my skin.

They were eating their strawberries when at last I decided the time had come. I took a deep breath and in a loud voice I said, "I'm afraid we'll have to have the lights on now. The candles are nearly finished. Mary," I called, "Oh Mary, switch on the lights will you please."

There was a moment of silence after my announcement. I heard the maid walking over to the door, then the gentle click of the switch and the room was flooded with a blaze of light. They all screwed up their eyes, opened them again, gazed about them.

At that point I got up from my chair and slid quietly from the room, but as I went I saw a sight that I shall never forget as long as I live. It was Janet, with both hands in midair, stopped, frozen rigid, caught in the act of gesticulating toward someone across the table. Her mouth had dropped open two inches and she wore the surprised, not-quite-understanding look of a person who precisely one second before has been shot dead right through the heart.

In the hall outside I paused and listened to the beginning of the uproar, the shrill cries of the ladies and the outraged unbelieving exclamations of the men; and soon there was a great hum of noise with everybody talking or shouting at the same time. Then—and this was the sweetest moment of all—I heard Lord Mulherrin's voice, roaring above the rest, "Here! Someone! Hurry! Give her some water quick!"

Out in the street the chauffeur helped me into my car, and soon we were away from London and bowling merrily along the Great North Road toward this, my other house, which is only ninety-five miles from Town anyway.

The next two days I spent in gloating. I mooned around in a dream of ecstasy, half drowned in my own complacency and filled with a sense of pleasure so great that it constantly gave me pins and needles all along the lower parts of my legs. It wasn't until this morning when Gladys Ponsonby called me on the phone that I suddenly came to my senses and realized I was not a hero at all but an outcast. She informed me—with what I thought was just a trace of relish—that everybody was up in arms, that all of them, all my old and loving friends were saying the most terrible things about me and had sworn never never to speak to me again. Except her, she kept saying. Everybody except her. And didn't I think it would be rather cozy, she asked, if she were to come down and stay with me a few days to cheer me up?

I'm afraid I was too upset by that time even to answer her politely. I put the phone down and went away to weep.

Then at noon today came the final crushing blow. The post arrived, and with it—I can hardly bring myself to write about it, I am so ashamed—came a letter, the sweetest, most tender little note imaginable from none other than Janet de Pelagia herself. She forgave me completely, she wrote, for everything I had done. She knew it was only a joke and I must not listen to the horrid things other people were saying about me. She loved me as she always had and always would to her dying day.

Oh, what a cad, what a brute I felt when I read this! The more so when I found that she had actually sent me by the same post a small present as an added sign of her affection—a half-pound jar of my favorite food of all, fresh caviar.

I can never under any circumstances resist good caviar. It is perhaps my greatest weakness. So although I naturally had no appetite whatsoever for food at dinner time this evening, I must confess I took a few spoonfuls of the stuff in an effort to console myself in my misery. It is even possible that I took a shade too much, because I haven't been feeling any too chipper this last hour or so. Perhaps I ought to go up right away and get myself some bicarbonate of soda. I can easily come back and finish this later, when I'm in better trim.

You know—now I come to think of it, I really do feel rather ill all of a sudden.

THE MOST DANGEROUS GAME

BY RICHARD CONNELL

❡ "OFF THERE to the right—somewhere—is a large island," said Whitney. "It's rather a mystery—"

"What island is it?" Rainsford asked.

"The old charts call it 'Ship-Trap Island,' " Whitney replied. "A suggestive name, isn't it? Sailors have a curious dread of the place. I don't know why. Some superstition—"

"Can't see it," remarked Rainsford, trying to peer through the dank tropical night that was palpable as it pressed its thick warm blackness in upon the yacht.

"You've good eyes," said Whitney, with a laugh, "and I've seen you pick off a moose moving in the brown fall bush at four hundred yards, but even you can't see four miles or so through a moonless Caribbean night."

"Nor four yards," admitted Rainsford. "Ugh! It's like moist velvet."

"It will be light enough in Rio," promised Whitney. "We should make it in a few days. I hope the jaguar guns have come from Purdey's. We should have some good hunting up the Amazon. Great sport, hunting."

"The best sport in the world," agreed Rainsford.

"For the hunter," amended Whitney. "Not for the jaguar."

"Don't talk rot, Whitney," said Rainsford. "You're a big-game hunter, not a philosopher. Who cares how a jaguar feels?"

"Perhaps the jaguar does," observed Whitney.

"Bah! They've no understanding."

"Even so, I rather think they understand one thing at least—fear. The fear of pain and the fear of death."

"Nonsense," laughed Rainsford. "This hot weather is making you soft, Whitney. Be a realist. The world is made up of two classes— the hunters and the hunted. Luckily, you and I are hunters. Do you think we've passed that island yet?"

"I can't tell in the dark. I hope so."

"Why?" asked Rainsford.

"The place has a reputation—a bad one."

"Cannibals?" suggested Rainsford.

"Hardly. Even cannibals wouldn't live in such a God-forsaken place. But it's got into sailor lore, somehow. Didn't you notice that the crew's nerves seem a bit jumpy today?"

"They were a bit strange, now you mention it. Even Captain Nielsen—"

"Yes, even that tough-minded old Swede, who'd go up to the devil himself and ask him for a light. Those fishy blue eyes held a look I never saw there before. All I could get out of him was, 'This place has an evil name among seafaring men, sir.' Then he said to me, very gravely, 'Don't you feel anything?'—as if the air about us was actually poisonous. Now, you mustn't laugh when I tell you this—I did feel something like a sudden chill.

"There was no breeze. The sea was as flat as a plate-glass window. We were drawing near the island then. What I felt was a—a mental chill—a sort of sudden dread."

"Pure imagination," said Rainsford. "One superstitious sailor can taint the whole ship's company with his fear."

"Maybe. But sometimes I think sailors have an extra sense that tells them when they are in danger. Sometimes I think evil is a tangible thing—with wave lengths, just as sound and light have. An evil place can, so to speak, broadcast vibrations of evil. Anyhow, I'm glad we're getting out of this zone. Well, I think I'll turn in now, Rainsford."

"I'm not sleepy," said Rainsford. "I'm going to smoke another pipe up on the after deck."

"Good night, then, Rainsford. See you at breakfast."

"Right. Good night, Whitney."

There was no sound in the night as Rainsford sat there, but the muffled throb of the engine that drove the yacht swiftly through the darkness, and the swish and ripple of the wash of the propeller.

Rainsford, reclining in a steamer chair, indolently puffed on his favorite brier. The sensuous drowsiness of the night was on him. "It's so dark," he thought, "that I could sleep without closing my eyes; the night would be my eyelids—"

An abrupt sound startled him. Off to the right he heard it, and his ears, expert in such matters, could not be mistaken. Again he heard the sound, and again. Somewhere, off in the blackness, someone had fired a gun three times.

Rainsford sprang up and moved quickly to the rail, mystified. He strained his eyes in the direction from which the reports had come, but it was like trying to see through a blanket. He leaped upon the rail and balanced himself there, to get greater elevation; his pipe, striking a rope, was knocked from his mouth. He lunged for it; a short, hoarse cry came from his lips as he realized he had reached too far and had lost his balance. The cry was pinched off short as the blood-warm waters of the Caribbean Sea closed over his head.

He struggled up to the surface and tried to cry out, but the wash from the speeding yacht slapped him in the face and the salt water in his open mouth made him gag and strangle. Desperately he struck out with strong strokes after the receding lights of the yacht, but he stopped before he had swum fifty feet. A certain cool-headedness had come to him; it was not the first time he had been in a tight place. There was a chance that his cries could be heard by someone aboard the yacht, but that chance was slender, and grew more slender as the yacht raced on. He wrestled himself out of his clothes, and shouted with all his power. The lights of the yacht became faint and ever-vanishing fireflies; then they were blotted out entirely by the night.

Rainsford remembered the shots. They had come from the right, and doggedly he swam in that direction, swimming with slow, deliberate strokes, conserving his strength. For a seemingly endless time he fought the sea. He began to count his strokes desperately; he could do possibly a hundred more and then—

Rainsford heard a sound. It came out of the darkness, a high, screaming sound, the sound of an animal in an extremity of anguish and terror.

He did not recognize the animal that made the sound; he did not try to; with fresh vitality he swam toward the sound. He heard it again; then it was cut short by another noise, crisp, staccato.

"Pistol shot," muttered Rainsford, swimming on.

Ten minutes of determined effort brought another sound to his ears—the most welcome he had ever heard—the muttering and growling of the sea breaking on a rocky shore. He was almost on the rocks before he saw them; on a night less calm he would have been shattered against them. With his remaining strength he dragged himself from the swirling waters. Jagged crags appeared to jut up into the opaqueness; he forced himself upward, hand over hand. Gasping, his hands raw, he reached a flat place at the top. Dense jungle came down to the very edge of the cliffs. What perils that tangle of trees and underbrush might hold for him did not concern Rainsford just then. All he knew was that he was safe from his enemy, the sea, and that utter weariness was on him. He flung himself down at the jungle edge and tumbled headlong into the deepest sleep of his life.

When he opened his eyes he knew from the position of the sun that it was late in the afternoon. Sleep had given him new vigor; a sharp hunger was picking at him. He looked about him, almost cheerfully.

"Where there are pistol shots, there are men. Where there are men, there is food," he thought. But what kind of men, he wondered, in so forbidding a place? An unbroken front of snarled and jagged jungle fringed the shore.

He saw no sign of a trail through the closely knit web of weeds and trees; it was easier to go along the shore, and Rainsford floundered along by the water. Not far from where he had landed, he stopped.

Some wounded thing, by the evidence a large animal, had thrashed about in the underbrush; the jungle weeds were crushed down and the moss was lacerated; one patch of weeds was stained crimson. A small, glittering object not far away caught Rainsford's eye and he picked it up. It was an empty cartridge.

"A twenty-two," he remarked. "That's odd. It must have been a fairly large animal, too. The hunter had his nerve to tackle it with a light gun. It's clear that the brute put up a fight. I suppose the first three shots I heard was when the hunter flushed his quarry and wounded it. The last shot was when he trailed it here and finished it."

He examined the ground closely and found what he had hoped to find—the print of hunting boots. They pointed along the cliff in the direction he had been going. Eagerly he hurried along, now slipping on a rotten log or a loose stone, but making headway; night was beginning to settle down on the island.

Bleak darkness was blacking out the sea and jungle when Rainsford sighted the lights. He came upon them as he turned a crook in the coast line, and his first thought was that he had come upon a village, for there were many lights. But as he forged along he saw to his great astonishment that all the lights were in one enormous building—a lofty structure with pointed towers plunging upward into the gloom. His eyes made out the shadowy outlines of a palatial château; it was set on a high bluff, and on three sides of it cliffs dived down to where the sea licked greedy lips in the shadows.

"Mirage," thought Rainsford. But it was no mirage, he found, when he opened the tall spiked iron gate. The stone steps were real enough; the massive door with a leering gargoyle for a knocker was real enough; yet about it all hung an air of unreality.

He lifted the knocker, and it creaked up stiffly, as if it had never before been used. He let it fall, and it startled him with its booming loudness. He thought he heard footsteps within; the door remained closed. Again Rainsford lifted the heavy knocker, and let it fall. The door opened then, opened as suddenly as if it were on a spring, and Rainsford stood blinking in the river of glaring gold light that poured out. The first thing Rainsford's eyes discerned was the largest man Rainsford had ever seen—a gigantic creature, solidly made and black-bearded to the waist. In his hand the man held a long-barrel revolver, and he was pointing it straight at Rainsford's heart.

Out of the snarl of beard two small eyes regarded Rainsford.

"Don't be alarmed," said Rainsford, with a smile which he hoped was disarming. "I'm no robber. I fell off a yacht. My name is Sanger Rainsford of New York City."

The menacing look in the eyes did not change. The revolver pointed as rigidly as if the giant were a statue. He gave no sign that he understood Rainsford's words, or that he had even heard them. He was dressed in uniform, a black uniform trimmed with gray astrakhan.

"I'm Sanger Rainsford of New York," Rainsford began again. "I fell off a yacht. I am hungry."

The man's only answer was to raise with his thumb the hammer of his revolver. Then Rainsford saw the man's free hand go to his forehead in a military salute, and he saw him click his heels together and stand at attention. Another man was coming down the broad marble steps, an erect, slender man in evening clothes. He advanced to Rainsford and held out his hand.

In a cultivated voice marked by a slight accent that gave it added precision and deliberateness, he said, "It is a very great pleasure and honor to welcome Mr. Sanger Rainsford, the celebrated hunter, to my home."

Automatically Rainsford shook the man's hand.

"I've read your book about hunting snow leopards in Tibet, you see," explained the man. "I am General Zaroff."

Rainsford's first impression was that the man was singularly handsome; his second was that there was an original, almost bizarre quality about the general's face. He was a tall man past middle age, for his hair was a vivid white; but his thick eyebrows and pointed military mustache were as black as the night from which Rainsford had come. His eyes, too, were black and very bright. He had high cheekbones, a sharp-cut nose, a spare, dark face, the face of a man used to giving orders, the face of an aristocrat. Turning to the giant in uniform, the general made a sign. The giant put away his pistol, saluted, withdrew.

"Ivan is an incredibly strong fellow," remarked the general, "but he has the misfortune to be deaf and dumb. A simple fellow, but I'm afraid, like all his race, a bit of a savage."

"Is he Russian?"

"He is a Cossack," said the general, and his smile showed red lips and pointed teeth. "So am I.

"Come," he said, "we shouldn't be chatting here. We can talk later. Now you want clothes, food, rest. You shall have them. This is a most restful spot."

Ivan had reappeared, and the general spoke to him with lips that moved but gave forth no sound.

"Follow Ivan, if you please, Mr. Rainsford," said the general. "I was about to have my dinner when you came. I'll wait for you. You'll find that my clothes will fit you, I think."

It was to a huge, beam-ceilinged bedroom with a canopied bed big enough for six men that Rainsford followed the silent giant. Ivan laid out an evening suit, and Rainsford, as he put it on, noticed that it came from a London tailor who ordinarily cut and sewed for none below the rank of duke.

The dining room to which Ivan conducted him was in many ways remarkable. There was a medieval magnificence about it; it suggested a baronial hall of feudal times with its oaken panels, its high ceiling, its vast refectory table where twoscore men could sit down to eat. About the hall were the mounted heads of many animals— lions, tigers, elephants, moose, bears; larger or more perfect specimens Rainsford had never seen. At the great table the general was sitting, alone.

"You'll have a cocktail, Mr. Rainsford," he suggested. The cocktail was surpassingly good; and, Rainsford noted, the table appointments were of the finest, the linen, the crystal, the silver, the china.

They were eating *borsch*, the rich, red soup with sour cream so dear to Russian palates. Half apologetically General Zaroff said, "We do our best to preserve the amenities of civilization here. Please forgive any lapses. We are well off the beaten track, you know. Do you think the champagne has suffered from its long ocean trip?"

"Not in the least," declared Rainsford. He was finding the general a most thoughtful and affable host, a true cosmopolite. But there was one small trait of the general's that made Rainsford uncomfortable. Whenever he looked up from his plate he found the general studying him, appraising him narrowly.

"Perhaps," said General Zaroff, "you were surprised that I recognized your name. You see, I read all books on hunting published in English, French, and Russian. I have but one passion in my life, Mr. Rainsford, and it is the hunt."

"You have some wonderful heads here," said Rainsford as he ate a particularly well cooked filet mignon. "That Cape buffalo is the largest I ever saw."

"Oh, that fellow. Yes, he was a monster."

"Did he charge you?"

"Hurled me against a tree," said the general. "Fractured my skull. But I got the brute."

"I've always thought," said Rainsford, "that the Cape buffalo is the most dangerous of all big game."

For a moment the general did not reply; he was smiling his curious red-lipped smile. Then he said slowly, "No. You are wrong, sir. The Cape buffalo is not the most dangerous big game." He sipped his wine. "Here in my preserve on this island," he said in the same slow tone, "I hunt more dangerous game."

Rainsford expressed his surprise. "Is there big game on this island?"

The general nodded. "The biggest."

"Really?"

"Oh, it isn't here naturally, of course. I have to stock the island."

"What have you imported, General?" Rainsford asked. "Tigers?"

The general smiled. "No," he said. "Hunting tigers ceased to interest me some years ago. I exhausted their possibilities, you see. No thrill left in tigers, no real danger. I live for danger, Mr. Rainsford."

The general took from his pocket a gold cigarette case and offered his guest a long black cigarette with a silver tip; it was perfumed and gave off a smell like incense.

"We will have some capital hunting, you and I," said the general. "I shall be most glad to have your society."

"But what game—" began Rainsford.

"I'll tell you," said the general. "You will be amused, I know. I think I may say, in all modesty, that I have done a rare thing. I have invented a new sensation. May I pour you another glass of port, Mr. Rainsford?"

"Thank you, General."

The general filled both glasses, and said, "God makes some men poets. Some He makes kings, some beggars. Me He made a hunter. My hand was made for the trigger, my father said. He was a very rich man with a quarter of a million acres in the Crimea, and he was an ardent sportsman. When I was only five years old he gave me a little gun, specially made in Moscow for me, to shoot sparrows with. When I shot some of his prize turkeys with it, he did not punish me; he complimented me on my marksmanship. I killed my first bear in the Caucasus when I was ten. My whole life has been one prolonged hunt. I went into the army—it was expected of noblemen's sons—and for a time commanded a division of Cossack cavalry, but my real interest was always the hunt. I have hunted every kind of game in every land. It would be impossible for me to tell you how many animals I have killed."

The general puffed at his cigarette.

"After the debacle in Russia I left the country, for it was imprudent for an officer of the Czar to stay there. Many noble Russians lost everything. I, luckily, had invested heavily in American securities, so I shall never have to open a tearoom in Monte Carlo or drive a taxi in Paris. Naturally, I continued to hunt—grizzlies in your Rockies, crocodiles in the Ganges, rhinoceroses in East Africa. It was in Africa that the Cape buffalo hit me and laid me up for six months. As soon as I recovered I started for the Amazon to hunt jaguars, for I had heard they were unusually cunning. They weren't." The Cossack sighed. "They were no match at all for a hunter with his wits about him, and a high-powered rifle. I was bitterly disappointed. I was lying in my tent with a splitting headache one night when a terrible thought pushed its way into my mind. Hunting was beginning to bore me! And hunting, remember, had been my life. I have heard that in America businessmen often go to pieces when they give up the business that has been their life."

"Yes, that's so," said Rainsford.

The general smiled. "I had no wish to go to pieces," he said. "I must do something. Now, mine is an analytical mind, Mr. Rainsford. Doubtless that is why I enjoy the problems of the chase."

"No doubt, General Zaroff."

"So," continued the general, "I asked myself why the hunt no longer fascinated me. You are much younger than I am, Mr. Rainsford, and have not hunted as much, but you perhaps can guess the answer."

"What was it?"

"Simply this: hunting had ceased to be what you call 'a sporting proposition.' It had become too easy. I always got my quarry. Always. There is no greater bore than perfection."

The general lit a fresh cigarette.

"No animal had a chance with me any more. That is no boast; it is a mathematical certainty. The animal had nothing but his legs and his instinct. Instinct is no match for reason. When I thought of this it was a tragic moment for me, I can tell you."

Rainsford leaned across the table, absorbed in what his host was saying.

"It came to me as an inspiration what I must do," the general went on.

"And that was?"

The general smiled the quiet smile of one who has faced an obstacle and surmounted it with success. "I had to invent a new animal to hunt," he said.

"A new animal? You are joking."

"Not at all," said the general. "I never joke about hunting. I needed a new animal. I found one. So I bought this island, built this house, and here I do my hunting. The island is perfect for my purposes—there are jungles with a maze of trails in them, hills, swamps—"

"But the animal, General Zaroff?"

"Oh," said the general, "it supplies me with the most exciting hunting in the world. No other hunting compares with it for an instant. Every day I hunt, and I never grow bored now, for I have a quarry with which I can match my wits."

Rainsford's bewilderment showed in his face.

"I wanted the ideal animal to hunt," explained the general. "So I said, 'What are the attributes of an ideal quarry?' And the answer was, of course, 'It must have courage, cunning, and, above all, it must be able to reason.' "

"But no animal can reason," objected Rainsford.

"My dear fellow," said the general, "there is one that can."

"But you can't mean—" gasped Rainsford.

"And why not?"

"I can't believe you are serious, General Zaroff. This is a grisly joke."

"Why should I not be serious? I am speaking of hunting."

"Hunting? Good God, General Zaroff, what you speak of is murder."

The general laughed with entire good nature. He regarded Rainsford quizzically. "I refuse to believe that so modern and civilized a young man as you seem to be harbors romantic ideas about the value of human life. Surely your experiences in the war—" He stopped.

"Did not make me condone cold-blooded murder," finished Rainsford stiffly.

Laughter shook the general. "How extraordinarily droll you are!" he said. "One does not expect nowadays to find a young man of the educated class, even in America, with such a naïve, and, if I may say so, mid-Victorian point of view. It's like finding a snuffbox in a limousine. Ah, well, doubtless you had Puritan ancestors. So many Americans appear to have had. I'll wager you'll forget your notions when you go hunting with me. You've a genuine new thrill in store for you, Mr. Rainsford."

"Thank you, I'm a hunter, not a murderer."

"Dear me," said the general, quite unruffled, "again that unpleasant word. But I think I can show you that your scruples are quite ill founded."

"Yes?"

"Life is for the strong, to be lived by the strong, and, if needs be, taken by the strong. The weak of the world were put here to give the strong pleasure. I am strong. Why should I not use my gift? If I wish to hunt, why should I not? I hunt the scum of the earth— sailors from tramp ships—lascars, blacks, Chinese, whites, mongrels —a thoroughbred horse or hound is worth more than a score of them."

"But they are men," said Rainsford hotly.

"Precisely," said the general. "That is why I use them. It gives me pleasure. They can reason, after a fashion. So they are dangerous."

"But where do you get them?"

The general's left eyelid fluttered down in a wink. "This island is called Ship-Trap," he answered. "Sometimes an angry god of the high seas sends them to me. Sometimes, when Providence is not so kind, I help Providence a bit. Come to the window with me."

Rainsford went to the window and looked out toward the sea. "Watch! Out there!" exclaimed the general, pointing into the night. Rainsford's eyes saw only blackness, and then, as the general pressed a button, far out to sea Rainsford saw the flash of lights.

The general chuckled. "They indicate a channel," he said, "where there's none: giant rocks with razor edges crouch like a sea monster with wide-open jaws. They can crush a ship as easily as I crush this nut." He dropped a walnut on the hardwood floor and brought his heel grinding down on it. "Oh, yes," he said casually, as if in answer to a question, "I have electricity. We try to be civilized here."

"Civilized? And you shoot down men?"

A trace of anger was in the general's black eyes, but it was there for but a second, and he said, in his most pleasant manner: "Dear me, what a righteous young man you are! I assure you I do not do the thing you suggest. That would be barbarous. I treat these visitors with every consideration. They get plenty of good food and exercise. They get into splendid physical condition. You shall see for yourself tomorrow."

"What do you mean?"

"We'll visit my training school," smiled the general. "It's in the cellar. I have about a dozen pupils down there now. They're from the Spanish bark *San Lucar* that had the bad luck to go on the rocks out there. A very inferior lot, I regret to say. Poor specimens and more accustomed to the deck than to the jungle."

He raised his hand, and Ivan, who served as waiter, brought thick Turkish coffee. Rainsford, with an effort, held his tongue in check.

"It's a game, you see," pursued the general blandly. "I suggest to one of them that we go hunting. I give him a supply of food and an excellent hunting knife. I give him three hours' start. I am to follow, armed only with a pistol of the smallest caliber and range. If my quarry eludes me for three whole days, he wins the game. If I find him—" the general smiled—"he loses."

"Suppose he refuses to be hunted?"

"Oh," said the general, "I give him his option, of course. He need not play that game if he doesn't wish to. If he does not wish to hunt, I turn him over to Ivan. Ivan once had the honor of serving as official knouter to the Great White Czar, and he has his own ideas of sport. Invariably, Mr. Rainsford, invariably they chose the hunt."

"And if they win?"

The smile on the general's face widened. "To date I have not lost," he said.

Then he added, hastily, "I don't wish you to think me a braggart, Mr. Rainsford. Many of them afford only the most elementary sort of problem. Occasionally I strike a tartar. One almost did win. I eventually had to use the dogs."

"The dogs?"

"This way, please. I'll show you."

The general steered Rainsford to a window. The lights from the windows sent a flickering illumination that made grotesque patterns on the courtyard below, and Rainsford could see moving about there a dozen or so huge black shapes; as they turned toward him, their eyes glittered greenly.

"A rather good lot, I think," observed the general. "They are let out at seven every night. If anyone should try to get into my house —or out of it—something extremely regrettable would occur to him." He hummed a snatch of song from the Folies Bergère.

"And now," said the general, "I want to show you my new collection of heads. Will you come with me to the library?"

"I hope," said Rainsford, "that you will excuse me tonight, General Zaroff. I'm really not feeling at all well."

"Ah, indeed?" the general inquired solicitously. "Well, I suppose that's only natural, after your long swim. You need a good, restful night's sleep. Tomorrow you'll feel like a new man, I'll wager. Then we'll hunt, eh? I've one rather promising prospect—"

Rainsford was hurrying from the room.

"Sorry you can't go with me tonight," called the general. "I expect rather fair sport—a big, strong black. He looks resourceful— Well, good night, Mr. Rainsford; I hope that you have a good night's rest."

The bed was good and the pajamas of the softest silk, and he was tired in every fiber of his being, but nevertheless Rainsford could not quiet his brain with the opiate of sleep. He lay, eyes wide open. Once he thought he heard stealthy steps in the corridor outside his room. He sought to throw open the door; it would not open. He went to the window and looked out. His room was high up in one of the towers. The lights of the château were out now, and it was dark and silent, but there was a fragment of sallow moon, and by its wan light he could see, dimly, the courtyard; there, weaving in and out in the pattern of shadow, were black, noiseless forms; the hounds heard him at the window and looked up, expectantly, with their green eyes. Rainsford went back to the bed and lay down. By many methods he tried to put himself to sleep. He had achieved a doze when, just as morning began to come, he heard, far off in the jungle, the faint report of a pistol.

General Zaroff did not appear until luncheon. He was dressed faultlessly in the tweeds of a country squire. He was solicitous about the state of Rainsford's health.

"As for me," sighed the general, "I do not feel so well. I am worried, Mr. Rainsford. Last night I detected traces of my old complaint."

To Rainsford's questioning glance the general said, "Ennui. Boredom."

Then, taking a second helping of crepes suzette, the general explained, "The hunting was not good last night. The fellow lost his head. He made a straight trail that offered no problems at all. That's the trouble with these sailors; they have dull brains to begin with, and they do not know how to get about in the woods. They do excessively stupid and obvious things. It's most annoying. Will you have another glass of Chablis, Mr. Rainsford?"

"General," said Rainsford firmly, "I wish to leave this island at once."

The general raised his thickets of eyebrows; he seemed hurt. "But, my dear fellow," the general protested, "you've only just come. You've had no hunting—"

"I wish to go today," said Rainsford. He saw the dead black eyes of the general on him, studying him. General Zaroff's face suddenly brightened.

He filled Rainsford's glass with venerable Chablis from a dusty bottle.

"Tonight," said the general, "we will hunt—you and I."

Rainsford shook his head. "No, General," he said. "I will not hunt."

The general shrugged his shoulders and delicately ate a hothouse grape. "As you wish, my friend," he said. "The choice rests entirely with you. But may I not venture to suggest that you will find my idea of sport more diverting than Ivan's?"

He nodded toward the corner to where the giant stood, scowling, his thick arms crossed on his hogshead of chest.

"You don't mean—" cried Rainsford.

"My dear fellow," said the general, "have I not told you I always mean what I say about hunting? This is really an inspiration. I drink to a foeman worthy of my steel—at last."

The general raised his glass, but Rainsford sat staring at him.

"You'll find this game worth playing," the general said enthusiastically. "Your brain against mine. Your woodcraft against mine. Your strength and stamina against mine. Outdoor chess! And the stake is not without value, eh?"

"And if I win—" began Rainsford huskily.

"I'll cheerfully acknowledge myself defeated if I do not find you by midnight of the third day," said General Zaroff. "My sloop will place you on the mainland near a town."

The general read what Rainsford was thinking.

"Oh, you can trust me," said the Cossack. "I will give you my word as a gentleman and a sportsman. Of course you, in turn, must agree to say nothing of your visit here."

"I'll agree to nothing of the kind," said Rainsford.

"Oh," said the general, "in that case— But why discuss it now? Three days hence we can discuss it over a bottle of Veuve Clicquot, unless—"

The general sipped his wine.

Then a businesslike air animated him. "Ivan," he said to Rainsford, "will supply you with hunting clothes, food, a knife. I suggest you wear moccasins; they leave a poorer trail. I suggest too that you avoid the big swamp in the southeast corner of the island. We call it Death Swamp. There's quicksand there. One foolish fellow tried it. The deplorable part of it was that Lazarus followed him. You can imagine my feelings, Mr. Rainsford. I loved Lazarus; he was the finest hound in my pack. Well, I must beg you to excuse me now. I always take a siesta after lunch. You'll hardly have time for a nap, I fear. You'll want to start, no doubt. I shall not follow till dusk. Hunting at night is so much more exciting than by day, don't you think? *Au revoir*, Mr. Rainsford, *au revoir.*"

General Zaroff, with a deep, courtly bow, strolled from the room.

From another door came Ivan. Under one arm he carried khaki hunting clothes, a haversack of food, a leather sheath containing a long-bladed hunting knife; his right hand rested on a cocked revolver thrust in the crimson sash about his waist. . . .

Rainsford had fought his way through the bush for two hours. "I must keep my nerve. I must keep my nerve," he said through tight teeth.

He had not been entirely clear-headed when the château gates snapped shut behind him. His whole idea at first was to put distance between himself and General Zaroff, and, to this end, he had plunged along, spurred on by the sharp rowels of something very like panic. Now he had got a grip on himself, had stopped, and was taking stock of himself and the situation.

He saw that straight flight was futile; inevitably it would bring him face to face with the sea. He was in a picture with a frame of water, and his operations, clearly, must take place within that frame.

"I'll give him a trail to follow," muttered Rainsford, and he struck off from the rude path he had been following into the trackless wilderness. He executed a series of intricate loops; he doubled on his trail again and again, recalling all the lore of the fox hunt, and all the dodges of the fox. Night found him leg-weary, with hands and face lashed by the branches, on a thickly wooded ridge. He knew it would be insane to blunder on through the dark, even if he had the strength. His need for rest was imperative and he thought, "I have played the fox, now I must play the cat of the fable." A big tree with a thick trunk and outspread branches was nearby, and, taking care to leave not the slightest mark, he climbed up into the crotch, and stretching out on one of the broad limbs, after a fashion, rested. Rest brought him new confidence and almost a feeling of security. Even so zealous a hunter as General Zaroff could not trace him there, he told himself; only the devil himself could follow that complicated trail through the jungle after dark. But, perhaps, the general was a devil—

An apprehensive night crawled slowly by like a wounded snake, and sleep did not visit Rainsford, although the silence of a dead world was on the jungle. Toward morning when a dingy gray was varnishing the sky, the cry of some startled bird focused Rainsford's attention in that direction. Something was coming through the bush, coming slowly, carefully, coming by the same winding way Rainsford had come. He flattened himself down on the limb, and through a screen of leaves almost as thick as tapestry, he watched. The thing that was approaching him was a man.

It was General Zaroff. He made his way along with his eyes fixed in utmost concentration on the ground before him. He paused, almost beneath the tree, dropped to his knees and studied the ground. Rainsford's impulse was to hurl himself down like a panther, but he saw that the general's right hand held something small and metallic—an automatic pistol.

The hunter shook his head several times, as if he were puzzled. Then he straightened up and took from his case one of his black cigarettes; its pungent incense-like smoke floated up to Rainsford's nostrils. Rainsford held his breath. The general's eyes had left the ground and were traveling inch by inch up the tree. Rainsford froze there, every muscle tensed for a spring. But the sharp eyes of the hunter stopped before they reached the limb where Rainsford lay; a smile spread over his brown face. Very deliberately he blew a smoke ring into the air; then he turned his back on the tree and walked carelessly away, back along the trail he had come. The swish of the underbrush against his hunting boots grew fainter and fainter.

The pent-up air burst hotly from Rainsford's lungs. His first thought made him feel sick and numb. The general could follow a trail through the woods at night; he could follow an extremely difficult trail; he must have uncanny powers; only by the merest chance had the Cossack failed to see his quarry.

Rainsford's second thought was even more terrible. It sent a shudder of cold horror through his whole being. Why had the general smiled? Why had he turned back?

Rainsford did not want to believe what his reason told him was true, but the truth was as evident as the sun that had by now pushed through the morning mists. The general was playing with him! The general was saving him for another day's sport! The Cossack was the cat; he was the mouse. Then it was that Rainsford knew the full meaning of terror.

"I will not lose my nerve. I will not."

He slid down from the tree, and struck off again into the woods. His face was set and he forced the machinery of his mind to function. Three hundred yards from his hiding place he stopped where a huge dead tree leaned precariously on a smaller, living one. Throwing off his sack of food, Rainsford took his knife from its sheath and began to work with all his energy.

The job was finished at last, and he threw himself down behind a fallen log a hundred feet away. He did not have to wait long. The cat was coming again to play with the mouse.

Following the trail with the sureness of a bloodhound came General Zaroff. Nothing escaped those searching black eyes, no crushed blade of grass, no bent twig, no mark, no matter how faint, in the moss. So intent was the Cossack on his stalking that he was upon the thing Rainsford had made before he saw it. His foot touched the protruding bough that was the trigger. Even as he touched it, the general sensed his danger and leaped back with the agility of an ape. But he was not quite quick enough; the dead tree, delicately adjusted to rest on the cut living one, crashed down and struck the general a glancing blow on the shoulder as it fell; but for his alertness, he must have been smashed beneath it. He staggered, but he did not fall; nor did he drop his revolver. He stood there, rubbing his injured shoulder, and Rainsford, with fear again gripping his heart, heard the general's mocking laugh ring through the jungle.

"Rainsford," called the general, "if you are within sound of my voice, as I suppose you are, let me congratulate you. Not many men know how to make a Malay man-catcher. Luckily for me, I too have hunted in Malacca. You are proving interesting, Mr. Rainsford. I am going now to have my wound dressed; it's only a slight one. But I shall be back. I shall be back."

When the general, nursing his bruised shoulder, had gone, Rainsford took up his flight again. It was flight now, a desperate, hopeless flight, that carried him on for some hours. Dusk came, then darkness, and still he pressed on. The ground grew softer under his moccasins; the vegetation grew ranker, denser; insects bit him savagely. Then, as he stepped forward, his foot sank into the ooze. He tried to wrench it back, but the muck sucked viciously at his foot as if it were a giant leech. With a violent effort, he tore his foot loose. He knew where he was now. Death Swamp and its quicksand.

His hands were tight closed as if his nerve were something tangible that someone in the darkness was trying to tear from his grip. The softness of the earth had given him an idea. He stepped back from the quicksand a dozen feet or so and, like some huge prehistoric beaver, he began to dig.

Rainsford had dug himself in in France when a second's delay meant death. That had been a placid pastime compared to his digging now. The pit grew deeper; when it was above his shoulders, he climbed out and from some hard saplings cut stakes and sharpened them to a fine point. These stakes he planted in the bottom of the pit with the points sticking up. With flying fingers he wove a rough carpet of weeds and branches and with it he covered the mouth of the pit. Then, wet with sweat and aching with tiredness, he crouched behind the stump of a lightning-charred tree.

He knew his pursuer was coming; he heard the paddling sound of feet on the soft earth, and the night breeze brought him the perfume of the general's cigarette. It seemed to Rainsford that the general was coming with unusual swiftness; he was not feeling his way along, foot by foot. Rainsford, crouching there, could not see the general, nor could he see the pit. He lived a year in a minute. Then he felt an impulse to cry aloud with joy, for he heard the sharp crackle of the breaking branches as the cover of the pit gave way; he heard the sharp scream of pain as the pointed stakes found their mark. He leaped up from his place of concealment. Then he cowered back. Three feet from the pit a man was standing, with an electric torch in his hand.

"You've done well, Rainsford," the voice of the general called. "Your Burmese tiger pit has claimed one of my best dogs. Again you score. I think, Mr. Rainsford, I'll see what you can do against my whole pack. I'm going home for a rest now. Thank you for a most amusing evening."

At daybreak Rainsford, lying near the swamp, was awakened by a sound that made him know that he had new things to learn about fear. It was a distant sound, faint and wavering, but he knew it. It was the baying of a pack of hounds.

Rainsford knew he could do one of two things. He could stay where he was and wait. That was suicide. He could flee. That was postponing the inevitable. For a moment he stood there, thinking. An idea that held a wild chance came to him, and, tightening his belt, he headed away from the swamp.

The baying of the hounds drew nearer, then still nearer, nearer, ever nearer. On a ridge Rainsford climbed a tree. Down a watercourse, not a quarter of a mile away, he could see the bush moving. Straining his eyes, he saw the lean figure of General Zaroff; just ahead of him Rainsford made out another figure whose wide shoulders surged through the tall jungle weeds; it was the giant Ivan, and he seemed pulled forward by some unseen force; Rainsford knew that Ivan must be holding the pack in leash.

They would be on him any minute now. His mind worked frantically. He thought of a native trick he had learned in Uganda. He slid down the tree. He caught hold of a springy young sapling and to it he fastened his hunting knife, with the blade pointing down the trail; with a bit of wild grapevine he tied back the sapling. Then he ran for his life. The hounds raised their voices as they hit the fresh scent. Rainsford knew now how an animal at bay feels.

He had to stop to get his breath. The baying of the hounds stopped abruptly, and Rainsford's heart stopped too. They must have reached the knife.

He shinned excitedly up a tree and looked back. His pursuers had stopped. But the hope that was in Rainsford's brain when he climbed died, for he saw in the shallow valley that General Zaroff was still on his feet. But Ivan was not. The knife, driven by the recoil of the spring tree, had not wholly failed.

Rainsford had hardly tumbled to the ground when the pack took up the cry again.

"Nerve, nerve, nerve!" he panted, as he dashed along. A blue gap showed between the trees dead ahead. Ever nearer drew the hounds. Rainsford forced himself on toward the gap. He reached it. It was the shore of the sea. Across a cove he could see the gloomy gray stone of the château. Twenty feet below him the sea rumbled and hissed. Rainsford hesitated. He heard the hounds. Then he leaped far out into the sea. . . .

When the general and his pack reached the place by the sea, the Cossack stopped. For some minutes he stood regarding the blue-green expanse of water. He shrugged his shoulders. Then he sat down, took a drink of brandy from a silver flask, lit a perfumed cigarette, and hummed a bit from *Madame Butterfly*.

General Zaroff had an exceedingly good dinner in his great paneled dining hall that evening. With it he had a bottle of Pol Roger and half a bottle of Chambertin. Two slight annoyances kept him from perfect enjoyment. One was the thought that it would be difficult to replace Ivan; the other was that his quarry had escaped him; of course, the American hadn't played the game—so thought the general as he tasted his after-dinner liqueur. In his library he read, to soothe himself, from the works of Marcus Aurelius. At ten he went up to his bedroom. He was deliciously tired, he said to himself, as he locked himself in. There was a little moonlight, so, before turning on his light, he went to the window and looked down at the courtyard. He could see the great hounds, and he called, "Better luck another time," to them. Then he switched on the light.

A man, who had been hiding in the curtains of the bed, was standing there.

"Rainsford!" screamed the general. "How in God's name did you get here?"

"Swam," said Rainsford. "I found it quicker than walking through the jungle."

The general sucked in his breath and smiled. "I congratulate you," he said. "You have won the game."

Rainsford did not smile. "I am still a beast at bay," he said, in a low, hoarse voice. "Get ready, General Zaroff."

The general made one of his deepest bows. "I see," he said. "Splendid! One of us is to furnish a repast for the hounds. The other will sleep in this very excellent bed. On guard, Rainsford. . . ."

He had never slept in a better bed, Rainsford decided.

THE LADY ON THE GREY

BY JOHN COLLIER

❦ RINGWOOD was the last of an Anglo-Irish family which had played the devil in County Clare for a matter of three centuries. At last all their big houses were sold up, or burned down by the long-suffering Irish, and of all their thousands of acres not a single foot remained. Ringwood, however, had a few hundred a year of his own, and if the family estates had vanished he at least inherited a family instinct, which prompted him to regard all Ireland as his domain, and to rejoice in its abundance of horses, foxes, salmon, game, and girls.

In pursuit of these delights Ringwood ranged and roved from Donegal to Wexford through all the seasons of the year. There were not many hunts he had not led at some time or other on a borrowed mount, nor many bridges he had not leaned over through half a May morning, nor many inn parlors where he had not snored away a wet winter afternoon in front of the fire.

He had an intimate by the name of Bates, who was another of the same breed and the same kidney. Bates was equally long and lean, and equally hard up, and he had the same wind-flushed bony face, the same shabby arrogance, and the same seignorial approach to the little girls in the cottages and cowsheds.

Neither of these blades ever wrote a letter, but each generally knew where the other was to be found. The ticket collector, respectfully blind as he snipped Ringwood's third-class ticket in a first-class compartment, would mention that Mr. Bates had traveled that way only last Tuesday, stopping off at Killorglin for a week or two after the snipe. The chambermaid, coy in the clammy bedroom of a fishing inn, would find time to tell Bates that Ringwood had gone on up to Lough Corrib for a go at the pike. Policemen, priests, bagmen, game-keepers, even the tinkers on the roads, would pass on this verbal *pateran*. Then, if it seemed his friend was on to a good thing, the other would pack up his battered kit bag, put rods and guns into their cases, and drift off to join in the sport.

So it happened that one winter afternoon, when Ringwood was strolling back from a singularly blank day on the bog of Ballyneary, he was hailed by a one-eyed horse dealer of his acquaintance, who came trotting by in a gig, as people still do in Ireland. This worthy told our friend that he had just come down from Galway, where he had seen Mr. Bates, who was on his way to a village called Knock-derry, and who had told him very particularly to mention it to Mr. Ringwood if he came across him.

Ringwood turned this message over in his mind, and noted that it was a very particular one, and that no mention was made as to whether it was fishing or shooting his friend was engaged in, or whether he had met with some Croesus who had a string of hunters that he was prepared to lend. "He certainly would have put a name to it if it was anything of that sort! I'll bet my life it's a pair of sisters he's got on the track of. It must be!"

At this thought, he grinned from the tip of his long nose like a fox, and he lost no time in packing his bag and setting off for this place Knockderry, which he had never visited before in all his roving up and down the country in pursuit of fur, feather, and girls.

He found it was a long way off the beaten track, and a very quiet place when he got to it. There were the usual low, bleak hills all around, and a river running along the valley, and the usual ruined tower up on a slight rise, girdled with a straggly wood and approached by the remains of an avenue.

The village itself was like many another: a few groups of shabby cottages, a decaying mill, half-a-dozen beer shops and one inn at which a gentleman, hardened to rural cookery, might conceivably put up.

Ringwood's hired car deposited him there, and he strode in and found the landlady in the kitchen and asked for his friend Mr. Bates.

"Why, sure, your honor," said the landlady, "the gentleman's staying here. At least, he is, so to speak, and then, now, he isn't."

"How's that?" said Ringwood.

"His bag's here," said the landlady, "and his things are here, and my grandest room taken up with them (though I've another every bit as good), and himself staying in the house best part of a week. But the day before yesterday he went out for a bit of a constitutional, and—would you believe it, sir?—we've seen neither hide nor hair of him since."

"He'll be back," said Ringwood. "Show me a room, and I'll stay here and wait for him."

Accordingly he settled in, and waited all the evening, but Bates failed to appear. However, that sort of thing bothers no one in Ireland, and Ringwood's only impatience was in connection with the pair of sisters, whose acquaintance he was extremely anxious to make.

During the next day or two he employed his time in strolling up and down all the lanes and bypaths in the neighborhood, in the hope of discovering these beauties, or else some other. He was not particular as to which it should be, but on the whole he would have preferred a cottage girl, because he had no wish to waste time on elaborate approaches.

It was on the second afternoon, just as the early dusk was falling, he was about a mile outside the village and he met a straggle of muddy cows coming along the road, and a girl driving them. Our friend took a look at this girl, and stopped dead in his tracks, grinning more like a fox than ever.

This girl was still a child in her teens, and her bare legs were spattered with mud and scratched by brambles, but she was so pretty that the seignorial blood of all the Ringwoods boiled in the veins of their last descendant, and he felt an overmastering desire for a cup of milk. He therefore waited a minute or two, and then followed leisurely along the lane, meaning to turn in as soon as he saw the byre, and beg the favor of this innocent refreshment, and perhaps a little conversation into the bargain.

They say, though, that blessings never come singly, any more than misfortunes. As Ringwood followed his charmer, swearing to himself that there couldn't be such another in the whole county, he heard the fall of a horse's hoofs, and looked up, and there, approaching him at a walking pace, was a grey horse, which must have turned in from some bypath or other, because there certainly had been no horse in sight a moment before.

A grey horse is no great matter, especially when one is so urgently in need of a cup of milk, but this grey horse differed from all others of its species and color in two respects. First, it was no sort of a horse at all, neither hack nor hunter, and it picked up its feet in a queer way, and yet it had an arch to its neck and a small head and a wide nostril that were not entirely without distinction. And, second—and this distracted Ringwood from all curiosity as to breed and blood line —this grey horse carried on its back a girl who was obviously and certainly the most beautiful girl he had ever seen in his life.

Ringwood looked at her, and as she came slowly through the dusk she raised her eyes and looked at Ringwood. He at once forgot the little girl with the cows. In fact, he forgot everything else in the world.

The horse came nearer, and still the girl looked, and Ringwood looked, and it was not a mere exchange of glances, it was wooing and a marriage, all complete and perfect in a mingling of the eyes.

Next moment the horse had carried her past him, and, quickening its pace a little, it left him standing on the road. He could hardly run after it, or shout; in any case he was too overcome to do anything but stand and stare.

He watched the horse and rider go on through the wintry twilight, and he saw her turn in at a broken gateway just a little way along the road. Just as she passed through, she turned her head and whistled, and Ringwood noticed that her dog had stopped by him, and was sniffing about his legs. For a moment he thought it was a smallish wolfhound, but then he saw it was just a tall, lean, hairy lurcher. He watched it run limping after her, with its tail down, and it struck him that the poor creature had had an appalling thrashing not so long ago; he had noticed the marks where the hair was thin on its ribs.

However, he had little thought to spare for the dog. As soon as he got over his first excitement, he moved on in the direction of the gateway. The girl was already out of sight when he got there, but he recognized the neglected avenue which led up to the battered tower on the shoulder of the hill.

Ringwood thought that was enough for the day, so made his way back to the inn. Bates was still absent, but that was just as well. Ringwood wanted the evening to himself in order to work out a plan of campaign.

"That horse never cost two ten-pound notes of anybody's money," said he to himself. "So she's not so rich. So much the better! Besides, she wasn't dressed up much; I don't know what she had on— a sort of cloak or something. Nothing out of Bond Street, anyway. And lives in that old tower! I should have thought it was all tumbled down. Still, I suppose there's a room or two left at the bottom. Poverty Hall! One of the old school, blue blood and no money, pining away in this God-forsaken hole, miles away from everybody. Probably she doesn't see a man from one year's end to another. No wonder she gave me a look. God! if I was sure she was there by herself, I wouldn't need much of an introduction. Still, there might be a father or a brother or somebody. Never mind, I'll manage it."

When the landlady brought in the lamp: "Tell me," said he. "Who's the young lady who rides the cobby-looking, old-fashioned-looking grey?"

"A young lady, sir?" said the landlady doubtfully. "On a grey?"

"Yes," said he. "She passed me in the lane up there. She turned in on the old avenue, going up to the tower."

"Oh, Mary bless and keep you!" said the good woman. "That's the beautiful Murrough lady you must have seen."

"Murrough?" said he. "Is that the name? Well! Well! Well! That's a fine old name in the west here."

"It is so, indeed," said the landlady. "For they were kings and queens in Connaught before the Saxon came. And herself, sir, has the face of a queen, they tell me."

"They're right," said Ringwood. "Perhaps you'll bring me in the whisky and water, Mrs. Doyle, and I shall be comfortable."

He had an impulse to ask if the beautiful Miss Murrough had anything in the shape of a father or a brother at the tower, but his principle was "least said soonest mended," especially in little affairs of this sort. So he sat by the fire, recapturing and savoring the look the girl had given him, and he decided he needed only the barest excuse to present himself at the tower.

Ringwood had never any shortage of excuses, so the next afternoon he spruced himself up and set out in the direction of the old avenue. He turned in at the gate, and went along under the forlorn and dripping trees, which were so ivied and overgrown that the darkness was already thickening under them. He looked ahead for a sight of the tower, but the avenue took a turn at the end, and it was still hidden among the clustering trees.

Just as he got to the end, he saw someone standing there, and he looked again, and it was the girl herself, standing as if she was waiting for him.

"Good afternoon, Miss Murrough," said he, as soon as he got into earshot. "Hope I'm not intruding. The fact is, I think I had the pleasure of meeting a relation of yours, down in Cork, only last month. . . ." By this time he had got close enough to see the look in her eyes again, and all this nonsense died away in his mouth, for this was something beyond any nonsense of that sort.

"I thought you would come," said she.

"My God!" said he. "I had to. Tell me—are you all by yourself here?"

"All by myself," said she, and she put out her hand as if to lead him along with her.

Ringwood, blessing his lucky stars, was about to take it, when her lean dog bounded between them and nearly knocked him over.

"Down!" cried she, lifting her hand. "Get back!" The dog cowered and whimpered, and slunk behind her, creeping almost on its belly. "He's not a dog to be trusted," she said.

"He's all right," said Ringwood. "He looks a knowing old fellow. I like a lurcher. Clever dogs. What? Are you trying to talk to me, old boy?"

Ringwood always paid a compliment to a lady's dog, and in fact the creature really was whining and whimpering in the most extraordinary fashion.

"Be quiet!" said the girl, raising her hand again, and the dog was silent.

"A cur," said she to Ringwood. "Did you come here to sing the praises of a half-bred cur?" With that she gave him her eyes again, and he forgot the wretched dog, and she gave him her hand, and this time he took it and they walked toward the tower.

Ringwood was in the seventh heaven. "What luck!" thought he. "I might at this moment be fondling that little farm wench in some damp and smelly cowshed. And ten to one she'd be sniveling and crying and running home to tell her mammy. This is something different."

At that moment, the girl pushed open a heavy door, and, bidding the dog lie down, she led our friend through a wide, bare, stone-flagged hall and into a small vaulted room which certainly had no resemblance to a cowshed except perhaps it smelt a little damp and moldy, as these old stone places so often do. All the same, there were logs burning on the open hearth, and a broad, low couch before the fireplace. For the rest, the room was furnished with the greatest simplicity, and very much in the antique style. "A touch of the Kathleen ni Houlian," thought Ringwood. "Well, well! Sitting in the Celtic twilight, dreaming of love. She certainly doesn't make much bones about it."

The girl sat down on the couch and motioned him down beside her. Neither of them said anything; there was no sound but the wind outside, and the dog scratching and whimpering timidly at the door of the chamber.

At last the girl spoke. "You are of the Saxon," said she gravely.

"Don't hold it against me," said Ringwood. "My people came here in 1656. Of course, that's yesterday to the Gaelic League, but still I think we can say we have a stake in the country."

"Yes, through its heart," said she.

"Is it politics we're going to talk?" said he, putting an Irish turn to his tongue. "You and I, sitting here in the firelight?"

"It's love you'd rather be talking of," said she with a smile. "But you're the man to make a blunder and a mockery of the poor girls of Eire."

"You misjudge me entirely," said Ringwood. "I'm the man to live alone and sorrowful, waiting for the one love, though it seemed something beyond hoping for."

"Yes," said she. "But yesterday you were looking at one of the Connell girls as she drove her kine along the lane."

"Looking at her? I'll go so far as to say I did," said he. "But when I saw you I forgot her entirely."

"That was my wish," said she, giving him both her hands. "Will you stay with me here?"

"Ah, that I will!" cried he in a rapture.

"Always?" said she.

"Always," cried Ringwood. "Always and forever!" for he felt it better to be guilty of a slight exaggeration than to be lacking in courtesy to a lady. But as he spoke she fixed her eyes on him, looking so much as if she believed him that he positively believed himself.

"Ah," he cried. "You bewitch me!" And he took her in his arms. He pressed his lips to hers, and at once he was over the brink. Usually he prided himself on being a pretty cool hand, but this was an intoxication too strong for him; his mind seemed to dissolve in sweetness and fire, and at last the fire was gone, and his senses went with it. As they failed he heard her saying "Forever! Forever!" and then everything was gone and he fell asleep.

He must have slept some time. It seemed he was wakened by the heavy opening and closing of a door. For a moment he was all confused and hardly knew where he was.

The room was now quite dark, and the fire had sunk to a dim glow. He blinked, and shook his ears, trying to shake some sense into his head. Suddenly he heard Bates talking to him, muttering as if he, too, was half asleep, or half drunk more likely. "You *would* come here," said Bates. "I tried hard enough to stop you."

"Hullo!" said Ringwood, thinking he must have dozed off by the fire in the inn parlor. "Bates? God, I must have slept heavy! I feel queer. Damn it—so it was all a dream! Strike a light, old boy. It must be late. I'll yell for supper."

"Don't, for Heaven's sake," said Bates, in his altered voice. "Don't yell. She'll thrash us if you do."

"What's that?" said Ringwood. "Thrash us? What the hell are you talking about?"

At that moment a log rolled on the hearth, and a little flame flickered up, and he saw his long and hairy forelegs, and he knew.

THE WAXWORK

BY A. M. BURRAGE

❡ WHILE the uniformed attendants of Marriner's Waxworks were ushering the last stragglers through the great glass-paneled double doors, the manager sat in his office interviewing Raymond Hewson.

The manager was a youngish man, stout, blond and of medium height. He wore his clothes well and contrived to look extremely smart without appearing overdressed. Raymond Hewson looked neither. His clothes, which had been good when new and which were still carefully brushed and pressed, were beginning to show signs of their owner's losing battle with the world. He was a small, spare, pale man, with lank, errant brown hair, and although he spoke plausibly and even forcibly he had the defensive and somewhat furtive air of a man who was used to rebuffs. He looked what he was, a man gifted somewhat above the ordinary, who was a failure through his lack of self-assertion.

The manager was speaking.

"There is nothing new in your request," he said. "In fact we refuse it to different people—mostly young bloods who have tried to make bets—about three times a week. We have nothing to gain and something to lose by letting people spend the night in our Murderers' Den. If I allowed it, and some young idiot lost his senses, what would be my position? But your being a journalist somewhat alters the case."

Hewson smiled.

From *Someone in the Room*, by Ex-Private X. Reprinted by permission of the author.

"I suppose you mean that journalists have no senses to lose."

"No, no," laughed the manager, "but one imagines them to be responsible people. Besides, here we have something to gain; publicity and advertisement."

"Exactly," said Hewson, "and there I thought we might come to terms."

The manager laughed again.

"Oh," he exclaimed, "I know what's coming. You want to be paid twice, do you? It used to be said years ago that Madame Tussaud's would give a man a hundred pounds for sleeping alone in the Chamber of Horrors. I hope you don't think that we have made any such offer. Er—what is your paper, Mr. Hewson?"

"I am free-lancing at present," Hewson confessed, "working on space for several papers. However, I should find no difficulty in getting the story printed. The *Morning Echo* would use it like a shot. 'A Night with Marriner's Murderers.' No live paper could turn it down."

The manager rubbed his chin.

"Ah! And how do you propose to treat it?"

"I shall make it gruesome, of course; gruesome with just a saving touch of humor."

The other nodded and offered Hewson his cigarette case.

"Very well, Mr. Hewson," he said. "Get your story printed in the *Morning Echo*, and there will be a five-pound note waiting for you here when you care to come and call for it. But first of all, it's no small ordeal that you're proposing to undertake. I'd like to be quite sure about you, and I'd like you to be quite sure about yourself. I own I shouldn't care to take it on. I've seen those figures dressed and undressed, I know all about the process of their manufacture, I can walk about in company downstairs as unmoved as if I were walking among so many skittles, but I should hate having to sleep down there alone among them."

"Why?" asked Hewson.

"I don't know. There isn't any reason. I don't believe in ghosts. If I did, I should expect them to haunt the scene of their crimes or the spot where their bodies were laid, instead of a cellar which happens to contain their waxwork effigies. It's just that I couldn't sit alone among them all night, with their seeming to stare at me in the way they do. After all, they represent the lowest and most appalling types of humanity, and—although I would not own it publicly—the people who come to see them are not generally charged with the very highest motives. The whole atmosphere of the place is unpleasant, and if you are susceptible to atmosphere I warn you that you are in for a very uncomfortable night."

Hewson had known that from the moment when the idea had first occurred to him. His soul sickened at the prospect, even while he smiled casually upon the manager. But he had a wife and family to keep, and for the past month he had been living on paragraphs, eked out by his rapidly dwindling store of savings. Here was a chance not to be missed—the price of a special story in the *Morning Echo*, with a five-pound note to add to it. It meant comparative wealth and luxury for a week, and freedom from the worst anxieties for a fortnight. Besides, if he wrote the story well, it might lead to an offer of regular employment.

"The way of transgressors—and newspaper men—is hard," he said. "I have already promised myself an uncomfortable night because your murderers' den is obviously not fitted up as a hotel bedroom. But I don't think your waxworks will worry me much."

"You're not superstitious?"

"Not a bit," Hewson laughed.

"But you're a journalist; you must have a strong imagination."

"The news editors for whom I've worked have always complained that I haven't any. Plain facts are not considered sufficient in our trade, and the papers don't like offering their readers unbuttered bread."

The manager smiled and rose.

"Right," he said. "I think the last of the people have gone. Wait a moment. I'll give orders for the figures downstairs not to be draped, and let the night people know that you'll be here. Then I'll take you down and show you round."

He picked up the receiver of a house telephone, spoke into it and presently replaced it.

"One condition I'm afraid I must impose on you," he remarked. "I must ask you not to smoke. We had a fire scare down in the

Murderers' Den this evening. I don't know who gave the alarm, but whoever it was it was a false one. Fortunately there were very few people down there at the time, or there might have been a panic. And now, if you're ready, we'll make a move."

Hewson followed the manager through half a dozen rooms where attendants were busy shrouding the kings and queens of England, the generals and prominent statesmen of this and other generations, all the mixed herd of humanity whose fame or notoriety had rendered them eligible for this kind of immortality. The manager stopped once and spoke to a man in uniform, saying something about an armchair in the Murderers' Den.

"It's the best we can do for you, I'm afraid," he said to Hewson. "I hope you'll be able to get some sleep."

He led the way through an open barrier and down ill-lit stone stairs which conveyed a sinister impression of giving access to a dungeon. In a passage at the bottom were a few preliminary horrors, such as relics of the Inquisition, a rack taken from a medieval castle, branding irons, thumbscrews, and other mementos of man's one-time cruelty to man. Beyond the passage was the Murderers' Den.

It was a room of irregular shape with a vaulted roof, and dimly lit by electric lights burning behind inverted bowls of frosted glass. It was, by design, an eerie and uncomfortable chamber—a chamber whose atmosphere invited its visitors to speak in whispers. There was something of the air of a chapel about it, but a chapel no longer devoted to the practice of piety and given over now for base and impious worship.

The waxwork murderers stood on low pedestals with numbered tickets at their feet. Seeing them elsewhere, and without knowing whom they represented, one would have thought them a dull looking crew, chiefly remarkable for the shabbiness of their clothes, and as evidence of the changes of fashion even among the unfashionable.

Recent notorieties rubbed dusty shoulders with the old "favorites." Thurtell, the murderer of Weir, stood as if frozen in the act of making a shopwindow gesture to young Bywaters. There was Lefroy the poor half-baked little snob who killed for gain so that he might ape the gentleman. Within five yards of him sat Mrs. Thompson, that erotic romanticist, hanged to propitiate British middle-class matronhood. Charles Peace, the only member of that vile company who looked uncompromisingly and entirely evil, sneered across a gangway at Norman Thorne. Browne and Kennedy, the two most recent additions, stood between Mrs. Dyer and Patrick Mahon.

The manager, walking around with Hewson, pointed out several of the more interesting of these unholy notabilities.

"That's Crippen; I expect you recognize him. Insignificant little beast who looks as if he couldn't tread on a worm. That's Armstrong. Looks like a decent, harmless country gentleman, doesn't he? There's old Vaquier; you can't miss him because of his beard. And of course this—"

"Who's that?" Hewson interrupted in a whisper, pointing.

"Oh, I was coming to him," said the manager in a light undertone. "Come and have a good look at him. This is our star turn. He's the only one of the bunch that hasn't been hanged."

The figure which Hewson had indicated was that of a small, slight man not much more than five feet in height. It wore little waxed mustaches, large spectacles, and a caped coat. There was something so exaggeratedly French in its appearance that it reminded Hewson of a stage caricature. He could not have said precisely why the mild-looking face seemed to him so repellent, but he had already recoiled a step and, even in the manager's company, it cost him an effort to look again.

"But who is he?" he asked.

"That," said the manager, "is Dr. Bourdette."

Hewson shook his head doubtfully.

"I think I've heard the name," he said, "but I forget in connection with what."

The manager smiled.

"You'd remember better if you were a Frenchman," he said. "For some long while that man was the terror of Paris. He carried on his work of healing by day, and of throat-cutting by night, when the fit was on him. He killed for the sheer devilish pleasure it gave him to kill, and always in the same way—with a razor. After his last crime he left a clue behind him which set the police upon his track. One clue led to another, and before very long they knew that they were on the track of the Parisian equivalent of our Jack the Ripper, and had enough evidence to send him to the madhouse or the guillo-tine on a dozen capital charges.

"But even then our friend here was too clever for them. When he realized that the toils were closing about him he mysteriously disappeared, and ever since the police of every civilized country have been looking for him. There is no doubt that he managed to make away with himself, and by some means which has prevented his body coming to light. One or two crimes of a similar nature have taken place since his disappearance, but he is believed almost for certain to be dead, and the experts believe these recrudescences to be the work of an imitator. It's queer, isn't it, how every notorious murderer has imitators?"

Hewson shuddered and fidgeted with his feet.

"I don't like him at all," he confessed. "Ugh! What eyes he's got!"

"Yes, this figure's a little masterpiece. You find the eyes bite into you? Well, that's excellent realism, then, for Bourdette practised mesmerism, and was supposed to mesmerize his victims before dis-patching them. Indeed, had he not done so, it is impossible to see how so small a man could have done his ghastly work. There were never any signs of a struggle."

"I thought I saw him move," said Hewson with a catch in his voice.

The manager smiled.

"You'll have more than one optical illusion before the night's out, I expect. You shan't be locked in. You can come upstairs when you've had enough of it. There are watchmen on the premises, so you'll find company. Don't be alarmed if you hear them moving about. I'm sorry I can't give you any more light, because all the lights are on. For obvious reasons we keep this place as gloomy as pos-sible. And now I think you had better return with me to the office and have a tot of whisky before beginning your night's vigil."

The member of the night staff who placed the armchair for Hew-son was inclined to be facetious.

"Where will you have it, sir?" he asked, grinning. "Just 'ere, so as you can 'ave a little talk with Crippen when you're tired of sitting

still? Or there's old Mother Dyer over there, making eyes and looking as if she could do with a bit of company. Say where, sir."

Hewson smiled. The man's chaff pleased him if only because, for
the moment at least, it lent the proceedings a much desired air of the
commonplace.

"I'll place it myself, thanks," he said. "I'll find out where the
drafts come from first."

"You won't find any down here. Well, good night, sir. I'm upstairs if you want me. Don't let 'em sneak up be'ind you and touch
your neck with their cold and clammy 'ands. And you look out for
that old Mrs. Dyer; I b'lieve she's taken a fancy to you."

Hewson laughed and wished the man good night. It was easier
than he had expected. He wheeled the armchair—a heavy one up-
holstered in plush—a little way down the central gangway, and deliberately turned it so that its back was toward the effigy of Dr. Bourdette. For some undefined reason he liked Dr. Bourdette a great deal
less than his companions. Busying himself with arranging the chair he
was almost lighthearted, but when the attendant's footfalls had died
away and a deep hush stole over the chamber he realized that he had
no slight ordeal before him.

The dim unwavering light fell on the rows of figures which were
so uncannily like human beings that the silence and the stillness
seemed unnatural and even ghastly. He missed the sound of breathing,
the rustling of clothes, the hundred and one minute noises one hears
when even the deepest silence has fallen upon a crowd. But the air
was as stagnant as water at the bottom of a standing pond. There
was not a breath in the chamber to stir a curtain or rustle a hanging
drapery or start a shadow. His own shadow, moving in response to a
shifted arm or leg, was all that could be coaxed into motion. All was
still to the gaze and silent to the ear. "It must be like this at the bottom of the sea," he thought, and wondered how to work the phrase
into his story on the morrow.

He faced the sinister figures boldly enough. They were only
waxworks. So long as he let that thought dominate all others he promised himself that all would be well. It did not, however, save him long
from the discomfort occasioned by the waxen stare of Dr. Bourdette,
which, he knew, was directed upon him from behind. The eyes of the

little Frenchman's effigy haunted and tormented him, and he itched
with the desire to turn and look.

"Come!" he thought, "my nerves have started already. If I turn
and look at that dressed-up dummy it will be an admission of funk."
And then another voice in his brain spoke to him.

"It's because you're afraid that you won't turn and look at him."
The two Voices quarreled silently for a moment or two, and at
last Hewson slewed his chair round a little and looked behind him.

Among the many figures standing in stiff, unnatural poses, the
effigy of the dreadful little doctor stood out with a queer prominence,
perhaps because a steady beam of light beat straight down upon it.
Hewson flinched before the parody of mildness which some fiendishly
skilled craftsman had managed to convey in wax, met the eyes for one
agonized second, and turned again to face the other direction.

"He's only a waxwork like the rest of you," Hewson muttered
defiantly. "You're all only waxworks."

They were only waxworks, yes, but waxworks don't move. Not
that he had seen the least movement anywhere, but it struck him
that, in the moment or two while he had looked behind him, there
had been the least, subtle change in the grouping of the figures in
front. Crippen, for instance, seemed to have turned at least one
degree to the left. Or, thought Hewson, perhaps the illusion was due
to the fact that he had not slewed his chair back into its exact original
position. And there were Field and Grey, too; surely one of them had
moved his hands. Hewson held his breath for a moment, and then
drew his courage back to him as a man lifts a weight. He remembered the words of more than one news editor and laughed savagely
to himself.

"And they tell me I've got no imagination!" he said beneath his
breath.

He took a notebook from his pocket and wrote quickly.

"Mem.—Deathly silence and unearthly stillness of figures. Like
being bottom of sea. Hypnotic eyes of Dr. Bourdette. Figures seem
to move when not being watched."

He closed the book suddenly over his fingers and looked round
quickly and awfully over his right shoulder. He had neither seen nor
heard a movement, but it was as if some sixth sense had made him

aware of one. He looked straight into the vapid countenance of Lefroy which smiled vacantly back as if to say, "It wasn't I!"

Of course it wasn't he, or any of them; it was his own nerves. Or was it? Hadn't Crippen moved again during that moment when his attention was directed elsewhere? You couldn't trust that little man! Once you took your eyes off him he took advantage of it to shift his position. That was what they were all doing, if he only knew it, he told himself; and half rose out of his chair. This was not quite good enough! He was going. He wasn't going to spend the night with a lot of waxworks which moved while he wasn't looking.

. . . Hewson sat down again. This was very cowardly and very absurd. They *were* only waxworks and they *couldn't* move; let him hold that thought and all would yet be well. Then why all that silent unrest about him?—a subtle something in the air which did not quite break the silence and happened, whichever way he looked, just beyond the boundaries of his vision.

He swung round quickly to encounter the mild but baleful stare of Dr. Bourdette. Then, without warning, he jerked his head back to stare straight at Crippen. Ha! he'd nearly caught Crippen that time! "You'd better be careful, Crippen—and all the rest of you! If I do see one of you move I'll smash you to pieces! Do you hear?"

He ought to go, he told himself. Already he had experienced enough to write his story, or ten stories, for the matter of that. Well, then, why not go? The *Morning Echo* would be none the wiser as to how long he had stayed, nor would it care so long as his story was a good one. Yes, but that night watchman upstairs would chaff him. And the manager—one never knew—perhaps the manager would quibble over that five-pound note which he needed so badly. He wondered if Rose were asleep or if she were lying awake and thinking of him. She'd laugh when he told her that he had imagined . . .

This was a little too much! It was bad enough that the waxwork effigies of murderers should move when they weren't being watched, but it was intolerable that they should *breathe*. Somebody was breathing. Or was it his own breath which sounded to him as if it came from a distance? He sat rigid, listening and straining, until he exhaled with a long sigh. His own breath after all, or—if not, Something had divined that he was listening and had ceased breathing simultaneously.

Hewson jerked his head swiftly around and looked all about him out of haggard and haunted eyes. Everywhere his gaze encountered the vacant waxen faces, and everywhere he felt that by just some least fraction of a second had he missed seeing a movement of hand or foot, a silent opening or compression of lips, a flicker of eyelids, a look of human intelligence now smoothed out. They were like naughty children in a class, whispering, fidgeting and laughing behind their teacher's back, but blandly innocent when his gaze was turned upon them.

This would not do! This distinctly would not do! He must clutch at something, grip with his mind upon something which belonged essentially to the workaday world, to the daylight London streets. He was Raymond Hewson, an unsuccessful journalist, a living and breathing man, and these figures grouped around him were only dummies, so they could neither move nor whisper. What did it matter if they were supposed to be lifelike effigies of murderers? They were only made of wax and sawdust, and stood there for the entertainment of morbid sightseers and orange-sucking trippers. That was better! Now what was that funny story which somebody had told him in the Falstaff yesterday? . . .

He recalled part of it, but not all, for the gaze of Dr. Bourdette, urged, challenged, and finally compelled him to turn.

Hewson half turned, and then swung his chair so as to bring him face to face with the wearer of those dreadful hypnotic eyes. His own eyes were dilated, and his mouth, at first set in a grin of terror, lifted at the corners in a snarl. Then Hewson spoke and woke a hundred sinister echoes.

"You moved, damn you!" he cried. "Yes, you did, damn you! I saw you!"

Then he sat quite still, staring straight before him, like a man found frozen in the Arctic snows.

Dr. Bourdette's movements were leisurely. He stepped off his pedestal with the mincing care of a lady alighting from a bus. The platform stood about two feet from the ground, and above the edge of it a plush-covered rope hung in arclike curves. Dr. Bourdette lifted up the rope until it formed an arch for him to pass under, stepped off the platform and sat down on the edge facing Hewson. Then he nodded and smiled and said, "Good evening.

"I need hardly tell you," he continued, in perfect English in which was traceable only the least foreign accent, "that not until I overheard the conversation between you and the worthy manager of this establishment, did I suspect that I should have the pleasure of a companion here for the night. You cannot move or speak without my bidding, but you can hear me perfectly well. Something tells me that you are—shall I say nervous? My dear sir, have no illusions. I am not one of these contemptible effigies miraculously come to life: I am Dr. Bourdette himself."

He paused, coughed and shifted his legs.

"Pardon me," he resumed, "but I am a little stiff. And let me explain. Circumstances with which I need not fatigue you, have made it desirable that I should live in England. I was close to this building this evening when I saw a policeman regarding me a thought too curiously. I guessed that he intended to follow and perhaps ask me embarrassing questions, so I mingled with the crowd and came in here. An extra coin bought my admission to the chamber in which we now meet, and an inspiration showed me a certain means of escape.

"I raised a cry of fire, and when all the fools had rushed to the stairs I stripped my effigy of the caped coat which you behold me wearing, donned it, hid my effigy under the platform at the back, and took its place on the pedestal.

"I own that I have since spent a very fatiguing evening, but fortunately I was not always being watched and had opportunities to draw an occasional deep breath and ease the rigidity of my pose. One small boy screamed and exclaimed that he saw me moving. I understood that he was to be whipped and put straight to bed on his return home, and I can only hope that the threat has been executed to the letter.

"The manager's description of me, which I had the embarrassment of being compelled to overhear, was biased but not altogether inaccurate. Clearly I am not dead, although it is as well that the world thinks otherwise. His account of my hobby, which I have indulged for years, although, through necessity, less frequently of late, was in the main true although not intelligently expressed. The world is divided between collectors and noncollectors. With the noncollectors we are not concerned. The collectors collect anything, according to their individual tastes, from money to cigarette cards, from moths to matchboxes. I collect throats."

He paused again and regarded Hewson's throat with interest mingled with disfavor.

"I am obliged to the chance which brought us together tonight," he continued, "and perhaps it would seem ungrateful to complain. From motives of personal safety my activities have been somewhat curtailed of late years, and I am glad of this opportunity of gratifying my somewhat unusual whim. But you have a skinny neck, sir, if you will overlook a personal remark. I should never have selected you from choice. I like men with thick necks . . . thick red necks. . . ."

He fumbled in an inside pocket and took out something which he tested against a wet forefinger and then proceeded to pass gently to and fro across the palm of his left hand.

"This is a little French razor," he remarked blandly. "They are not much used in England, but perhaps you know them? One strops them on wood. The blade, you will observe, is very narrow. They do not cut very deep, but deep enough. In just one little moment you shall see for yourself. I shall ask you the little civil question of all the polite barbers: Does the razor suit you, sir?"

He rose up, a diminutive but menacing figure of evil, and approached Hewson with the silent, furtive step of a hunting panther.

"You will have the goodness," he said, "to raise your chin a little. Thank you, and a little more. Just a little more. Ah, thank you! . . . *Merci, m'sieur . . . Ah, merci . . . merci. . . .*"

Over one end of the chamber was a thick skylight of frosted glass which, by day, let in a few sickly and filtered rays from the floor above. After sunrise these began to mingle with the subdued light from the electric bulbs, and this mingled illumination added a certain ghastliness to a scene which needed no additional touch of horror.

The waxwork figures stood apathetically in their places, waiting to be admired or execrated by the crowds who would presently wander fearfully among them. In their midst, in the center gangway, Hewson sat still, leaning far back in his armchair. His chin was up-tilted as if he were waiting to receive attention from a barber, and although there was not a scratch upon his throat, nor anywhere upon his body, he was cold and dead. His previous employers were wrong in having him credited with no imagination.

Dr. Bourdette on his pedestal watched the dead man unemotionally. He did not move, nor was he capable of motion. But then, after all, he was only a waxwork.

THE DUMB WIFE

BY THOMAS BURKE

❧ DARK IS THIS TALE of love with woe as dark as the brooding arches that shut out light from the streets about the waterside. In these streets it is always chilly afternoon, gray hued and empty of happy noise and welcoming windows. Here the narrow curbs make boundaries for the puckered lives of their people; and feet fall without echo upon their stones.

Yet, though all else perish here, beauty and love and sacrifice survive. In these waste places below London River mean iniquities propagate and flourish, and curl their soiling arms about all that would be brave and beautiful. Yet beauty persists. Even in the heart of darkness love takes root and spreads therein its eternal enchantments of gardens and moonrise and April airs and song.

In one of these infelicitous streets, some distance from the main Chinese quarter, stood a small Chinese laundry. At an upper window of this laundry sat, for many years, a woman of semi-Oriental features. Day by day, month by month, she sat there, the object of that pity which those deep in misfortune bestow so largely upon others in misfortune. Part of her story was known. She was the wife of the owner of the laundry, Ng Yong; and she was dumb.

Throughout the hours of light she sat at her window, her naturally placid face now coldly blank by her affliction; staring at nothing, hearing nothing; silent and still; a piece of Chinese carving. And deep in her narrow eyes lay a crouching horror, so that strangers, passing that window, quickened their steps to the friendly main road.

What passed each day behind that rigid face may not be known; can only be conjectured. What hate—what fear—what resolution of vengeance and escape—what vacillation—what dark ideas and darker memories gathered there—these things are not to be told.

Upon recurring occasions she would, without warning, shed her impassivity, and a scene would follow. She would run to the door and strive for speech to the point of paroxysm, and utter anomalous noises, and make wild gestures in the direction of West India Dock. Then her husband would hasten to her. He would take her in hand, sadly, and lead her, with kind firmness, back to seclusion; and the neighbors would murmur in sympathy with him and his forbearance under his trials.

He had early explained to them the misfortune that had befallen his house, and they had often aided him in quieting the sufferer. On her rare walks he went always with her, the ministering husband; and when she turned and turned from street to street, as though in search of one desired spot, and stopped passers-by with her pleading face and working jaws, he would make forlorn play with his hands, and strangers would draw away, and those who knew would gather about him.

This much was known. Here is the full story.

When Moy Toon was born in Poplar of an English mother and a Chinese father there was no warm place for her with her father's people, and none at all with her mother's. Her father's people, however, finding her lying about unclaimed, and holding something of grace within them, did provide her with bare necessities. Left motherless in her early years, she was received into a teahouse in the colony to do the rough work. In this teahouse she spent many tedious years whose days she scarcely counted. She had little capacity for thought; felt little; asked little; was as content as the slave born in slavery and untaught. Her birth had given her a larger share of Oriental compliance than of Western skepticism and challenge. Things were what they were, and she accepted them. She grew up in the promiscuous company of the docks. Of moral training she had little, and no learning beyond that given of custom to the Chinese woman of the coolie class. So she passed her young years in a kind of somnambulism.

Then one night there came to the teahouse, in the fourth stage of inebriety, a young second mate. She had seen him many times about the streets; and, in her aimless way, had admired his happy stride and clear, sea-brightened face. On this occasion the wavering charm of the girl, unsettled between English mobility and Eastern gravity, captivated his beer-bound senses, and he made proposals to her. He had but to invite, and she went, her warped spirit mildly pleased at the attention from this man-wonder.

Well, that night was the first of many. He made a fuss of her, and called her Baby Doll and other babbling names, and brought cheap gifts for her. On his next time ashore he again sought her out, and pleased himself with her simple company. Some months later he made a definite parting from her, telling her only that he was about to marry and settle down in another part of London; and she saw him no more. She took her dismissal placidly, without rancor, as she took all things, whether blows or endearments, and asked nothing of him.

Later came the baby. The restaurant keeper was a little cha-grined at this clumsy misdemeanor, but he gave her rough attention, and the child was placed with an old woman, known to the Chinese colony, who lived at Blackwall. Now Moy Toon became quite silly about that baby. It was her living memory of the one adventure of her life, and she worshiped it. At first she clung to it defiantly, as a gesture of disdain against those about her who so lightly esteemed her wonderful achievement of motherhood. But in a more sober mo-ment she saw that in their advice lay her best course. With the child, she could not hope to earn even the scanty living that her abilities and known story permitted her to command today; and she had no taste for the life which other girls of her birth and class affected. She had had her one adventure, and desired, for the child's sake, to walk se-curely. She preferred the rough comfort of the teahouse to the dolorous enterprise of the streets. She knew that the child would receive, un-der other protection, at least the essentials of life, which she herself could not faithfully promise him. So she let wisdom beat down her sentiment, and surrendered the child, with the condition that she should see it from time to time as she wished.

For six years, then, she followed her arid course, mother and no mother, accepting, without question or conjecture, the untoward-ness of her circumstance; rather giving thanks that her course was broken, week by week, by visits to the boy. Often during these years her pillow shook to the vibrations of her sobbing breast, as she recalled the young strength and delicate small ways of him, and reached vain arms through the darkness to the child she might not openly claim. In the rough-and-tumble of the dockside alleys he had grown into a wiry, alert urchin, big and bold for his age; and delicious afternoons she spent with him, dressing him in a travesty of seaman's uniform—reefer jacket and gilt buttons, with peaked cap and much cheap braid about it—and calling him "Mother's Sailor Boy"; afternoons that compensated for the lonely nights.

Then old Ng Yong appeared. He had bought the laundry business of a compatriot who was returning to his own country, and he was doing very well with it. But, looking round the fittings of the house, which he had bought with the business, he felt that something was lacking, and discovered that it lacked a woman. He felt that a woman would be an agreeable piece of furniture, and would finish off the establishment. He looked about for one, and at the teahouse of the Hundred Gilded Dragons he found Moy Toon. Moy Toon seemed to him to be just the article. He inquired of the keeper of the house concerning her, and found that she was available, and was in the gift of the keeper.

Now Ng Yong was very strict on the sanctity of womanhood (from the prospective purchaser's point of view) and put to the keeper voluminous questions upon her life and behavior. These the man behind the Gilded Dragons answered freely: not entirely truthfully, but freely, with an engaging air of candor. When Ng Yong demanded assurances of the unblemished character of the goods, these also he freely gave. No gentleman of commerce has yet been known to cry down his wares; and he knew that the disclosure of a certain adventure would appreciably lower the price of the article to that of shop-soiled.

Moy Toon was privately told of the opening of negotiations, and was shown, by reports of Ng Yong's prosperity, how largely her situation should be uplifted by an alliance with him, and how necessary it was that the existence of the boy should be kept secret. It was urged upon her that she should renounce forever any further part in him; but to that she answered nothing. To the proposed union she offered no objection. Ng Yong was old, but she was not repelled on that ground: she was sufficiently Chinese to regard the difference in ages as fitting. She saw here a chance of helping herself, and, indirectly, the boy, and was prepared to take it without a second thought. She never doubted her ability to keep her own secret.

So, some nights later, she was inspected and questioned by Ng Yong, who expressed himself as satisfied with her person and with her demeanor of modesty. But he did not let the serious occasion of wife-taking pass without administering a sharp lecture on wifely deportment. He sat before her in the kitchen of the teahouse, his fleshy hands splayed upon his knees, his old head wagging, the secrets of his eyes shaded from the groping minds of his fellows. Ng Yong's wife, he told her, must be obedient; must give unquestioning and unceasing service to her lord; must give ready and regular attention to household duties; must sever all connection with the people about the teahouse; and, above all, must be honest and faithful. She must be all his and his alone. He quoted passages from the Four Books concerning the Virtuous Wife, and the others; and his voice dropped to a muttered monotone as he spoke of the punishment befitting the wife who failed in the first law.

To this homily Moy Toon listened perfunctorily, and answered casually, with modest and low-toned responses. So the business proceeded, through many evenings of bargaining, until at last a middle price was agreed, the money paid to the Gilded Dragons, and Moy Toon lifted over the threshold of Ng Yong.

All that he required of her in service and obedience she gave him. But she would not renounce her boy. Her heart had not been asked of her, and that she kept; and in it, guarded from all profane contact, rested the boy. He was her joss, and through him and before him she worshiped. For the rest, she served Ng Yong well. She had no desire to do else. She was scrupulous in anticipating his wishes, studious in attending the house, and looked at no other man.

Of this she had but little chance, for her husband was ever about her. Maybe her demeanor of modesty had not wholly convinced him. He watched her with vigilant eyes; never was she free from him; and even when she was out on shopping business she felt that she was under his regard.

Her meetings with her boy became, therefore, matters of deli-cacy. To go to the house in Canning Town, each Thursday, as she had done these six years, would at once arouse suspicion. He would note these regular, recurring disappearances; he would question her and perhaps not be satisfied by her answers; he would follow her or have her followed, and discover her secret; and then the pavement would receive her, and she and the boy would starve.

She considered carefully new arrangements, and decided that future meetings must be haphazard, snatched at odd moments, and a different rendezvous must be appointed for each meeting. Discretion warned her to follow the Dragon's advice and abandon wholly these meetings. She was safe now and comfortable, and her daily life was well set. Better to take the chance of seeing the boy at a distance, without speech, or of getting word of his welfare from independent parties, than to risk all her present security and well-being for the idle whim of fondling him and talking with him. For discovery meant banishment from the house of Ng Yong and consequent privation and misery. Beyond that her mind did not travel. Of the words of his homily on wifely decorum she remembered nothing: they had gone, as the phrase is, in at one ear and out at the other. He would be angry and kick her out, and she and the boy would suffer. And suffer-ing of any kind she could not face. She hated it and feared it.

Yet, upon a night in the first month of marriage, as she lay awake, she thought of the boy, and fancied his small arms about her, and his voice whispering childish prayers for pennies in her ear. Her boy. Next morning she managed to pass the word, through many chan-nels, to the woman who had charge of him, that she should bring him, the following afternoon, to Tunnel Gardens. There she could sit with him and the woman, and hear him talk; and if Ng Yong or any friend of his should see her thus engaged, she could reply, quite suit-ably, that the woman and the boy were strangers; that the child at play had attracted her and she had spoken to him and his mother. No harm in that. So it was done, without misadventure.

For the next meeting, a fortnight later, she appointed a sweet-stuff shop near Blackwall, where the boy was fed with cakes and ginger beer. She spent an hour with him here, and when she returned, Ng Yong, who was customarily superintending the laundry at that hour, was awaiting her upstairs. He told her that she had been long gone; and she answered that she had gone to the cheaper market at Shadwell, and had been delayed because the road was under repair. He looked strangely and closely at her, but she caught nothing of the look. Her eyes were full of her boy—how bonny he was looking and how pert of manner.

The next meeting she fixed, after some thought, for a morning in a disused cellar in a remote corner near West India Dock. She had discovered this cellar some years ago, and it was today much as it was then. She and her sailor had spent some hours there one wet evening of summer, when he had been unable to find other temporary accommodation. It was easily entered, and, as it held nothing that could be stolen, was never under observation. It had lain abandoned since the river first entered it and swamped its contents. Repairs had been attempted, but the river persisted; and at every high tide it was waist deep in water. It was entered from a narrow passage by a flight of broken steps so hidden that none could without guidance discover them.

Hither, then, the boy was brought. The cellar, lit by Moy Toon's electric torch, did not daunt him. He was a lad of his father's spirit, she told herself, for he was delighted with the adventure, and trotted about the place, prying here and there, and nourishing his mother's heart with smiles. She stood by him, blooming with pride and encouraging his tricks, careless of all save the small circle in which he moved. But in the midst of his gamboling the woman who had brought him lifted a nervous finger.

"Listen! Quiet!"

He stopped suddenly, and Moy Toon gathered him against her skirt. They listened.

"Oo—er!" croaked the woman. "Someone comin'. I was afraid we'd get into trouble comin' 'ere. What'll we do? Where shall we go? Oo—er. I'm gointer get outer this. It's your affair. I ain't in it. I ain't gointer be mixed up in no—"

With a whirl of worried skirts and cumbrous boots, she pounded up the steps. Moy Toon, below, heard a sound as of a dull impact, and a shrill "Oo—er!" followed by "Look out, gel!"

It was a moment of panic. The woman had seen something to

affright her, and Moy Toon's first instinct was the boy. At that moment she was without power of thought. She saw three feet from her an alcove in which the boy had been exploring. It was guarded by a heavy door with a great iron hasp and lock. She grabbed the boy by the arm, and put her mouth to his ear.

"In there, darling. Quick—in there. Don't make a sound. It's for Mummy."

The boy understood and hopped into the alcove. She swept the door upon him and snapped it closed. She turned from it to reach the torch and extinguish it; and turned to see Ng Yong descending the last step to the cellar, with hand outstretched in command which she instinctively obeyed. He reached the bottom, and stood motionless, looking about him, right and left. The sudden shock of his arrival, and the closing of the door, had left her breathless, incapable of act or word. She leaned against the wall, panting, her slow mind rolling round one idea: "What did he see? What did he see?" Through his silence she prayed for him to speak.

At last he spoke, quietly. "So this is where you meet your lover? Let us see him."

"Lover? Me? No, I don't. Oh no—no—I don't. What d'you mean?"

She knew that she was speaking stupidly, unconvincingly, but delight at his mistake about a lover made her careless. Inside herself she laughed. If she had to suffer his wrath, she would suffer; but at least the boy was safe, while the lover idea remained.

"Where is your lover?"

"Lover? Ha-ha! I ain't got no lover."

"What then would you be doing here?"

"But—I mean—don't be silly! Lover? I come 'ere to—"

"So you come to this place—this place—to gossip with old women, huh? Bring out your lover."

"But I ain't—" She saw suddenly that her best plan, for the boy's sake, was to hold the idea of a lover, to develop it.

"Well, I mean, suppose I—"

He raised a hand. "Look at me!"

The instinct of obedience raised her eyes, and she looked full at him, and what she saw in his face turned her sick. She gibbered.

"But I ain't—I ain't—"

"You—you to whom I gave my trust. Oh, child of a dog!"

"But I mean—I—"

A snarl broke from his lips. His hand dipped to his inner pocket. She watched it, with foolish eyes, fumbling under his canvas coat. She saw it come out, holding a long curved knife, the blade dulled by long disuse. He held it by the ivory hilt, directed the point upon her, horizontally, and slowly, quietly approached her. Like dropping water, the words of his homily on the Virtuous Wife dropped through her mind.

"You have chosen your place well. We are safe here. I told you how I would punish unfaithfulness."

With each step forward he took, she took one backward, shrinking from him. He followed her. She drew back, shuddering, arms extended, pressing herself against the wall as if she would force herself into it. He followed her. Pat-pat, pat-pat, they moved softly along the damp floor. She continued to step slow paces backward, eyes fixed on him. He followed her. He followed her until she had reached the far wall, where an iron grating gave out to the river. There she stood, mouthing at him, cornered; fascinated, rabbit-like, by the dull tongue of steel that slowly floated toward her breast. Nearer and nearer it came. She felt the touch of it upon her corsage; then the prick of it upon her skin; and at this she opened wide her throat to scream: "Mercy! Mercy! I ain't got no lover!"

But, though she opened her throat, none of these words came. Her mouth opened and shut, and her teeth came together and flew apart; but no sound could she utter. The knife rose and fluttered half an inch from her throat. Then Ng Yong dropped it to his waist, and drew back. He looked long at her before he spoke again.

"Where is this lover?"

Her lips moved, and she made meaningless noises, and shook her head and prayed with her hands. Ng Yong replaced the knife in his coat, and nodded gravely. The shock of discovery and the threatened punishment had taken punishment from his hands. His wife was punished by an instrument keener than any blade of steel. She was struck dumb.

He took her by the arm. She shrank from the touch, and he

smiled upon her. He drew her to the steps leading to the alley. As he led her away, she struggled, and pointed to the great door of the alcove, and made low noises: "Myw! Myw!"

Ng Yong, too, looked at the door, and gave a smile of understanding. With easy force he compelled her up the steps. She beat against his bent arm, and strove with hands and lips, as one explaining. But he led her away, quietly, down that narrow passage, so that none noted their going until they reached the main road. And he led her home, and told sympathetic inquirers how his wife had suffered a sad shock from a street accident, which had deprived her of speech and made her foolish of mind.